D0470586

organic kitchen

organic kitchen
making the most of fresh and seasonal produce

Ysanne Spevack

METRO BOOKS
NEW YORK

Dedicated to my mom, Coral,
for all her inspiration both in and out of the kitchen,
to Steve, for his support throughout the writing of this book,
and to John at the Organic Delivery Company, for his fantastic fruits and vegetables.

This 2008 edition published by Metro Books, by arrangement with Anness Publishing Ltd

Publisher: Joanna Lorenz
Managing Editor: Linda Fraser
Senior Editor: Margaret Malone
Editor: Joy Wotton
Copy Editors: Jenni Fleetwood and Jane Bamforth
Editorial Reader: Jan Cutler
Indexer: Hilary Bird
Designer: Nigel Partridge
Photographers: Peter Anderson and Simon Smith
Home Economist: Annabel Ford
Stylist: Helen Trent
Production Controller: Wendy Lawson

Metro Books
122 Fifth Avenue
New York, NY 10011

ISBN-13: 978-1-4351-0456-3
ISBN-10: 1-4351-0456-0

Printed and bound in China

1 3 5 7 9 10 8 6 4 2

NOTES
Standard spoon and cup measures are level.

Large eggs are used unless otherwise stated.

Electric oven temperatures in this book are for conventional ovens. When using a fan oven, the temperature will probably need
to be reduced by about 20–40°F. Since ovens vary, you should check with your manufacturer's instruction book for guidance.

CONTENTS

INTRODUCTION

Organic food is the fastest growing sector of the entire food industry. Step into any supermarket and you will see an impressive array of organic produce, not tucked away at the end of an aisle, but proudly and prominently displayed. This is often the first point of contact for shoppers unfamiliar with organic food, but after experiencing the superior flavors and learning of the undeniable health benefits, many people go on to investigate home delivery, farmers' markets featuring organic produce, and small, local organic suppliers.

Interest in organic food and farming is at an all-time high. This is partly due to the fact that people are better informed about nutrition, more concerned about the environment, and more cautious about the short- and long-term effects of diet on health than at any time in the past, but there are also more fundamental reasons, such as flavor. To put it simply, we appreciate good food. This generation is more widely traveled than any previous one, and is discovering

Below: Organic sheep and lambs graze on unsprayed grass, free of pesticides.

exotic cuisines and exciting new tastes from all over the world. People eat out more, and are more adventurous when cooking at home. As palates become increasingly sophisticated, we demand more from the ingredients that make up our meals, so it is hardly surprising that we increasingly favor organic food.

But What Is Organic Food?

Organic farming is the cultivation of crops and rearing of livestock with natural soil fertility at the heart of the system. Organic farmers believe that by working hard to maintain and encourage good soil structure on their land, the crops and livestock grown and bred there will flourish. They work with nature, instead of trying to bend nature to their own purpose, so produce is grown without the routine use of pesticides or artificial fertilizers, and animals are reared without being treated with growth promoters or unnecessarily dosed with antibiotics.

If this sounds like a return to the way things used to be, it is, but only to a point. Modern organic farming is highly scientific and makes considerable use of

Above: Organic pumpkins and squash are grown free of artificial fertilizers.

technology. Research into more efficient organic farming methods is ongoing. For food to be labeled organic, it must have been produced according to strict guidelines, which are rigidly regulated.

Soil fertility is promoted by crop rotation, composting, and planting crops that supply specific nutrients. Farmers encourage predator insects, such as ladybugs, to visit by planting their favorite flowers. They may also sometimes introduce other predators to control pests biologically. When coupled with preventative methods, such as growing in plastic tunnels, where insects can be kept out, the need to use agrochemical pesticides is avoided.

Agrochemical Farming

The cultivation of crops and rearing of livestock using agrochemicals was first promoted on a large scale in the 1950s, in response to widespread food shortages during and immediately after World War II. This was a period of modernism, with technologies of all kinds being optimistically embraced. Agrochemicals held the promise of maximizing food production, so they were universally adopted. They achieved

Right: Organic cattle are less susceptible to disease because they are always free-range and have access to the outdoors.

their immediate objectives, but at a cost to the environment that is only now beginning to be fully appreciated.

Yields from organic and agrochemical farms are now almost identical, and organic yields continue to grow as a result of continued research into intensive organic agriculture. Organic farmers also benefit from access to much wider seed banks than those customarily used by agrochemical farmers, so they can select the best varieties of crops for their climate and terrain.

Organic farming now utilizes some of the same noninvasive technology as agrochemical farming. Satellites, for example, are used to predict weather patterns or map insect migrations.

The Cost of Going Organic

If yields are improving and organic food production is becoming steadily more efficient, why does organic food tend to cost more than agrochemical food? The answer lies in outdated government subsidy plans, which are based on the aspirations and knowledge of post-World War II policymakers. Agrochemical farmers receive a much higher amount of taxpayers' money than organic farmers. Historically, this was because farmers were encouraged to experiment with chemicals to increase yields. Thinking has changed radically since those days, but subsidizing policy has not altered for the last fifty years.

Farmers are actively encouraged to spray their fields with chemical pesticides and fertilizers. When these chemicals run off farms and pollute the water table, huge sums of money must be spent internationally in cleanup operations. It is not the chemical companies or the farmers who pay for this pollution management; it is the taxpayer.

Consumers pay for agrochemical products three times. First at the checkout, then—about half the price of the item again—through taxes as a subsidy to agrochemical farmers, and,

finally, through further taxes to clean up the water table. This economic breakdown does not include any costs incurred to industry through the ill health of agrochemical farm workers who have been exposed to toxins.

Organic food will continue to be marginally more expensive than agrochemical food until government policies change. However, the difference in food quality that organic food offers more than justifies this price premium. An organic apple contains more vitamins, minerals, and phytonutrients than a nonorganic apple. It also contains about 25 percent less water. It is likely to be a more interesting variety, will almost certainly taste better, and will have a

more enjoyable texture. Most importantly, it will not be coated in an untested cocktail of up to twenty artificial chemicals and waxes.

Organic Livestock

Animal welfare is a fundamental principle of organic livestock, poultry, and dairy farming. Organic animals are always free range. Because they have access to the outdoors and are not intensively reared in enclosed spaces, they are less susceptible to disease and, although farmers will take appropriate action if an animal becomes unwell, there is no need for the routine administration of antibiotics that is standard preventive practice on agrochemical farms.

Above: These cows are being reared organically, free from hormones that increase milk production or encourage growth.

Organic farmers will often use alternative medicines, such as homeopathic treatments, to cure a sick animal and inject antibiotics only as a last resort when other treatments have failed.

Organic farmers are not allowed to use hormones to encourage animal growth or increase milk production. In countries where growth hormones, such as BST (bovine somatotropin), are administered, dairy cows often have intense pain from unnaturally swollen udders. Their milk—and dairy products produced from it—contains the same hormones, increasing the consumer's risk of multigenerational cancers and hormone disruption disorders.

Fish

Organic fish, whether wild or farmed, should come from sustainable fisheries and farms, and be caught using fishing practices that protect the environment.
Wild Fish Logic dictates that all wild fish are organic, since they swim and eat where they will. However, pollution, insensitive fishing methods, and proximity

to major shipping lanes all have a detrimental effect on wild fish stocks, and there is no standard for organics in wild fish. The Marine Stewardship Council is an international organization offering an accreditation plan for sustainable wild fisheries.
Farmed Fish The conditions under which fish are farmed vary widely. For farmed fish to be labeled organic, they must be reared responsibly. This means giving them adequate room to move, letting them grow and develop naturally, and giving them organic feed. This is not the case on many agrochemical fish farms, where fish populations can be so high and intensive that infestation and disease are commonplace and chemical pesticides must be used liberally to control them. Pesticides, waste fish food, and sewage from agrochemical fish farms frequently pollute rivers and waterways, and it is not just these substances that escape. Fish get under the wire, too. In Europe, four out of every five salmon caught in rivers originated on an agrochemical farm.

Farmed fish are bred to mature later and be less aggressive than their wild counterparts in order to produce a greater yield and be easier to manage.

The damage from wild and farmed salmon interbreeding is immense, with natural fish stocks at ever increasing risk. Intensive fish farms are beginning to address these problems in many areas of the world, but to be sure that your farmed fish is produced responsibly, make sure it carries the mark of an organic certification body that you trust.

Hemp

This is a wonder crop that puts more nutrients back into the soil than it needs to grow. It is, therefore, ideal for farmers who are converting their land to organic methods. The conversion period required for organic certification can be a difficult time financially for farmers. While the land is renewing itself, farmers may not sell their produce as organic even though they are not using agrochemicals. Hemp can usefully bridge the gap by providing a crop that can be sold while improving soil fertility.

The applications of hemp are extraordinary. The ropes and sails used on the ships that first charted our seas were made of hemp. So was the first pair of Levi's jeans. Hemp also made the paper on which the original American Constitution was written. Hemp is the most versatile organic crop we have. You

Below: Organic fish are farmed carefully for the environment.

Above: Organic fruit contains more vitamins, minerals, and phytonutrients than nonorganic fruit. It also tastes better.

can make cosmetics from its oil, power cars with it, and even use it for making plastics. In fact, hemp can do anything that a hydrocarbon can do. In these times of dwindling fossil fuel reserves, hemp is potentially a major part of the solution because it actually reduces greenhouse gases, it manufactures oxygen when it grows, and it can easily be processed into a powerful fuel source to rival oil.

Hemp seed is the only complete vegetable protein known, with a nutritional makeup that is even more balanced than soya. Sixty-five percent of the protein in hemp is in globular edestin form, which is the most easily digestible form of protein. The typical oil content of hemp seeds consists of 60 percent Omega-6; 20 percent Omega-3 and 10 percent Omega essential fatty acids (EFAs). This is seen as the most suitable ratio of dietary fat for long-term human consumption. Hemp seed oil also contains GLA, the active constituent of evening primrose oil. This makes the oil ideal for the treatment of PMS, eczema, joint conditions and even some cancers.

NOT EVERYTHING ORGANIC IS FOOD!

Nonorganic cotton and tobacco are two pesticide-dependent crops grown widely in the Americas and in developing countries. Dangers to the consumer from agrochemicals used in the cultivation of nonfood crops are minimal, but when the soil's natural fertility is undermined by artificial fertilizers, farmers become reliant on agrochemicals. Concerns are high for farm workers in developing countries exposed to pesticides deemed too strong for use on food crops. Where protective clothing is absent, they have a higher than average incidence of cancers and respiratory conditions. There is also a high rate of early mortality among the farmers themselves.

Organic cotton and tobacco are available. The Scandinavian Oeko-Tex mark is an assurance that fabrics are organic or sustainable. The American Spirit tobacco company manufactures organic cigarettes.

Seeds and garden flowers are two more areas of environmental concern. Because it is vital that no weed seeds contaminate the product, agrochemical seed producers spray their crops liberally with herbicides.

Cut flowers are not regulated as stringently as food crops, so farm workers and the environment can lose out. Buying organically grown flowers benefits both the people who grew them and the planet.

Left: Hemp products include beauty products, such as soaps, moisturizers, and loofahlike scrubs.

Organically grown grape hyacinths

WHY GO ORGANIC?

There are dozens—many would say hundreds—of excellent reasons for choosing the organic option. Apart from benefits to the individual in terms of health, avoidance of chemicals and the sheer enjoyment of eating food that is full of flavor, there are environmental issues to consider, as well as moral questions, such as animal welfare, the health of farm workers, and fair trade.

Improved Health

All organic food is good for you. Fresh organic produce contains more vitamins, minerals, enzymes, and other micronutrients than intensively farmed produce. It also tastes better. Organic fruits and vegetables are full of juice and flavor, and there are many different

Below: Organic cauliflower, cabbage, broccoli, and Brussels sprouts are high in glucosinolates, which help prevent cancer.

varieties to try. Organic meat, poultry, and dairy produce are of excellent quality and usually lower in saturated fat.
Vitamins and Minerals The reason why fresh organic produce contains more vitamins and minerals than the agrochemical equivalent is largely due to the method of cultivation. Unlike agrochemical fruits and vegetables, which are sprayed with artificial fertilizers that force the plants to grow quickly, even in inferior soil, organic fruits and vegetables are allowed to grow and ripen more naturally in richer soil, obtaining the maximum variety of micronutrients.

These micronutrients are also more concentrated in organic fruits and vegetables because they contain much less water than agrochemical produce.
Phytonutrients Organic produce is rich in naturally occurring chemical compounds known as phytonutrients. These are found in fresh fruits and vegetables and

help to fight disease and promote good health. More research is needed to pinpoint the precise benefits of all these compounds, but much is already known. Glucosinolates in cabbage, broccoli, cauliflower, and Brussels sprouts help to prevent cancer. Flavonoids are powerful antioxidants. The strongest flavonoids are found in onions and garlic. Eating onions and garlic regularly significantly reduces the risk of heart disease and the spread of cancer.

While all fresh produce contains phytonutrients, organic produce contains more than its nonorganic equivalent. This is because all plants produce phyto-nutrients as part of their natural defense against pests. If a plant is protected from pests by agrochemicals, there is no need for it to produce phytochemicals in the same quantity. Also, studies have found that when plants take up high levels of nitrogen from the soil, they produce

Above: Just some of the fruits available organically: apples, grapes, pineapple, oranges, kiwi, and passion fruit.

fewer and less diverse phytonutrients. Agrochemical crops are liberally sprayed with nitrogen fertilizers to make them grow quicker, whereas organic crops are grown in more balanced and less nitrogen-rich soil.

Fats Hydrogenated fats are oils that have had hydrogen added to them so that they become solid or semisolid at room temperature. They are widely used in the food industry despite the fact that nutritionists universally agree that they are a major cofactor in heart disease, cancer, diabetes, and obesity. The best way to remove hydrogenated fats from your diet is to go organic. Organic food regulations throughout the world prohibit the use of hydrogenated fats.

Eating too much saturated fat is a contributing factor in cardiovascular diseases, such as heart attacks and stroke. Saturated fat is present in organic beef as well as in intensively reared beef, but the percentage is likely to be lower. Saturated fat is also easier to remove from organic beef. In intensively reared cattle, saturated fat is more evenly distributed, so is harder to cut away when you are preparing the meat for cooking. Because it clogs up your arteries, the more saturated fat you can remove from your food the better.

Meat, poultry, eggs, and milk from grass-fed animals also contain more conjugated linoleic acid, or CLA. This substance helps those who consume it to maintain a healthy weight, and studies have shown that it reduces the risk of heart disease and may help to prevent cancer. So although organic meat contains saturated fat, it also contains CLA to balance it.

The Balanced Diet
A wholesome, organic diet provides balanced nutrition, including a healthy range of vitamins, minerals, and phytonutrients. This is an important consideration in a world where many people opt for convenience foods that are often high in fat and sugar and offer little in terms of nutrition. The body craves the nutrients it lacks, and this can drive people to overeat, yet remain malnourished. There is a direct correlation between overconsumption malnutrition trends in industrialized nations and eating nonorganic food. Obesity epidemics have occurred in countries that rely on agrochemicals to grow and process their foods.

Improved Immunity There is evidence to suggest that people who eat organic food build up a stronger immunity to disease than those who consistently eat food that is laden with chemicals. Eating overprocessed, nonorganic junk food puts a strain on immune systems already compromised by living in a polluted world, forcing the liver and kidneys to work harder to remove the toxins they frequently contain.

A New Zealand report into the possible benefits of an organic diet suggested that people who follow an organic diet benefit from a very marked decline in influenza and experienced far fewer colds and catarrhal problems than other members of the population. Further reported benefits included clear, healthy skin, improved dental health, and excellent general health.

Below: Organic eggs are high in linoleic acid, which helps maintain a healthy weight.

Above: Eating an organic diet before conception and during pregnancy will help rid the body of toxins.

Increased Fertility Studies appear to support a link between organic diets and increased fertility in men. The World Health Organization estimates that the average sperm count for male adults is about 66 million/ml. Two recent studies recorded that men who eat organic food have between 99 and 127 million sperm/ml. More research is needed to confirm these findings. However, the fact that a balanced organic diet is more nutritionally sound and contains fewer chemicals or artificial hormones than a nonorganic diet is bound to offer the best option for men—and women—wanting to support their sexual health and improve their chances of conceiving.

Avoiding the Chemical Cocktail

The average adult living in one of the industrialized nations has between 300 and 500 agrochemical pesticides in his or her body at any one time. Each of these toxic chemicals is stored in body fat, and each is toxic enough to kill insects. In combination, they are

certainly more poisonous. Pesticides can remain stored in body fat for many years. No long-term studies have truly evaluated the damage to our health that these chemicals pose, but there is evidence to suggest that they exacerbate chronic conditions and seriously undermine health.

Children are particularly susceptible to agrochemical toxins. They have a higher intake of food than adults in relation to their body weight, and their bodies are less efficient at eliminating toxins. Breast milk from mothers whose diets are not organic generally contains concentrations of pesticides. These have been shown to adversely affect brain development in babies. Ideally, a woman planning to conceive a child should adopt an organic diet at least one year before becoming pregnant. This gives her body time to detoxify, helping to create a healthier environment for the fetus to grow in and then purer breast milk for the baby once it has been born.

Artificial Additives Every year, the average American eats more than four pounds of chemical food additives. Seven thousand artificial additives are permitted to be used in conventional food. Only seven of these—the most innocuous—are allowed to be used in processed organic food. Artificial additives are used by manufacturers to improve the shelf life, flavor, color, sweetness, and saltiness of nonorganic

Below: Organic fruits and vegetables, on sale at a local farmers' market, are fresh and full of goodness.

processed foods. Flavor enhancers may be added to disguise inferior quality ingredients. Although some artificial additives are absolutely harmless, many undermine our health. Generally, they are used in combination, unleashing an unresearched toxic combination upon the consumer, which may well have implications in terms of cancer, asthma, liver disease, and osteoporosis.

When food deteriorates naturally, you can see at a glance when it is past its best. Preservatives may artificially prolong a food's shelf life, but they do not prolong the life of all the nutrients within the product. When preservatives are banned, as in processed organic food, you can be sure that as long as the food is fresh, it is full of goodness.

Antibiotics and Hormones Intensively reared livestock are routinely fed and injected with antibiotics to keep them healthy. These substances pass into their meat. People who eat this meat develop reduced immunity through over-exposure to antibiotics. On the other hand, bacteria that become overexposed to antibiotics become increasingly resistant to them. The British Medical Association has stated that: "The risk to human health of antibiotic resistance…is one of the major health threats that could be faced in the twenty-first century."

Hormones and endocrine disrupting chemicals (EDCs) also pose a threat to health. Five out of the twelve most commonly used pesticides in the world are known to be EDCs. This means that they are known to affect the delicate balance of human hormones. Some women in Hawaii have extremely high rates of breast cancer. Hawaii also has a high rate of zenoestrogens from pesticides in its groundwater. A Danish scientific study, which tracked more than seven hundred Hawaiian women over twenty years, concluded that there is a probable link between the pesticides in the water and breast cancers.

There is also evidence that growth hormones from intensively farmed meat can lead to a wide variety of human endocrine disorders, from obesity to multigenerational cancers.

Food Safety

All organic animals that are naturally vegetarian are fed only vegetarian food. This was a huge benefit during Britain's BSE (Bovine Spongiform Encephalopathy) crisis. BSE was caused and spread because cows were fed contaminated food, which was itself animal in origin. All organic farms are completely BSE-free because organic cows are always fed food that is 100 percent vegetarian.

Organic meat and dairy produce is free from genetically modified organisms, or GMOs, because all food for organic animals must be GMO-free by law. The diet of organic animals is also solvent-free. This may seem obvious until it is considered that nonorganic animals regularly eat food contaminated with solvents. Nonorganic cooking oil is usually produced by soaking oil-rich vegetable matter in solvents. The oil is then extracted from the liquid, and the remaining solid matter is used for animal feed. Solvent-extracted animal feed is banned from organic farms.

Natural Flavors

During 2000, 43 percent of consumers who bought organic food in Britain declared that they did so because they thought it tasted better than nonorganic

Above: Heirloom and rare varieties of potatoes are appearing at markets as organic farmers seek out new crops.

food. Tastes vary from person to person, but there are sound reasons why organic food tastes better.

Most agrochemical crops are grown from seeds bred to produce a high yield. Organic fresh produce, however, comes from seeds bred primarily for flavor. Many organic farmers take pride in growing heirloom crops. These crops were once highly prized but have been overlooked in recent years because they were less commercially profitable than modern varieties. Organic growers in industrialized nations regularly produce about a hundred different kinds of potato. This is considerably fewer than the thousand or more varieties on sale at the farmer's market in the town of Cuzco in Peru, but at least five times more than the twenty or so varieties of agrochemically grown potatoes on sale in the United States or Britain.

The slower growth rates of organic crops allow more time for flavor to develop naturally. Phytonutrients often help to flavor the fresh produce in which they occur so, as well as being good for health, high levels of certain

Above: *Flowers planted among vegetables encourage the predator insects that control pests in an environmentally friendly fashion.*

phytonutrients boost the taste factor. Sugar levels are often slightly higher in organic fresh produce than in nonorganic varieties; this is particularly obvious in carrots and apples. Organic fruit is more likely to be allowed to ripen naturally on the tree, granting more time for flavors and sweetness to develop.

The lower percentage of water in organic fresh produce concentrates the nutrients and intensifies the flavor. If you were to evaporate all the water from an agrochemical carrot and an organic carrot of equal weight, the remaining dry matter from the organic carrot would be some 26 percent heavier.

Food animals raised organically also benefit from growing more slowly than their agrochemical equivalents, and their meat becomes more flavorsome during the lengthy process. Another reason why meat from organic farms tastes better is because flavor is an important factor in selecting which type of animal to raise, and farmers are increasingly choosing the

Right: *Fresh produce grown in an organic vegetable garden is an excellent option for the health-conscious consumer.*

traditional heritage breeds that are noted for the tastiness of their meat above yield.

Organic prepared foods are allowed to contain very few of the chemical flavorings and flavor enhancers found in nonorganic foods. Monosodium glutamate, for instance, is outlawed in organic food. This substance, commonly known as MSG, has been linked to nausea, dizziness, and even asthma attacks. Organic foods taste so good that they do not need flavor enhancers.

Although much organic produce is currently grown a long way from the point of sale, it is best to buy it fresh from local producers. Not only will it have the finest flavor and highest concentration of nutrients, it will not contribute to pollution by having to be transported long distances. The range of fruits and vegetables may not be as great as that available in supermarkets, but the pleasure of enjoying seasonal treats, such as strawberries in summer, is more than adequate compensation.

Animal Welfare

Organic farm animals and poultry are treated with respect, without recourse to artificial hormones, antibiotics, or routine drug therapies. Inhumane practices, such as overcrowded poultry houses, are banned. Dairy cows raised

organically have, on average, 50 percent more room in their barns than nonorganic cows, and unlike the latter, they are always provided with bedding. They also enjoy much more time outdoors. The same holds true for organic poultry.

Wildlife and the Environment

Our environment is under immense threat. Over the last thirty years, intensive farming in many countries has led to dramatic erosion of the soil. Bird populations have declined, and some species of butterflies, frogs, grass snakes, and wild mammals have been brought near extinction. Wild flowers and shrubs that once flourished in the fields are now seldom seen. In Britain, intensive farmers dug up ancient hedges that surround their fields to allow access for their giant machinery.

Organic farmers actively promote biodiversity by cherishing hedges, not just for their natural beauty, but for the practical support they offer. They play a vital role in supplying a habitat for the birds and insects that an organic farm needs in order to function. Wild flowers at the edge of a field attract butterflies and useful predators to the crop, so organic farmers always keep a strip of wild land around a field. Intensive farmers destroy resources such as these, either mechanically or by using

Above: A willow fence forms a natural field boundary and encourages butterflies.

pesticides. Many chemical pesticides are directly related to nerve gases. They are designed to kill. Those pests that survive being drenched with pesticides may develop immunity. Stronger pesticides must be developed and this leads to an ever-increasing cycle.

Although agrochemical farmers use pesticides to target specific pests, they are toxic to many creatures. Small mammals and birds are often killed or weakened by agricultural pesticides. Equally damaging are agrochemical seeds that have been treated with organochlorides in an attempt to prevent them from being eaten. These highly poisonous chemicals, which last for years in the environment, kill many birds and animals every year.

Chemicals sprayed on crops eventually either penetrate the plants or trickle down into the soil, polluting the land and draining into the water table. The poisons then flow into streams and rivers, polluting the ecosystem. Agrochemical fertilizers are just as damaging to the ecosystem as pesticides. Nitrate-based fertilizers also seep out of the fields into the water system. In rivers and lakes, they stimulate the growth of algae. Excessive algae throws the whole ecosystem out of balance, poisoning waterways.

Farm Workers' Health and Fair Trade

On agrochemical farms, especially those in such developing countries as India, workers are often at direct risk from pesticide pollution. Protective clothing and machinery is expensive, whereas pesticide chemicals are relatively cheap. The result is that many farm workers are forced to apply these poisons to crops while unprotected. It is not only the farm workers themselves who are at risk—pesticides also endanger the general population.

Many farm workers in developing nations are exposed to horrifying amounts of poisons every day from childhood onward. Pesticide exposure can lead to multigenerational diseases and cancers. The children of farm workers are more likely to have genetic defects that continue to successive generations. The workers often receive only subsistence wages for working long and back-breakingly hard days. In some countries, the average age of death for farm workers is around fifty.

Going organic avoids supporting these types of injustices. Using spending power sensitively is a direct way of working toward a fairer trading world. Many organic products are fairly traded, which means that a buyer will offer a reasonable price for crops. The majority

of trading between the developed and the developing world does not currently follow this principle. A cash-poor farmer may be forced to sell his crop for less than its worth because he does not have the bargaining power of a multinational company. For assurance that an organic product is fairly traded, look out for the Fairtrade seal and consult your supplier or storekeeper.

Packaging

While packaging provides a valuable method of food preservation without the use of additives, unnecessary packaging is wasteful and environmentally insensitive. Many smaller organic companies are beginning to use recycled and recyclable containers for their products, but too many organic foods are still wrapped in the same plastics and bleached non-recycled papers as nonorganic products.

Lobbying these organic companies to change their practices can help, but it is equally vital that organic consumers make every effort to recycle their waste. Glass, aluminum, and paper are all candidates for recycling. Shopping bags can be reused, and a compost container is ideal for disposing of waste organic matter.

Below: Recycling organic waste matter in by composting is good for the environment and enriches the soil of any garden.

THE ORGANIC KITCHEN

The organic cook has a vast array of ingredients, from fresh fruits and vegetables to fine quality meat and pantry staples. Take the same care with preparation as you do with selection and storage and you'll be rewarded with delicious dishes. Exploring the range of organic fresh and pantry items is a rewarding experience. If you buy fresh produce direct from the grower, ask the names of varieties so you can seek out your favorites. The selection that follows is not intended to be an exhaustive guide to every organic item, but it does introduce some of the best buys from organic growers and producers around the world.

FRESH PRODUCE

Good fruits and vegetables are at the heart of organic cuisine. The main point of agreement between health experts and nutritionists throughout the world is that we need to eat more fruits and vegetables. The United Nations World Health Organization has stated that if you eat five portions of fresh produce every day, you halve your chances of getting cancer.

If you can't afford to buy organic produce every day, it is better for you to supplement your diet with nonorganic alternatives than to cut back on fruits and vegetables. Organic fresh produce is, however, nutritionally richer, tastier, and more diverse. As well as the usual varieties on sale, you will find rare heirloom types of fruits and vegetables.

There is a huge global market for both organic and agrochemical produce,

Below: Stock up on fresh organic vegetables at local farmers' markets.

and imported fruits and vegetables often travel thousands of miles before they reach our shores. Because demand for organic produce is growing at such a high rate in industrialized countries, many organic fruits and vegetables are likely to have been transported long distances.

Local Produce
If you can get it, it is better to buy locally grown produce. There are two main reasons why this is superior to imported organic fruits and vegetables: nutrition and the need to avoid increasing pollution.

Locally grown food is more nutritious than food that has been flown in from another country. Fruits and vegetables for export are often picked before they are fully ripe and kept chilled to avoid spoilage. This means that they fail to develop the complex flavors and nutritional compounds available in produce that has been allowed to ripen naturally and has been freshly picked

Above: Growing your own organic herbs will add taste and nutrition to your cooking.

and transported no farther than to the nearest farmers' market. Also, organic standards vary in different countries. Some are not as stringent as others in terms of conversion periods from agrochemical to organic farming, or in nurturing natural soil fertility.

The other major advantage of buying locally grown organic produce is to avoid contributing to pollution. Long-distance transportation of food, whether it be organic or agrochemical, currently uses enormous quantities of petrochemicals, to fuel airplanes, ships, or road vehicles. Burning fossil fuels is the antithesis of the organic ideal. Major ecological advances, such as fuel cell technology, are in the pipeline for green transportation. However, as long as petrochemicals power organic food imports, it is preferable to buy locally grown organic produce where possible.

That said, buying imported organic fruit is sometimes the only option. Citrus trees do not grow outdoors in cool climates, and date palms prefer arid climates to wet ones. Supplementing locally grown organic produce in season with the occasional imported organic treat is probably a good balance for most organic connoisseurs.

Growing and Buying
The best way to take advantage of the hundreds of different varieties of organic fruits and vegetables is to grow your own. Whether you have a couple of tubs on the patio, a vegetable plot or an impressive garden, preparing the soil,

Above: Freshly dug organic potatoes have a flavor all of their own.

nurturing the plants, and then reaping the harvest is richly rewarding. The pleasures of gardening aside, the fresher the produce, the tastier and more nutritious it will be.

If you don't have a green thumb, the best way to ensure that vegetables and fruits are fresh is to buy them from a local farmers' market or through a home-delivery plan. Such plans are operated by small individual growers or cooperatives. Customers opt for regular deliveries, either specifying which seasonal vegetables and fruits they would like to receive, or paying a set amount each week and leaving the selection of produce to the grower. The arrival of the delivery is then a delightful surprise, and often there will be extras, such as a few fresh herbs, a small box of berries, or some garlic.

Buying Direct

One key benefit of buying fruits and vegetables direct from the grower is to maintain a valid connection with our food. Purchasing vegetables from the man who grew them allows information about the produce to be exchanged. Stories about an individual crop can be passed on and cooking tips and recipes shared. A farmer might also welcome feedback on a new variety that he is experimenting with, and customers can let him know which fruits or vegetables they have particularly enjoyed.

Children who have watched carrots being lifted or have sifted through sacks of potatoes with soil still clinging to

them, will soon make the connection between their food and the place it comes from, and will be much more likely to enjoy their organic greens.

Farmers get a better deal selling their organic food directly. Not only do they get a better price at a farmers' market than they would from the supermarket, but they enjoy the contact with the townsfolk who tuck into their produce. Never before has the connection between urban and rural societies been so weak. Farmers' markets and home deliveries help to bridge the gap.

Supermarkets

It is possible, of course, to shop at the supermarket. While it is heartening that supermarkets are providing greater access to organic fresh produce than before, it is useful to be aware of a couple of negative aspects. Supermarkets generally spray nonorganic produce with pesticides after it has left the field to ensure that stores remain free of insects. And, to avoid contamination of organic produce, they have to protect it in plastic packaging. This does not alter the organic status of the produce but the packaging does contribute to the environmental pollution that organic farming techniques aim to minimize. With increased public pressure, larger supermarket chains are likely to address this issue.

Another point to consider is that of food miles. Supermarkets tend to pool their products at central depots. This makes for easier distribution, but can be very wasteful of fuel and energy. An organic potato grown near Town A might have been driven to a central washing plant hundreds of miles away, near Town B. It may then be driven to the central supermarket distribution depot a similar distance away in Town C, only to be transported back to Town A for sale in the supermarket there.

Right: Some packaging, such as this mug and spoon made out of recycled paper, is not harmful to the environment.

CONVENIENCE FOODS

Enthusiastic organic cooks would doubtless prefer always to buy and cook fresh ingredients, but there are occasions when it is useful to have ready-made meals and frozen foods at hand. The wide range of organic convenience foods extends to pasta sauces, soups, TV dinners, and freshly prepared sandwiches.

Organic convenience products are unlikely to be as tasty or nutritionally balanced as organic foods prepared at home, but they are better for you than the nonorganic alternative. They contain only a small number of artificial additives and are prohibited from containing hydrogenated fats. Such foods may not be irradiated and are not allowed to contain genetically modified ingredients.

Many nonorganic processed foods contain excessive levels of refined white sugar and salt, both of which should be avoided. The quick energy rush provided by white sugar is followed always by energy depletion. Complex, natural unrefined sweeteners, such as organic fruit syrups, produce a far more balanced response from the body. Too much salt raises blood pressure, increasing the risk of heart disease and strokes. The majority of organic prepared foods offer a safe level of salt, but it is important to check the salt and sugar content on the label of all convenience products.

The good news is that some convenience foods, such as frozen organic fruits and vegetables, can be more nutritious than the fresh nonorganic equivalent. This is because produce is frozen within hours of being picked, whereas fresh nonorganic produce may have been picked many days before.

Storing Fresh Fruits and Vegetables

It is very important to store organic produce carefully because it will not keep as long as nonorganic examples.

Store ripe fruit in a cool place, away from direct sunlight. Green bananas will ripen within a couple of days if they are stored in a plastic bag with an overripe banana. Some fruits, such as tomatoes, kiwis, and avocados, can be placed on a sunny windowsill to help them ripen. This also brings out the flavor and encourages their natural juices to flow.

Most fresh vegetables are best stored in the refrigerator. Salad greens, including lettuce, arugula, and spinach, should be eaten within a few days of purchase. Root vegetables should be left unwashed because the soil or mud coating helps to keep them fresh. Moisture is retained within the root or tuber, so unwashed carrots, turnips, and potatoes keep for much longer than the shiny, scrubbed vegetables that look so pretty but perish so much quicker.

Right:: Making flavorful juices from fresh fruits and vegetables is easy and delicious, as in this power booster mix of apple, carrot, and beet (back). Blend cucumber, tomatoes, garlic, and lemon juice for an energizing summer drink (front).

Cooking Organic Fruits and Vegetables

Cooking fruit reduces valuable vitamins and minerals, so, if you can, eat it raw. Overcooking vegetables depletes their nutritional value, destroys their texture, impairs their flavor, and spoils their natural color. It is always advisable to steam vegetables instead of boil them. Boiling vegetables destroys up to half their nutrients, although this figure can be reduced if the vegetables are cooked whole and sliced afterward. Better still, serve vegetables raw. They will contain many more enzymes than if cooked. Enzymes help us to digest the micronutrients in fresh produce, so, apart from potatoes, aim to cook for as short a time as possible.

Juicing

If you need to use up a stock of fruits or vegetables quickly, simply juice them. This is the most direct way of accessing the nutrients. Any vegetables can be mixed together satisfactorily, but apples are the only fruit that work well with vegetables. By the same token, any combination of fruits can be juiced, but if you want to add a vegetable, make it a carrot. Following these rules ensures that juices do not curdle and are refreshing, delicious, and nutritious.

Preserving

For added variety during the winter months, you can preserve organic fruits. Marmalades and jams are easy to make. Drying slices of fruit, such as apples, by baking them overnight in the oven on a very low heat maintains much of the nutritional value while concentrating the taste. It is important to use organic fruits when preserving, because the peel is included. All kinds of organic dried fruits can be bought, from apricots to bananas and mangoes. Nonorganic dried fruits are generally treated with sulfur, fungicides, and mineral oils, whereas organic varieties are preserved naturally.

Left: Pickling is a great way to preserve extra stocks of all kinds of vegetables, including garlic, small onions, and shallots.

ONIONS

This family of plants includes onions, leeks, chives, and garlic, all of which owe their characteristic odor and flavor to a compound called allicin. Organic onions contain more allicin than their nonorganic counterparts, so have stronger flavors and more health benefits. Organic onions are sweeter, and organic garlic is more pungent. Unfortunately, allicin is also the constituent in onions that makes us cry, so organic onions should be chopped at arm's length—or by someone else!

Onions help to lower cholesterol. They also have antibacterial qualities and can help to relieve asthma, bronchitis, and other sinus and chest ailments. The cycloallin they contain is an anticoagulant, which thins the blood and helps to protect the heart. Onions also have antifungal properties; the juice can be rubbed onto the skin to relieve fungal infections. Garlic is the most powerful healer of the onions and has been praised for its medicinal powers for hundreds of years, but all members of the family contain some allicin, so they all have beneficial qualities.

All onions should be stored in a cool place. It is important to keep them dry or they will begin to sprout. Organic onions keep just as well as nonorganic ones. The wide variety of onions can be enjoyed raw or cooked and, with garlic, add flavor to many dishes.

Below: Red onions have been shown to cut cholesterol radically.

Above: A bunch of baby leeks is a bonus in the fall.

Above: Scallions are at their most nutritious when they are raw.

Onions
These are indispensable in the organic kitchen and form the basis of innumerable savory dishes, including salads, stews, soups, and gravies. There are many varieties, including big Bermuda onions and small, sweet red onions. Add onions on the side when making a classic organic cooked breakfast. Not only do they taste delicious with bacon and sausages, but they have been shown to cut cholesterol radically.

Garlic
Although it is the most powerful healer of the onion family, this is not garlic's only attribute. It also has a superb flavor. Both hardneck (or topsetting) and softneck varieties are on sale in the organic market, and there is a wealth of taste and color to explore. Hardneck garlic has a central woody stem surrounded by five to ten easy-to-peel cloves. It has a richer, more rounded flavor than softneck garlic, which is the type you often find twisted together, French fashion, to form braids. Softneck garlic has a spicy flavor. Each bulb contains a seemingly endless amount of increasingly smaller cloves.

This type of garlic can be stored for up to a year, unlike hardneck garlic, which must be used within six months. Fresh organic garlic is available but it is at its best when dried and cured. When the thin skin is papery dry, the cloves are mature and will burst with flavor. Look for a firm head when buying garlic.

Above: Garlic

Leeks
A bunch of sweet, young leeks is a bonus in the fall. Although they are good enough to eat raw, they also taste great when lightly steamed or sautéed with garlic.

Scallions and Chives
These vegetables taste delicious, especially when raw, which is also when they are at their most nutritious. Organic growers often sell bunches of thin, young scallions, which make delicious snacks.

TUBERS

Whether you are shopping for potatoes, yacons, or Jerusalem artichokes, you'll be spoiled for choice because there are many more varieties of organic tubers available than the few agrochemical types.

Potatoes

A farmers' market or home-delivery box plan will provide opportunities to sample unusual types of organic potatoes. There are huge variations in the size and flavor of potatoes, and colors include yellow, red, pink, purple, and black. There are two textures: waxy and starchy. Common waxy varieties include new potatoes, White Rose, and Rose Fir. Russet Burbank and other russets are starchy. Yukon Gold and Alaskan Sweetheart are also good.

All potatoes are a good source of vitamin C and the B group vitamins.

Organic potatoes are helpful in supporting the body's natural resistance and keeping energy levels steady. Their peel can safely be eaten, boosting fiber levels, nutrition, and flavor.

Waxy potatoes are ideal for frying and steaming, while starchy potatoes are better for mashing or creaming. Use starchy potatoes in leek and potato soup or for French fries that are soft in the middle, and waxy new potatoes as a springtime accompaniment for lamb chops. Potatoes should be stored in a dark, cool place that is perfectly dry.

Jerusalem Artichokes

Widely available in the fall months, these delicious vegetables have an unusual, slightly bitter yet buttery flavor, and are excellent served alone or added to dishes. Their bitterness is due to the presence of a compound called cynarine. This is a powerful liver stimulant, so eating Jerusalem artichokes will

Above: Jerusalem artichokes help detoxify the body.

support liver action, helping to detoxify the body. Organic Jerusalem artichokes also help to alleviate rheumatism and arthritis. Try Jerusalem artichokes lightly steamed with fish, or mashed with potatoes and rutabagas.

Sweet Potatoes

When cooked, sweet potatoes become sticky and soft with a gorgeous, smooth taste. Organic varieties are particularly sweet and are an excellent source of vitamins, including vitamins C, E, and betacarotene, which helps to prevent cancer. They encourage eye and skin health, too. Because organic sweet potatoes are free of fungicides, they can be scrubbed and cooked whole for a wonderfully caramelized alternative to the ubiquitous baked potato. They are also good when steamed and mashed in the same way as regular potatoes.

Yacon Tubers

Almost all yacon tubers are organic. A staple food of the people of the Andes, they can be savored cooked or raw. They are a good source of complex carbohydrates, with a lot of vitamins and minerals. Their crunchy flesh is sweet and juicy like that of a water chestnut or jicama. Try them sliced or grated in leaf or rice salads. When steamed or roasted, the yacon becomes even sweeter. Yacons are not widely available, but can be found through box plans and at farmers' markets. Store them in the vegetable drawer of the refrigerator.

Above: Sweet potatoes are a good source of vitamins, including vitamins C, E, and betacarotene.

Below: Organic farmers produce many varieties of white and red potatoes.

ROOTS

The roots are a plant's powerhouse, and root vegetables provide us with a delicious way of tapping into this energy store. Organic root vegetables are often more knobbly and curly than agrochemically grown root vegetables. They deliver more nutrition and flavor than their more uniform counterparts, as well as being more individual in appearance.

All root vegetables should be stored unwashed. As with tubers, a layer of soil helps to seal moisture and nutrients into the roots.

Below: Rutabaga contains vitamins A and C.

Carrots
Organically grown carrots are extremely high in betacarotenes, giving them a rich orange color. Celebrate this with a sweet Middle Eastern salad. Grate four small carrots and mix with the juice of one orange, a few sesame seeds, and 1 teaspoon of honey. Or simply steam lightly or add to stews and stir-fries.

Below: Turnips are credited with soothing aching joints.

Parsnips
Organic parsnips are fragrant and intense. When roasted, they caramelize more successfully than non-organic ones because they are sweeter. Their flavor concentrates and the texture becomes chewy, with a crunch at the tip.

Rutabaga and Turnips
There is nothing more comforting on a cold winter night than mashed rutabaga with a little butter and seasoning. Organic turnips have a subtle flavor, underpinned with a bitter edge that people love or hate. They are delicious lightly steamed and served as a side dish for fish. Turnips deliver calcium and potassium and are credited with soothing aching joints.

Beets
Organic beets come in an amazing variety of types. From yellow mangels to the chioggia beet, these are the most colorful root vegetables. Young beets taste very good when served raw and grated. Alternatively, roast them with a medley of other root vegetables.

Left: Radishes are a good source of anticancer phytochemicals.

Radishes
When grown organically, radishes are very hot and spicy. They also have more concentrated amounts of anticancer phytochemicals. Traditionally, radishes are eaten to stimulate the gall bladder to manufacture digestive juices. The many varieties range from Japanese daikon to the classic red cherry belle. As with all root vegetables, any sign of springiness indicates that a radish is not fresh. Radishes are delicious sliced raw in salads, especially with watercress or arugula, and are also good in stir-fries.

MAKING A BASIC VEGETABLE STOCK
Homemade stock is a healthier option than the store-bought version and is easy to make. It can be stored in the refrigerator for up to four days. Alternatively, prepare it in large quantities and freeze.

INGREDIENTS
1 tablespoon olive oil
1 potato, chopped
1 carrot, chopped
1 onion, chopped
1 celery stalk, chopped
2 garlic cloves, peeled
1 sprig thyme
1 bay leaf
a few stalks of parsley
2½ cups water
salt and freshly ground pepper

1 Heat the oil in a large pan. Add the vegetables and cook, covered, for 10 minutes, or until softened, stirring occasionally. Stir in the garlic and herbs.

2 Pour the water into the pan, bring to a boil, and simmer, partially covered, for 40 minutes. Strain, season with salt and pepper, and use as required.

PUMPKINS and SQUASHES

Organic farmers grow many more varieties of pumpkins and squashes than agrochemical farmers. Summer squashes include the thin-skinned zucchini, which can be allowed to grow extra large, and patty pans, while winter brings the heavyweights, such as pumpkins and acorn squashes, with their glowing colors, thick skins, and superb keeping properties. The natural sweetness of these vegetables makes them a favorite with small children. To cook, simply cut open, scoop out the seeds, slice into cubes, and steam or roast until soft.

Right: Organic large zucchini and other summer squashes have a pleasant mild flavor.

Zucchini and Summer Squash

Organic zucchini and other summer squashes range in color from pale yellow to deep green. They are easy to grow in a garden or on a balcony, and are readily available in stores and farmers' markets. Slice them into salads, or fry with onions, garlic, coriander, and paprika for a quick side dish. Large summer squashes are best baked. Try stuffing them with brown rice, almonds, onions, and cheese.

Summer squashes are effective diuretics and their potassium content helps to relieve high blood pressure.

Right: Zucchini can help to relieve high blood pressure.

Pumpkins

Classic round orange pumpkins are full of betacarotene. This has been proven scientifically to help prevent cancer, particularly lung cancer. Pumpkin seeds can be washed, seasoned, and roasted for a delicious snack that is rich in protein, minerals, and the B vitamins. Shell them after roasting to enjoy their nutty flavor, and reap the benefits of their protective action on the human reproductive system.

Above: Pumpkins are full of betacarotene, which has been scientifically proven to help prevent cancer.

ROASTING SQUASH

Cooking squash in this way brings out its flavor and retains its goodness.

1 Preheat the oven to 400°F. Cut the squash in half, scoop out the seeds, and place it cut side down on an oiled baking sheet.

2 Bake for 30 minutes, or until the flesh is soft. Serve in the skin, or remove the flesh and mash with butter and seasoning.

GREENS

Green-leaf vegetables, such as cabbages, broccoli, chard, Brussels sprouts, and cauliflower, are among the best sources of phytochemicals when organic. They help to defend the body against cancer, and should be eaten every day if possible. Leaf vegetables are a rich source of vitamins and minerals, too, including vitamin C, calcium, iron, and betacarotene.

Agrochemical green-leaf vegetables are heavily sprayed with the strongest fungicides, insecticides, and herbicides. Some include a compound, lindane, which is banned in the United States but still used in other countries. Organic vegetables are not sprayed in this way. They are nutritionally richer, with a more complex phytochemical profile and a more complex flavor. Lightly steamed or freshly stir-fried, they are full of color, crunch, and vitality.

Below: Organic cabbages are among the best sources of phytochemicals.

Cauliflowers

When grown organically, cauliflowers are often small, around the size of tennis balls. Try to find vegetables that still have their outer leaves. The leaves should be green instead of yellow to indicate freshness, and they are a usable part of the cauliflower. Remove them from the cauliflower head and steam for a few minutes.

Above: Organic cauliflowers are often small, which was how they looked when they were first cultivated.

Below: Spinach is high in folic acid.

Swiss Chard and Spinach

Vegetarians and vegans are advised to eat chard and spinach regularly. Swiss chard is a rich, deep green with bright red or creamy white veins, and is almost exclusively found organically grown. Rich in iron, calcium, vitamins A and C, and carotenes, Swiss chard is excellent for menstruating women and also as a treatment for anemia.

Organic spinach is available as savoy (crinkled), semi-savoy, or smooth. A superb source of chlorophyll and folic acid, it is an excellent food for preconception and pregnancy.

To prepare, cut chard leaves away from their stems. Steam the stems for two to three minutes, adding the leaves at the end for only a few seconds. Likewise, steam spinach for only 20 to 30 seconds because the delicate leaves wilt almost immediately. Alternatively, lightly fry the leaves in organic olive oil or butter for a few moments, or eat smooth spinach leaves raw in a salad.

Cabbages

These versatile vegetables come in a variety of organic types, from wrinkly Savoy King to smooth purple red cabbages. Some have tight, compact heads; while others are loose-leaved. Thinly sliced cabbage makes a very good salad or coleslaw. Stir-frying cabbage leaves brings out their natural sweetness.

SALAD VEGETABLES

Fresh vegetables are at the heart of organic cuisine, and the most nutritious way to eat them is in salads. Most vegetables, with the exception of potatoes, can be used raw in salads, but some are particularly well suited to this treatment.

Lettuce
Along with other salad greens, lettuce is the classic basis of a salad, and organic ones are extremely tasty and nutritious. All lettuce contains tiny quantities of opiates, which give the vegetable relaxing qualities that help to relieve stress and relax the lungs. It is these compounds that contribute the characteristic, slightly bitter taste. Organic lettuces contain more phytochemical compounds than agrochemical examples. Nutritionally, lettuce is best eaten raw, but it can also be braised or steamed.

Asian Greens
Pak choi, bok choy, Chinese mustard greens, mizuna, and tatsoi are just some of the Asian greens grown organically. Try raising lettuce and Asian greens from seeds. They are easy to grow all year round on a windowsill,

or outside in spring and fall. When buying prepared salad greens, it is absolutely essential to choose organic. Non-organic prepared greens are washed in chlorine to prevent the leaves from going brown. This is why a home-prepared salad composed of similar ingredients will not last as long. Packaged organic salads and precut vegetables are simply preserved by oxygen exclusion as well as modern refrigeration methods.

Below: Lettuce is easy to grow all year round on a windowsill or outside in the spring and fall.

Left: Organic pak choi is free from harmful chemical pesticides and fertilizers.

Cucumbers
Organically grown cucumbers are full of flavor and there are a lot of different kinds. The tiny lemon cucumber looks similar to its namesake. Yellow in color, it is so short and plump that it is almost round. These cucumbers have an extraordinary ability to absorb radiation, an attribute that was underlined during experiments with organic lemon cucumbers at the Los Alamos nuclear research center in the United States. Lemon cucumbers are just one of the many traditional and heirloom varieties of cucumbers that are grown organically alongside the more familiar long, green cucumbers. With their refreshing, mild flavor, cucumbers are perfect in salads.

Below: Traditional cucumbers are available in organic varieties.

Celery helps to flush out excess fluid from the body and is a useful remedy for constipation. It is great in a mixed vegetable juice or stock. When finely sliced, fresh celery adds crunch to a Waldorf salad. Celery is also delicious braised and will add flavor to a stuffing for roast chicken.

Above: Watercress helps to relieve the symptoms of lung cancer and skin complaints.

Avocados

These are possibly the most indulgent of vegetables. Many dieters are deterred from eating these delicious vegetables because of their relatively high calorie content, but they are packed with the right kinds of fats—essential fatty acids. Non-organic avocados are often picked while they are still bullet hard and ripened artificially, whereas organic avocados ripen naturally over a longer period. The result is creamy flesh that relieves PMS, is great for the skin, and helps prevent cancer. Slice or cube avocado for salads, or mash with lemon juice and chile for an instant guacamole dip. You can even use the empty avocado skins to moisturize your skin.

Above: Avocados contain essential fatty acids.

Watercress and Celery

Unless they are organic, watercress and celery are generally both treated heavily with pesticides and fertilizers. Because it has a high water content, agrochemical watercress can be particularly toxic and could well be laced with nitrates.

Organic watercress may be smaller but the flavor is sharper and more concentrated. The pungent taste is due to an antibacterial phytonutrient, so watercress works well against bacterial disorders, such as food poisoning. It is also believed to protect against—and relieve the symptoms of—lung cancer and skin complaints. It can be used in smaller quantities than agrochemical watercress because of its intensity. Try it in salads, or make it into a peppery soup with onions, cream, and nutmeg.

PREPARING FENNEL

With a sharp knife, cut the fennel bulb in half lengthwise, then either cut into quarters or slice thinly.

Fennel

The aromatic fennel bulb has a very similar texture to celery and is topped with edible feathery fronds. Organic fennel is smaller and tastier than non-organic fennel, with essential oils that help combat digestive complaints, such as flatulence. Its distinctive aniseed flavor is most potent when eaten raw in salads. This tasty vegetable can also be braised, when it acquires a delicious sweetness. Fennel is at its best when it is fresh and should be eaten as soon as possible after purchase.

Below: Fennel contains essential oils that can help combat digestive disorders.

VEGETABLE FRUITS

Tomatoes, eggplants, bell peppers and chiles are treated as vegetables in cooking, however, they are classified botanically as fruit.

Tomatoes

There is simply no comparison between the flavor of a freshly picked organic tomato that has been allowed to ripen naturally and the taste of an artificially ripened tomato. Organic growers select the sweetest, tastiest varieties, and whether you buy tiny cherry tomatoes or big beefsteaks, you won't be disappointed.

In terms of nutrition, tomatoes contain a beneficial carotenoid called lycopene. This important micronutrient helps to protect the body from cancer, especially cancers of the gastrointestinal tract, breast, cervix, and prostate. Lycopene is present in the fresh fruit and is released from the skin when fresh tomatoes are cooked. This means that levels of lycopene are even higher in canned or processed products, such as tomato paste, canned tomatoes, ketchup, and pasteurized tomato juice, than they are in fresh tomatoes. However, fresh tomatoes are

Left: Chadwick tomatoes are sweet and juicy.

higher in vitamin C, which is destroyed in cooking. It is absolutely essential to buy organic tomato products since almost all nonorganic prepared tomato products contain GMO tomatoes.

Chiles

Fresh chiles come in a wide variety of shapes, sizes, and colors, with flavors ranging from mild and fruity to intensely fiery. Organic growers like to experiment with the rarer varieties, so you may find unusual types at a farmers' market. More than 200 different types of chiles are available and they now form an integral part of very many cuisines, including Indian, Thai, Mexican, South American, and African.

Right: Serrano chiles contain capsaicin, a phytochemical that is essential for heart health.

CHILE BOOST

For an instant uplift, sprinkle some organic crushed chile on your food. The chile will stimulate the release of endorphins, which are the body's "feel-good" chemicals.

Handle chile peppers with care—they can irritate the skin and eyes. Wear gloves when preparing chiles.

Chiles are the concentrated relations of bell peppers, and there are some wonderful stories concerning their heart-strengthening abilities. They also have antibacterial properties and help respiration and chest complaints.

Like peppers, chiles contain capsaicin. In chiles, however, it is concentrated and accounts for their heat. Handle them with care, because the capsaicin can damage sensitive skin, especially around the lips and eyes. The hottest part of a chile is the white membrane that connects the seeds to the flesh. Removing this membrane and the seeds removes most of the heat. The heat can also be moderated and the sweetness released if chiles are roasted or broiled until charred, and then peeled in the same way as peppers. Chiles prepared in this way freeze well.

Above: Naturally ripened organic tomatoes contain a beneficial carotenoid called lycopene, which helps protect the body from cancer.

Left: Organic eggplants are meaty and delicious.

Eggplants

Organic eggplants are both meaty and delicious. They come in a range of beautiful varieties, from the pretty dappled pink 'Listada de Gandia' to the creamy 'Chinese White Sword'. The phytochemical that gives eggplants their bitter flavor helps to prevent and cure the common cold. If you prefer a less bitter taste, slice each vegetable and sprinkle it with salt. Leave for about an hour and the salt will leach out the bitterness, then rinse thoroughly and pat dry before cooking. This also prevents the absorption of excessive oil when frying.

A great way to release the sweetness of eggplants is to bake them. Simply put them, on a baking sheet, in an oven preheated to 350°F. Cook for about 30 minutes, or until tender, then peel the skin from the flesh, chop them, and serve drizzled with olive oil, tahini, and lemon juice. This popular dish is known as baba ganoush. Eggplants are also delicious when roasted, griddled, and pureed into garlic-laden dips.

Bell Peppers

Agrochemical bell peppers are often grown hydroponically, which is why they tend to taste inferior to organic ones. Organic bell peppers are full of vitamin C and contain the phytochemical capsaicin that is great for heart health. Green bell peppers are fully developed but less ripe than other examples, which can make them hard to digest. They have refreshing juicy flesh with a crisp texture. In addition to being more mature, orange, red, and purple bell peppers have sweeter flesh and are more digestible than less ripe green bell peppers. Roasting or chargrilling bell peppers enhances their sweetness. They are also delicious when served stuffed, sliced into salads, or steamed.

Below: Bell peppers are members of the capsicum family. The very best organic peppers are firm and glossy with unblemished skins.

PEELING BELL PEPPERS

1 Roast the peppers under a hot broiler for 12–15 minutes, turning regularly, until the skin chars.

2 Alternatively, place the peppers on a baking sheet and roast in a preheated 400°F oven for 20–30 minutes, until the skin blackens and blisters.

3 Put the peppers in a plastic bag and let cool. The steam will encourage the skin to come away from the flesh easily.

4 Peel away the skin, then slice in half. Remove the core and scrape out any remaining seeds. Slice or chop according to your recipe.

MUSHROOMS

Nonorganic mushrooms are subjected to vast amounts of chemicals, on the crop itself and to sterilize the straw on which they grow. Fungicides and insecticides are sprayed over them and their growing sheds are regularly bleached. Organic mushrooms have no such hazards. They are also much tastier than most non-organic varieties, whether simply sliced raw in a salad or fried with tamari or soy sauce.

Most organic mushrooms do not contain a wealth of nutrients, but are a useful source of B vitamins, potassium, iron, and niacin. Organic shiitake mushrooms, however, are fantastic for the immune system, and they have been prized for centuries in Japan for their medicinal properties. They are also a good source of phytochemicals and other nutrients. Dried shiitake mushrooms are readily available in organic stores.

White, cap, and flat mushrooms are the most common cultivated variety of mushrooms. They are all one type of mushroom in various stages of maturity, from small white mushrooms, through cap mushrooms to the largest, strongest-flavored flat mushrooms. Flat mushrooms are good broiled or baked on their own or with stuffing.

Left: Fresh and dried shiitake mushrooms are fantastic for the immune system.

Although cremini mushrooms look similar to white, mushrooms, they have brown caps and a nutty flavor. Portabello mushrooms are wild and have an intense, rich flavor that makes them ideal for broiling and stuffing. Chanterelles are a pretty yellow color, with a funnel shape and a fragrant but delicate flavor. Available dried as well as fresh, they are delicious sautéed, baked, or added to sauces.

Store fresh organic mushrooms in paper bags in the refrigerator, and use within a few days of purchase. When you are ready to eat them, wipe the mushrooms gently with damp paper towels and trim the stems. Wild mushrooms often harbor grit and dirt and may need to be rinsed briefly under cold running water, but they must be dried thoroughly. Never soak fresh mushrooms or they will become soggy.

PREPARING DRIED SHIITAKE MUSHROOMS

Dried shiitake mushrooms are a useful pantry standby. However, before they can be used in cooking, they must be rehydrated.

1 Quickly wash off any dirt under cold running water, then soak dried shiitake mushrooms in tepid water for 2–3 hours, or overnight. If you are in a rush, soak them for at least 45 minutes before cooking.

2 Remove the shiitake from the soaking water, and gently squeeze out any excess water. With your fingers or a knife, trim off the stem and then slice or chop the caps to use in cooking. Add the stems to soups or stock. Don't discard the soaking liquid; instead, drain it through cheesecloth, then use it in soups or stews or for simmering vegetables.

Left: This mixed selection of organic mushrooms is a useful source of B vitamins, iron, potassium, and niacin.

PEAS, BEANS, and CORN

These popular organic vegetables can be bought frozen as well as fresh, so you can enjoy them all year round. They are frozen within hours of being picked, so they are still high in nutritional value.

Left: Organic corn cobs have sweet kernels.

Peas and Beans
Organic farmers often rely on legume crops to keep their fields fertile, so there is usually an abundant and varied supply of peas and beans, from sweet snow peas to meaty fava beans. Early summer brings the first green peas, so sweet and tender that you can eat them raw, straight from the pod. This season is short, but other delights lie ahead. Crisp green beans, sugar snaps, and runner beans soon appear on organic market stalls.

Shelled peas are best eaten lightly steamed or added to sauces and stews in the last few minutes of cooking. Snow peas and beans can be sliced raw into salads, stir-fried, or lightly steamed as a side dish. Store fresh peas and beans in the vegetable compartment of the refrigerator and use them within a week to ensure the best taste.

Corn
Organic corn cobs are often smaller and paler than the agrochemical equivalent, but the kernels are beautifully tender and sweet. Corn cobs are best eaten soon after picking, before their natural sugars start to convert into starch, the kernels begin to toughen, and their flavor fades. Remove the green outer leaves and cook whole, or slice off the kernels with a sharp knife. Baby corn can be eaten raw, and are also good in stir-fries. One delicious way to serve corn on the cob is to fry it whole in hot olive oil for just a few minutes. The heat will be just enough to release the natural sweetness and caramelize the exterior.

Left: Organic snow peas and sugar snap peas have a fresh flavor.

Edamame
These are fresh soyabeans. They are widely available in Japan and in many parts of the United States. Edamame deliver a complete balance of protein and phytochemicals that are good for maintaining healthy hormone levels.

PREPARING EDAMAME
This is a good way to appreciate young soy beans in the pod.

1 Separate the pods from the stalks, if they are still attached, and trim off the stem end. Sprinkle the pods generously with salt and rub the salt into the pods with your hands. Let stand for 15 minutes.

2 Boil plenty of water in a large saucepan, add the beans, and boil over a high heat for 7–10 minutes, or until the beans are tender but still crunchy. Drain immediately and refresh briefly under running water.

3 Serve hot or cold in a basket or a bowl with drinks. To eat, squeeze the pods with your teeth to push out the beans into your mouth.

SEA VEGETABLES

Also known as seaweeds, these amazing vegetables, with unusual, tangy flavors and exotic colors, provide our strongest natural source of minerals and trace elements. Nori, wakame, and hijiki are the richest sources of minerals. Nori is also the best source of protein.

Although Japan and China are the countries best known for their use of sea vegetables, seaweeds have been collected all over the world for centuries.

One interesting property of seaweeds is their ability to detoxify the body, thanks to the alginic acid they contain. When we ingest this substance, it binds with heavy metals in our intestines and allows them to be released, cleansing the body. Nori, laver, dulse, kombu, wakame, and arame are all types of seaweeds with these detoxifying properties.

Fresh seaweed requires little preparation. Having been gathered in clean and unpolluted water, it needs to be rinsed in fresh water before being dried in the sun or in an oven on a very low heat. It can also be chopped and frozen.

Most seaweeds are only available dried. Once reconstituted they can be used as substitutes for fresh green vegetables; toasted and crumbled over soups, salads, or stir-fries; or used in sushi. Unopened packages of dried seaweeds keep well for several months if stored in a cool place. Canned organic seaweeds often taste stronger than the dried versions.

Nori

The traditional sushi wrap, nori is one sea vegetable that does not require soaking. It comes in purple-black sheets, which, when toasted for use as a garnish, turn translucent green.

Above: Dried and cut wakame can be used in stews and salads.

Below: Toasted nori sheets add crunch when used as a garnish.

TOASTING NORI

This brings out the flavor and makes nori crispy. Take care not to scorch the nori sheets—or your fingers.

I Hold a sheet of nori with a pair of tongs about 2 inches above a gas burner for about I minute, moving it around so it toasts evenly and turns bright green and crisp.

2 Let the nori cool for a few moments. Crumble between your fingers and sprinkle over soups, salads, or stir-fries, or use in sushi.

Wakame

A dark-colored seaweed with a delicate flavor, wakame adds body to stews and can also be used in salads. A small strip, cooked with beans and legumes, will help to soften them. Prepare it in the same way as arame.

Kombu

A strongly flavored seaweed with flat fronds, kombu, or kelp as it is also known, is used in slowly cooked dishes. It is an essential ingredient in the Japanese stock, dashi.

1 Rinse the hijiki in a sieve under
cold, running water, then place in a
bowl and cover with tepid water.
Let soak for 15 minutes—it will
expand to several times its dried
volume. Drain and place in a pan.

2 Add fresh water to cover the
hijiki and bring to a boil. Simmer
for about 20 minutes, until tender.

Dulse
A purple-red sea vegetable, dulse has
a chewy texture and spicy flavor
when cooked. It can be
added to salads. In the
United States, Canada,
Wales, and Ireland, dulse is
gathered in summer and sold
in health food stores and fish
markets. It is great in noodle
dishes and soups or toasted and
crumbled for a nourishing garnish.

Right: Dulse has a spicy flavor.

*Above: Hijiki requires longer
cooking than most sea vegetables.*

*Below: Laver is
high in minerals
and vitamins.*

Arame
Mild-tasting arame is a good sea
vegetable to try if you haven't tasted
these vegetables before. It must be
soaked in warm water for 20 minutes
before using in salads or stir-fries, but it
can be added straight from the package
to slow-cooked noodle dishes and soups.

Hijiki
This twiggy, black sea vegetable looks
similar to arame but is thicker and has
a stronger flavor. It requires longer
cooking than most sea vegetables.

Laver
Commonly found around the shores of
Great Britain, laver is used in regional
dishes, such as Welsh laverbread, where
it is combined with oatmeal. It can be
added to sauces and stuffings.

Agar-agar
A setting agent, derived
from a type of
seaweed called
"rock flower
vegetable" in
China, agar-agar
is an ideal
vegetarian alternative
to gelatin. Available in
strips or as powder, it can
be used to make excellent
gelatin-based dishes.

HERBS and EDIBLE FLOWERS

Fresh and dried herbs have been prized by cooks for centuries for their ability to enhance the flavor of any ingredient they accompany and enliven even the simplest meal. It is a bonus that many herbs have remarkable healing qualities.

Typically, organic herbs have stronger flavors than nonorganic ones because they have a higher concentration of phytochemicals. These active components are the main source of a herbal plant's flavor and health-promoting properties. Nonorganic herbs all have the medicinal and taste benefits of organic herbs, but often contain much smaller amounts of the essential oils vital for these purposes. Because it is rare for cooks to wash fresh herbs thoroughly before use, pesticide residues on nonorganic herbs can be inadvertently included in a meal. Dried nonorganic herbs carry the same risk.

Another big plus when buying herbs from organic growers is the sheer variety and number of plants available, including unusual and heirloom varieties, such as apple mint, purple basil, and Chinese chives. By shopping from organic growers direct, or sourcing organic seeds, the organic cook will have access to a much broader selection of flavors.

Growing Herbs

It is essential to use fresh herbs before they start to wilt, and the best way to guarantee freshness is to grow your own herbs in containers or in a window box. Good herbs that grow all year round are parsley, thyme, chives, marjoram, winter savory, sorrel, and tarragon. These perennials are difficult to grow from seeds, so they are best bought as young plants.

Annual herbs, such as mint or basil, can be grown from seeds sown from late March onward. They should be sown in seed-starting mix in shallow trays and transferred to bigger containers after about a month. Herbs should always be grown outside, and stone or terra-cotta flowerpots are best. Traditional herb pots not only look attractive, with their little pockets on the sides, but also work well. Keep all herbs under cover on the coldest nights of winter, but otherwise they can stay outside on a windowsill or balcony, or in the garden.

Right: Basil is said to have a calming effect on the stomach, easing constipation, nausea, and cramps, and aiding digestion.

Culinary Combinations

The reason why particular herbs are traditionally added to certain dishes has something to do with complementary flavors, but there are other practical considerations, too. For example, the combination of fried lamb's liver with sage not only tastes superb, but the sage helps the body to digest the meat. Organic rosemary contains powerful essential oils that stimulate the digestive system to make extra bile. This makes it the perfect partner for lamb and chicken dishes. Bay leaves added to bolognese sauce aid the digestion of a pasta meal, and the mint tea that customarily concludes the meal in many countries helps to counter indigestion. It also sweetens the breath and because it is a mild stimulant, the diner is less likely to fall asleep on a full stomach.

Preparing Leafy Herbs

Organic herbs do not need to be washed, but different herbs should be prepared in different ways. Such woody-stemmed herbs as sage and thyme need their leaves removed from the stems before adding to dishes. Large leaves can be picked off with the fingers. For small leaves, hold a sprig of herb at the tip and strip off the leaves with a fork.

Soft leafy herbs, including parsley, can simply be chopped once any coarse stalks have been removed. Cutting herbs with a knife or scissors damages the essential oils from the plant, making them taste more bitter. Try tearing the delicate leaves and stems to encourage a sweeter flavor.

Lightly crushing, or bruising, whole leaves or sprigs of herbs with a mortar and pestle helps to release their flavor into dishes that are cooked quickly.

Use herbs as soon as possible after picking. If you must store them briefly, do so in the refrigerator, wrapped in foil or paper, or chop and freeze them.

Herb Oils

Flavored oils are delicious for cooking chicken and fish or drizzling over roasted vegetables. Strongly flavored herbs, such as thyme, bay, basil, rosemary, marjoram, and tarragon, are best suited to flavoring oils. Push several sprigs into a clean, empty bottle. Fill with light olive or sunflower oil and store in a cool place for two weeks. Then strain through cheesecloth into clean bottles. Herb oils will keep for three to six months.

Edible Flowers

Whole flowers or individual petals can enhance savory and sweet dishes with their delicate flavors. The visual appeal of adding whole flowers or individual petals to a recipe is immediate and wonderful. Flowers from plants with other culinary uses usually taste like a milder version of that plant.

Cooking with organic flowers instead of nonorganic flowers is much preferable because they are more likely to be strongly scented and, therefore, strongly flavored. They are available in a fantastic range of species.

Cut deep pink carnation petals from the bitter base of each flower and soak in white wine for half an hour.

Left: Chives and bay leaves add flavor to any organic meal.

Above: Rosemary and sage

Pour the mixture over a fruit salad. Raw sunflower petals add vibrancy to stir-fries. Deep blue cornflowers and bright orange calendula petals transform a green salad, and nasturtiums add peppery bite. Passion flowers, fuchsias, pansies, and violas are a dramatic garnish for cakes. Violet and rose petals are traditionally used throughout Europe candied as cake decorations. Lavender and rose waters are made by steeping the flowers in hot water until it cools, then straining the mixture. In Eastern Europe and the Middle East, dried rose petals and rose water are mixed into such dishes as couscous and tagines.

APPLES and PEARS

Few sights are more pleasing than an orchard of mature organic apple and pear trees in summer. Fallen white and pink blossoms litter the grass like confetti, and birds and bees dart between the branches overhead. The fruit begins to form. Soon it will start to swell and ripen, the fragrance redolent of times in childhood spent climbing trees and scraping knees. Later, in fall, the ants and other insects on the ground might be lucky with a windfall. But we will be luckier still. The fruit grown in an organic orchard form delicious, self-packaged parcels of vitamins, minerals, and phytochemicals.

Agrochemical pears and apples are grown in startlingly different circumstances from the organic ideal described above. Single species trees grow in regimented rows, over-laden with fruit that is systematically sprayed with toxic

Above: This selection of organic apples includes Granny Smith and Spartan.

fungicides, herbicides, insecticides, and growth-regulating hormones. The insecticides are often organophosphate-based products, similar to nerve gases. Before going on sale, the fruit may be treated with preservatives. This process lengthens its shelf life but does nothing to preserve the natural nutrients within the product. Because the fruit is picked before it is ripe, its nutritional value is further undermined. If you buy nonorganic apples and pears, peel them to remove the chemical covering. The paradox is that the skin is the most nutritious part of the fruit.

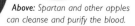

Above: Spartan and other apples can cleanse and purify the blood.

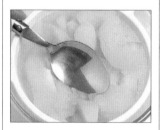

Apples

Rich in pectin and potassium, apples are a good general tonic for the immune system. While an agrochemical apple might look fresh, it could have lost many of its most valuable active vitamins and compounds.

Organic apples can be found in a wealth of varieties, from classic heirloom fruit to modern hybrids. Some varieties, including Granny Smith, are particularly good for cooking and make wonderful pies and desserts or chips. The variety is particularly tasty—and even more nutritious—when mixed with oats, ground almonds, and cinnamon to make a dessert topping. Eating apples, such as Cox's Orange Pippin and Spartan, are often favored for cooking, too. Their slices stay whole when baked.

Classic apples grown organically include the sweet-flavored Gala, one of the most popular apples. Modern apples range from the sweet and juicy Japanese Fuji to Pink Lady, which are similar to Gala but have a meater flesh and softer taste. Look out for unusual varieties at farmers' markets that you can experiment with at home.

Above: Pears are good at lowering cholesterol as well as easing constipation.

Below: 'Red Bartlett' pears are high in soluble fiber.

Pears

Most pears are all-purpose—they can be eaten fresh or cooked. Popular varieties include Comice, Bartlett, Anjou, Bosc, and Seckel. It is best to buy pears slightly under-ripe, because they will ripen over a few days on a sunny windowsill. Like organic apples, pears are a good source of soluble fiber and great at lowering cholesterol as well as easing constipation.

Eating and Storing

When eaten fresh, organic apples and pears should be cut immediately before serving to limit oxidization. Some varieties of apples do not go brown as quickly as others when exposed to air, especially Ginger Gold. Apples and pears can also be eaten cooked or dried. They are both ideal for making juice, too, and the juice can be frozen for a few months without losing its nutrient content and flavor. Store apples and pears in a cool, dark place and do not let them touch each other. Check them frequently, especially the pears, because they tend to spoil more quickly than agrochemical fruit.

PITTED FRUITS

The delicate juicy sweetness of organic pitted fruit is one of the greatest joys of the summer months. Like all fruit, these are best home-grown and in season.

Cherries and Plums
From pale yellow varieties to dark-red morellos, cherries are the prettiest of fruits. Plums are just as varied, from small European Green Gage plums to regal dark purple Japananese plums. Agrochemical plums and cherries are treated with differing levels of respect by the farmers who grow them, from widespread use of agrochemicals in

Above: Cherries are high in phytochemicals.

some countries to near abstinence in others. Unless you can be certain that no agrochemicals have been used, it is safer to choose organic plums and cherries to eat unpeeled.

Both plums and cherries are a good source of phytochemicals and may help to prevent cancer and relieve rheumatism and arthritis. Plums contain malic acid and betacarotene, which provides protection against heart disease and circulatory disorders. Plums also relieve fluid retention and are good for digestion.

Plums can be sweet and juicy or slightly tart; the latter are best cooked in pies and cakes or made into a jam. Sweet plums can be eaten as they are but are also good in fruit salads and pies. There are also two types of cherries: sweet and sour. Some, such as the popular Bing, are best eaten raw, while others, such as Morello, are best cooked.

Peaches, Nectarines and Apricots
Organic peaches, nectarines, and apricots tend to be smaller and more intensely colored than nonorganic fruit, and are much sweeter and tastier. They help to regulate the system and ease constipation. Ripe peaches and apricots should be stored in the refrigerator but brought to room temperature before eating.

*Above:
Elegant
peaches*

Above: Organic plums contain malic acid and betacarotene, which protect against heart disease.

Below: Plums may help relieve rheumatism and arthritis.

PITTING A PEACH

1 Slice through the seam line around the peach.

2 Twist the two halves in opposite directions to separate them.

3 Lever out the pit with a knife.

BERRIES and CURRANTS

Among the most popular of all fruits are berries and currants, with their glowing colors and sweet, scented juices. Strawberries, raspberries, currants of all colors, cranberries, blackberries, and blueberries are just some of the delights that are sold throughout the summer. These are strictly seasonal crops. Buy them out of season and they will be inferior in terms of taste, texture, and nutrition, and they will almost certainly have been brought great distances by air.

Berries are delicate fruit. Washing them can spoil their texture and flavor. This is just one of the reasons why it is best to buy organic. It is perfectly safe to pop an organic berry into your mouth, whereas the agrochemical fruit will have been heavily sprayed with herbicides, fungicides, insecticides, and slug deterrents. Organic berries are smaller and sweeter than nonorganic ones.

Strawberries

From organic growers, strawberries are naturally sweet and delicious. Their flavor is concentrated in smaller, less watery fruit. As with all berries and grapes, they are high in vitamin C. Strawberries are also rich in soluble fiber and betacarotene and contain phytochemicals that help to ease arthritis.

Below: Organic strawberries are naturally firm and delicious.

Above: Organic blueberries are strong cancer-preventing berries.

Above: Cranberries are a good source of vitamins A and C and potassium.

Blackberries

These high-fiber berries contain a wealth of minerals, including iron, magnesium, and calcium. They are rich in the bioflavonoids, which act as antioxidants, inhibiting the growth of cancer cells and protecting against cell damage by carcinogens.

Raspberries

These soft and fragrant berries are effective in removing toxins from the body. To make an uncooked puree or coulis, process some raspberries in a food processor or blender until smooth. Sweeten with maple syrup to taste and add a splash of lemon juice to bring out the flavor. For a smooth puree, press through a nylon sieve. Store raspberries in the refrigerator for up to two days.

Right: Raspberries are high in vitamin C.

Blueberries

These are providing considerable interest in terms of cancer research, being rich in anthocyanidins, the phytochemicals that give them their blue color. The consensus is that they can help prevent cancer.

Cranberries

An excellent source of vitamin C, cranberries also provide potassium and vitamin A. Cranberry juice is effective in treating infections of the urinary tract, such as cystitis.

Red Currants

These pretty, delicate berries are rich in antioxidants, carotene, and vitamins A and C.

Below: Red currants

Below: Blackberries

GRAPES, MELONS, and FIGS

Some of the first fruits ever cultivated, grapes, melons and figs are now available in an enormous range of shapes, colors, and sizes. They are excellent sources of essential nutrients.

Grapes
There are hundreds of different kinds of organic grapes available, from the largest black sweet varieties through to tiny seedless white ones. Wine grapes are often fragrant and remarkably differing in taste, texture, size, consistency, and acidity. Semillon grapes are a classic variety from South West France, now grown from Australia to California. They have a honeylike taste. *Vitis routndifolia* Magnolia is a sweet, bronze colored grape suitable for wine. Baco Noir is a French-American hybrid that produces bluish-black fruit. Seyval Blanc is a disease-resistant hybrid that provides large crops of white grapes.

Right: Delicious raw, organic figs can also be poached or baked.

Below: Grapes are high in vitamin C and carbohydrates.

Organic grapes are naturally high in antioxidants. They provide the perfect pick-me-up for convalescents, being a good source of carbohydrates and vitamin C. Grapes are easy to eat and taste delicious. Eat them at any time except after a big meal—they tend to ferment and upset the stomach if it is full. They are best eaten straight off the bunch, or chopped into fruit salads, and taste excellent in green salads.

Figs
The wonderful squashy texture of organic figs's flesh is the perfect foil for its crispy seeds, and the delicate fruit has a fantastically sweet and toffeelike flavor. Figs can be eaten raw but are also delicious poached or baked. Figs are a great cure for constipation and, since they are high in iron, they can help protect the body against anemia.

Melons
There are two kinds of melons: muskmelons and watermelons. Muskmelons include the honeydew, crenshaw, and casba varieties. Their flesh is typically sweet. Watermelons include the classic pink-fleshed and deep-green-skinned varieties, as well as paler versions such as Yellow Baby, with its yellow flesh and striped skin.

Agrochemically grown melons are sprayed with particularly noxious chemicals, including lindane and paraquat. The danger of ingesting these chemicals through a melon's skin is low, because only the inside flesh is eaten. However, if a melon plant is sprayed with pesticides and then watered, it is possible that some of the agrochemical will be diluted in the water. Melons are storehouses of the water used to irrigate them.

Organic melons are refreshing and cleansing, easing fluid retention and urinary problems. Try serving them cubed on sticks or simply serve a crescent in its skin, decorated with smaller fruits. Melons are also delicious in sweet and savory salads.

Left: Organic watermelons are filled with the unpolluted water used to irrigate them.

CITRUS FRUITS

Native to every warm to tropical country, citrus fruit is the most ubiquitous of tropical fruits and is enjoyed throughout the globe, from northern Europe to the southern tip of Chile. Oranges, grapefruit, lemons, limes, pomelos, tangerines, satsumas, kumquats, and mandarins are all grown organically and should be strongly favored over cheaper agrochemical alternatives.

Agrochemical citrus fruits are heavily treated with a huge range of powerful agrochemical toxins. Over one hundred different agrochemicals are permitted for use on citrus orchards in the United States, with a potentially higher and more dangerous toxic cocktail applied to citrus crops in the developing world. Organic citrus fruit is not dyed, whereas many agrochemically grown ones are injected with artificial colorings.

All of the members of the organic citrus family benefit from being grown as nature intended. Vitamin and mineral levels are boosted and the fruit is packed with bioflavonoids. The benefits of wax-free citrus peel are obvious to jam makers, with organic marmalade being the best choice by far. All citrus fruit is great for preventing or treating colds and sore throats and generally raising immunity.

Lemons
Smaller and more irregularly shaped than agrochemical lemons, organic lemons are juicy and tart. Although all citrus fruit contains citric acid, lemons have an amazing property that allows them to work as an alkaline food. When the human body digests lemon juice, a by-product is potassium carbonate. This salt actually neutralizes the digestive system, creating a beneficial balance.

In the kitchen, lemons have limitless uses. From soups to sorbets, there is scarcely a dish that does not benefit from a squeeze of lemon juice or a sprinkling of grated rind. When lemon juice is squirted over cooked meats, fish, and vegetables, the lemon juice caramelizes to crisp the main ingredient.

Organic lemons are not dyed and they are sometimes greener than agrochemical ones. Ripe lemons will yield to the touch when you squeeze them lightly. Rolling a lemon firmly over a work surface or in the palms of your hands will help you extract the maximum amount of juice.

Unwaxed, organic lemon rind adds an understated warmth to the dish and contributes bacteria-fighting limonine oils. The juice itself is packed with vitamin C and numerous phytochemicals, supporting the development of general health, and will help the body to build a strong immune system.

Below: Organic oranges

Below: Unwaxed organic lemons

Oranges and Grapefruits
Organic citrus fruit has more vitality—grapefruits are tarter and oranges are rounder in flavor. Like many other agrochemical citrus crops, nonorganic oranges and grapefruits are routinely coated with antifungal waxes that would contaminate any dishes prepared with citrus rind or peel. If the skin of the fruit is matte, not shiny, this is evidence that it has not been waxed. Both fruits are high in vitamin C and grapefruits offer valuable support for gum health. Try squeezing grapefruit juice into a fruit cocktail to add zest, or simply halve the fruit and eat it with a spoon.

Limes
Once considered an exotic fruit, limes are now a part of every modern cook's kitchen. The juice has a sharper flavor than that of lemons, so use less juice if you substitute limes for lemons in a recipe. Limes are an essential part of organic holistic cancer treatment.

Left: Organic limes

TROPICAL FRUITS

Organic kiwis, pineapples, papaya, and mangoes are abundant sources of vitamin C. All of these fruits tend to be smaller than their nonorganic equivalents, with denser and sweeter flesh. They also have higher levels of micronutrients, which result in rounded, more intense flavors.

Left: Kiwis contain as much fiber as pears.

Most tropical fruits are naturally high in sugar and should be picked and eaten as soon as they are ripe. Because they are often transported vast distances, this creates a temptation for agrochemical growers to pick under-ripe fruit for shipment. Organic farmers, however, allow fruit to ripen naturally for longer, which improves the nutritional content and flavor. When fully ripe, organic mangoes, kiwis, and papayas all feel slightly soft when squeezed. Organic tropical fruits should be eaten as soon as they are ripe—they have a short shelf life.

Mangoes
Organic mangoes are rich in vitamin C and carotene and are also reputed to cleanse the blood. To make an exotic tropical fruit salad, cube mangoes, papayas, kiwis, and pineapple and drizzle them with some freshly squeezed orange juice and a little maple syrup.

Kiwis
Packed with potassium, organic kiwis can alleviate depression and fatigue and help control high blood pressure. Kiwis contain similar amounts of vitamin C to lemons, and about the same amount of fiber as pears. Organic kiwis are smaller and furrier than nonorganic ones, with darker and less watery flesh.

Papayas
The enzyme papain contained in organic papayas cleanses the digestive tract and aids general immunity and health. Papaya seeds are crunchy and spicy. Try eating them sprinkled on savory green salads to add bite.

Papayas (above) and mangoes (below) are rich in vitamin C and carotene.

PREPARING A MANGO

1 Place the mango narrow side down on a cutting board. Cut off a thick lengthwise slice, keeping the knife as close to the pit as possible. Turn the mango around and repeat on the other side. Cut off the flesh adhering to the pit and scoop the flesh from the mango slices.

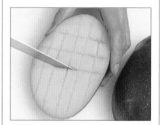

2 To make a crisscross pattern, prepare the mango as above and then score the flesh on each thick slice with crisscross lines at ½ inch intervals, being careful not to cut through the skin.

3 Carefully turn the mango halves inside out and serve.

Left: Bananas are high in dietary fiber and a major source of potassium, which can relieve high blood pressure.

Below: Pineapples have an enzyme called bromelain, which is good for the digestive system.

Bananas

Like kiwis, organic bananas are a major source of potassium. They are also very good for the digestion. It is well known that eating ripe bananas eases constipation, but they are also good for curing diarrhea. Agrochemical bananas can contain pesticides, so choose organic fruit when feeding children.

Pineapples

Organic pineapples are prized for their high enzyme content. One of these, bromelain, acts as a deep cleanser for the digestive system, improving the uptake of all nutritional compounds. They are also fantastic for the complexion, especially when applied topically.

Dates

Organic dates are a rich source of dietary fiber, potassium, and folic acid. Their extremely sweet taste makes dates wonderful to bake with. You can add them chopped to fruit cakes or eat them whole. They can be given to children instead of sugary candies, and they are a useful food for people needing extra energy, including sportsmen and women, pregnant women, and the elderly. Nonorganic dates are often soaked in syrups and oils, but you will find that organic dates are naturally sweet.

Left: Organic dates are naturally sweet and high in energy.

DRIED FRUIT

When dried, many of the nutrients in a fruit are concentrated, as are the natural sugars, but, unfortunately, so are pesticide residues. Nonorganic dried figs, for instance, not only contain more pesticides weight for weight than fresh figs, but they also contain added fungicides. Organic dried fruit is clearly a better option.

Dried apricots are particularly useful, not only for eating out of the hand, but also for baking or in jam. They are a rich source of carotenes and, when eaten in quantity, contain useful quantities of vitamin C. As such, they are the staple and only protection from scurvy available to many people in remote mountain communities, such as the Himalayan area of Ladakh. Organic dried apricots have also been credited with helping to reduce high blood pressure, protecting against cancer and supporting clear, naturally beautiful skin.

MEAT, POULTRY, and GAME

Meat and poultry that has been farmed organically is the prime choice for cooks whose criteria are good-quality, fine taste and texture, and whose concerns include basic levels of animal welfare. Intensively produced meat from nonorganic farms is almost always bland, watery, fatty, and laced with unnatural hormones, antibiotics, and drugs. Welfare conditions for the animals that provide nonorganic meat are often horrific, from their rearing to slaughter. Although there are some excellent small nonorganic meat farms, choosing organic meat and poultry is the only option that fully addresses the issues.

Organic meat labeled as such by a recognized certifying body is also the only option if you want to avoid genetically modified organisms, because about 99 percent of all nonorganic meat is produced from animals whose feed contains some GMOs.

Above: Animals raised on organic farms enjoy a healthy, stress-free lifestyle.

Farming Methods

Nonorganic, intensively farmed animals and birds are taken away from their mothers within a few days of birth and reared in huge herds and flocks. Most of their lives are spent indoors, and they are fed unnatural dried food pellets laced with growth hormones. Antibiotics are used routinely as a safeguard against the diseases and parasites that flourish in the cramped and stressful conditions in which they are kept. Animals and birds are brought to maturity as quickly as possible, by feeding them growth hormones, which speed up the process.

When intensively farmed livestock are ready for slaughter, they generally travel long distances in cramped transportation to the abattoir. In 2001, the European Union exported about 965,000 tons of live cows and beef to the rest of the world. At the same time, about 187,000 tons of live cows and beef were imported into Europe from Argentina, Botswana, Poland, and Brazil. The growth of intensive meat farms has eradicated small local abattoirs, with huge centralized slaughterhouses replacing them for the processors' convenience.

Animal welfare is at the heart of organic animal husbandry. Animals are allowed to feed more freely and grow naturally, resulting in meat and poultry that tastes very much better.

The absolute freedom of game's wild existence means that it cannot be classified as organic. However, truly wild game from unpolluted countryside areas is an excellent choice for anyone who supports animal welfare and freedom. Farmed game that is organically certified is delicious and sustainable.

Biodynamic farming really comes into its own for meat products. Biodynamic animals live extremely comfortable lives, from birth to the abattoir. Many different kinds of heirloom and rare breed animals are free to mingle under cover or outdoors, in scenes reminiscent of an old-fashioned dream of how an animal farm should be. In the Great Britain, regional species of pig, such as the Tamworth porke,r are reared biodynamically, whereas this breed is almost unheard of on commercial intensive meat farms. While organic farm animals that are unwell may be treated with chemical medicines if homeopathy

and other alternative treatments do not work, biodynamic animals must be entirely chemical free. Meat is always hung after slaughter, which helps the flavor to develop. While this process occurs with all quality organic and nonorganic meats, biodynamic meat is guaranteed to benefit from this traditional treatment.

Buying Organic Meat

Everybody who wants to eat delicious organic meat and poultry is encouraged to experiment with different stores or direct buying plans. It is convenient to be able to obtain organic meat from the supermarket, but it is worth considering what is available from organic suppliers and farmers' markets as well as local home-delivery plans.

All organic meat tastes good because the animals are free range and feed on grass. The best organic meat tastes even better, however, because the carcasses are hung in the traditional manner after slaughter. Organic meat from a local supplier or supplied from a home-delivery box plan sometimes come with cooking tips as part of the service. Another important advantage of buying meat either direct or from a specialized outlet is that the purchaser can often order an old-fashioned cut or ask for meat to be prepared in a particular way.

Organic kosher meat is available through mail order. Check local Jewish journals or search the Internet for details of a supplier near you.

Biodynamic and organic meats may be more expensive than intensively farmed meat, but this is not necessarily a bad thing. Reducing the quantity of meat we consume is recommended by doctors and nutritionists. When meat becomes an occasional treat, the cost is not so relevant, especially when the quality is first rate. Occasional meat eating is much more in line with man's original diet than daily hamburgers. Enjoyed weekly or biweekly, organic meat will regain its special place in our diet.

Beef and Veal
Organic beef contains a much better balance of good and bad cholesterol than meat from intensively reared cows. This is because the animals' diet includes a high content of grass, whereas many intensively reared cattle are fed dry food almost exclusively. Some good-quality nonorganic beef cattle benefit from a free-range, grass-

fed existence, but buying organic beef ensures that this happens.

For a classic roast beef, use either sirloin or prime rib. Top round is excellent slow roasted. When broiling or frying steaks, use sirloin, porterhouse, or beef tenderloin. Shank and chuck are good for stews, whereas chuck and sirloin are best for casseroles where whole slices are needed. Use brisket cuts for a pot roast, because these need to be cooked slowly over a long period. Chuck and flank are good for making ground beef for bolognese sauces and meat pies. Chuck and flank are also great for hamburgers and steak tartare. Shank makes a good filling for slow-cooked pies.

If you buy veal make sure that it is organic. It will not be as pale as intensively farmed veal, however you will have the satisfaction of knowing that it has come from a calf that has been reared with its mother, instead of being removed when only a few days old, which causes both animals great distress. Veal steaks are best simply pan-fried to seal in their flavor.

Above: Organic lamb is especially tender and full of flavor.

Lamb
Most good supermarkets offer organic lamb, but usually only as chops and ground lamb. Organic lamb is tender and full of flavor. The fat is clearly visible and can be removed easily. Organic mutton is harder to find but some organic butchers may stock it. It is invaluable for many authentic dishes, especially stews with an Arabic flavor. Ground lamb, which comes from shoulder, belly, or leg meat, can be used instead of ground beef.

For a classic roast lamb, use leg, shoulder, loin, or rack. If you like your lamb pink, you should choose loin, or rack of lamb. Broil or fry leg steaks, or loin or sirloin chops or cutlets. The rarer the meat, the more tender and flavorsome it will be. Lamb can be fatty, however the meat can easily be trimmed. You can make kebabs from shoulder or breast and butterflied or cubed leg. Use shoulder meat in casseroles to make classic dishes, such as navarin of lamb.

Above: Organic beef is a healthier choice.

Right: Organic pork loin is a popular cut for roasting.

Pork

There are a lot of delicious organic pork products available, including traditional homemade sausages, honey roasted hams, gammon, and bacon. Most organic and nonorganic bacon is cured with saltpeter. Although this helps to preserve the pinkish color of the meat, there are some concerns about whether this traditional process is entirely healthy. A few organic and biodynamic pork farms now offer fine-quality pork products that do not contain this ingredient. The meat they sell is darker, with a brown instead of red tinge, but it tastes just as delicious. High-quality organic pork sausages are widely available in supermarkets and delicatessens, but as with all organic meat products, traditional organic farmers' markets and delivery services offer an even more extensive range. Look out for pork sausages with apple, sage, or other seasonings, as well as preserved salamis and saucissons.

Pork is a tender meat, which is suitable for

Above: Organic chile and pepper salami (left) and hot salami are available from speciality organic butchers and organic stores.

all forms of cooking. Leg is a popular cut for roasting, as is blade, which can be roasted on the bone or boned and stuffed. For a truly succulent roast, try sparerib. Perhaps the most popular cut for roasting is loin, which provides the best crackling. To achieve this, score the fat deeply, rub salt into the cuts, and roast the joint dry. When broiling pork chops or steaks, it is essential to watch them carefully. They must be cooked throughly, because underdone pork can cause infection, but they should not be allowed to dry out.

Pork tenderloin is the best choice for frying. For braising, choose pork chops, steaks, spareribs, blade, or loin meat. Shoulder meat is a large cut that can be cubed and cooked in tender pork casseroles and stews.

Poultry

Organic poultry tends to be less fatty than intensively reared equivalents because the birds have more freedom to exercise and are not fed growth hormones. Because it is less fatty, the meat benefits from being cooked slowly.

Organic chicken, duck, goose, and turkey are easy to obtain, but goose and turkey tend to be more seasonal, their availability linked to festivals, such as Christmas, Easter, and Thanksgiving. As well as whole birds, poultry portions are available. They may be on the bone or boneless. Buying whole birds and cutting them up is not difficult, however, and provides the perfect opportunity for making homemade stock.

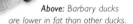

Above: Barbary ducks are lower in fat than other ducks.

Duck and Goose These are fatty birds with dark meat that has plenty of flavor. The fat helps to keep the meat moist during cooking. Goose is nearly always roasted, but the legs may be added to casseroles. Ducks are generally roasted whole or cut up for frying or casseroling.

American Long Island ducks have pale, tender meat with a significant proportion of fat and a rich flavor. Fresh duck is available in regions where they are raised in late spring to early winter. Ducks are sold young, with broilers and fryers less than eight weeks old; roasters are no more than four months old.

Unlike other domesticated poultry, geese have defied all attempts to rear them intensively. They are not prolific layers and are one of the few remaining sources of seasonal food. Goose fat is used in traditional cooking across central and Eastern Europe and in Scandinavia.

Chicken and Turkey Organic birds are raised in humane conditions, fed on a natural and (usually) traditional-style diet. They do not have lurid-colored skin. The skeleton of an organic bird is bigger and stronger, and the legs are longer. When cooked, the flesh is less uniform in color and texture; the breast meat is paler and the leg darker. Standards and conditions relating to the terms by which the birds are classified as organic are usually outlined on the packaging.

As well as whole birds, chicken and turkey are available in a wide choice of portions. Look for birds with a clear, soft skin, with no bruises or blemishes. The tougher the skin, the older the bird.

Organic chicken and turkey need to be cooked slower and longer than non-organic poultry to get the best flavor and texture. When roasting, try stuffing the cavity with grains and herbs, or with fresh fruits and spices for an aromatic dish. Rub the skin with sea salt and different vinegars for added crispiness and zest. Stock made from the carcass of an organic bird will be incomparably richer in flavo and color and will set to a firmer gelatin.

Game

Some game is farmed organically, including rabbit and venison. In a few parts of the world, other types of game, such as elk and wild boar, are seasonally available, either from rural farmers' markets, or speciality suppliers. Animals and birds that are truly wild cannot be classified as organic because their habitat and diet is not controlled or able to be inspected by an organic certifier. Wild game from areas with low agrochemically managed farmlands is unlikely to be contaminated with chemical pollutants.
Venison The term venison is used not only for meat from deer but also from elk, moose, reindeer, caribou, and antelope. Deer are now farmed organically, but the demand for most farmed game animals is still too slow to stimulate a market.

Venison is a dark, close-textured meat with very little fat; what there is should be firm and white. If it is in good condition and a prime cut, such as

haunch, loin, tenderloin, or rack, it will be juicy and tender and is best served rare. Other cuts, such as shoulder and shank, are often marinated and benefit from long and gentle cooking to bring out the flavor of the meat.
Rabbit Fresh rabbit is a delicate well-flavored meat, pale and mild in color. It is high in protein, low in cholesterol, and particularly low in fat. Organically farmed rabbit may be bought all year round. It can be broiled, fried, roasted, or stewed. Baste it well so that the meat does not dry out.
Wild Boar The meat of wild boar has a strong taste. It is dark in color and, because there is little fat, it can be dry and tough, but the flavor is excellent. For this reason, wild boar is usually marinated. Cook it in the same way as pork.
Game Birds Fresh game birds are only available during the hunting season, which varies from bird to bird and from country to country. In some countries frozen game is stocked all through the year. Simple

Above: Organic turkeys are free to exercise and are not fed growth hormones.

cooking methods are often the best for game birds: plain roasting for tender birds and simple casserole cooking for tougher birds. Organic butchers and direct suppliers will be able to provide useful cooking advice.

Pheasants are the most plentiful game birds and are often sold in a brace: a pair of birds that includes a male and a female. The hen is smaller and more tender than the cock. Organic partridge, grouse, and quail are also available. Scottish grouse has a wonderful, rich flavor from feeding on the highland heather of Scotland, where it is native.

There are two types of partridge, the French, or red-legged partridge, and the English, or gray-legged partridge. The red-legged bird is bigger but the flavor of the gray bird is often preferred.

Below: Wild boar has a strong taste and little fat.

FISH and SHELLFISH

Organic fish is a delicious source of protein and can be prepared and cooked very easily. Fresh fish is versatile and great for your health. Omega-3 essential fatty acids found naturally in oily fish help to lower cholesterol levels, protecting the heart and circulation system. Eating fish also reduces the risk of developing high blood pressure during pregnancy, and can help to prevent premature births. However, environmentally aware cooks need to shop with care.

Many fish are either caught using deeply environmentally insensitive methods or raised in unsustainable farms. Organic cooks should buy organically farmed fish or wild fish from sustainable farms and fisheries. If you have doubts about the source or sustainability of fish

Below: Organic fish is farmed using environmentally sensitive methods.

that you want to buy, write to or e-mail the head office of the retailer or processor to find out more. Every time an organization receives a letter of interest from a consumer, it is more likely to improve the sustainability of its practices. For information on the Internet, visit the websites of organic certification bodies. You can ask a good fish store or your local restaurateurs about the seafood they prepare, or contact an organization, such as the Marine Stewardship Council.

Farmed Fish

Organic fish farms are clean and humane. Chemicals are not permitted to be used routinely, although they may occasionally be administered if infection occurs. Many intensive fish farms need to douse their fish regularly in chemicals simply

Above: Pale, organically farmed salmon

because they are so intensive. The more fish are crammed into a body of water, the easier diseases, such as furunculosis, and parasites, such as fish lice, can spread. Organic fish farmers keep numbers lower and the result is a radical reduction in disease and pestilence. There are some nonorganic fish farms that do maintain healthier numbers, but buying organically farmed fish is the best way of being sure that the fish have been managed well.

Despite the many advantages, organic fish farming poses great challenges to pioneering organic aquaculture experts. To be certified as organic, fish must be fed fishmeal that is half a by-product of fish for human consumption, and half from sustainable sources. The trouble is, most fish by-products are from white fish, such as cod. Farmed fish, including salmon, do not easily digest this sort of fishmeal, so there can be a lot of wasted food, which then pollutes surrounding waters. Also, fishmeal from white fish has relatively low levels of fatty acids, so organically farmed fish can have relatively low levels of Omega-3 oils unless they are very carefully managed by an expert organic fish farmer. On the plus side, organically farmed fish are not permitted to be fed any genetically modified foods, so buying organic fish is the only way you can be certain that your farmed fish dinner is GM free.

Although good-quality nonorganic salmon usually has relatively low levels of chemical residues, organically farmed salmon has even less. Organically farmed

Right: Seawater fish farms produce excellent sea trout.

fish are generally top class in terms of taste and texture, whereas intensively farmed fish are often bland and fatty. Organically farmed fish also have paler flesh. The stronger color of nonorganic farmed salmon is due to a diet based on fishmeal with added carotenoids. Although these are the same as the beneficial compounds found in carrots, organic cooks will prefer the more natural paler color of organically farmed salmon.

Salmon, trout, and carp taste wonderful broiled, steamed, or fried in olive oil, especially when they are served with a generous squeeze of fresh lemon juice. Smoked in the traditional way, organically farmed fish have incomparable flavor, so different from the bland nonorganic product, which is prepared using artificial wood smoke flavoring.

Below: MSC-certified halibut harvested by methods that protect the seabed.

Seawater Fish Farms

Organic seawater fish farms are beginning to rear many more breeds of fish. These include organic sea trout, bass, cod, and halibut. Humane and causing the minimum impact on the marine environment, organic sea fish farming is still in its infancy. As wild fish stocks come under increasing threat, this area of organic farming is set to grow.

There are currently only a few experimental organic shrimp farms, but this sector is certain to increase exponentially. Nonorganic farmed shrimp tend to be the antithesis of the organic ideal, and have devastated large areas of the tropical world from the Indian Ocean to the mangroves of Honduras. Abusing the rights of local farmers who rear the crop, the shrimp industry often replaces rural diverse communities with a single polluting monoculture. To avoid adding to this type of situation, do not buy farmed shrimp unless they are certified as organic.

Shellfish, such as mussels, scallops, and oysters are sometimes farmed in enclosures around coastal seawaters. They feed on naturally occurring plankton and are a healthy source of food whose production has a low impact on the environment. Mussels and oysters are also a good source of betaine, a substance that helps to protect against heart attacks. These

FAST FISH

We are constantly advised to eat more fish, especially oily varieties rich in Omega-3 oils. Here are some suggestions for quick and easy meals.
• Make a fish stew or soup using large chunks of haddock, cod, or bass with garlic, onion, herbs, and red wine or stock.
• Thread cubes of hake with squares of red bell pepper, brush with olive oil, and broil until tender.
• Make a quick summer salad from smoked fish, new potatoes, and arugula. Make sure the fish is a naturally wood-smoked product for an authentic taste and to avoid added chemicals.
• Serve pickled herrings with a mixture of mayonnaise and crème fraîche for a quick appetizer.
• Make your own gravlax from wild salmon and fresh dill.
• Stuff whole mackerel with herbs and pan-fry in olive oil or butter.

shellfish are easy to prepare and make nutritious, high protein meals. Oysters should simply be pryed open with a knife and eaten whole, with a squirt of lemon. Clean mussels by scrubbing them in fresh water and pulling off any fibrous "beards" that sprout between the two halves of the shell. Always discard any mussels that are open or fail to snap shut when tapped with a knife.

Left: Organic mussels and other shellfish are increasingly farmed in enclosures around coastal seawaters.

MAINTAINING STANDARDS
There is no organic standard for wild fish. However, the MSC—Marine Stewardship Council—is a certifying body that is beginning to address the issue. It is a leading voice in the sustainable fishing debate, and offers practical guidance to consumers, fishermen, and governments alike.

When certifying a fishery, the MSC looks at three areas of activity. First, the state of the fish stocks in the locality is assessed to determine whether fishing is being carried out sustainably. The fishery's effect on the marine ecosystem is also looked at. One major problem of modern fishing methods is catching fish other than the target species—the "by-catch." The MSC standard is only awarded if levels of by-catch for the fishery are acceptable. Finally, management systems are examined to satisfy the MSC that good practice is being maintained.

Fishermen often work under an umbrella organization, which may be a government body, that regulates the area of the sea they harvest. If good management is in place, their practices can be coordinated to ensure sustainable fishing.

Buying MSC-certified Fish
A secondary certification plan traces all fish certified to the MSC standard from the fishery to the retailer, so consumers can buy wild fish with confidence if it carries the MSC logo. You will find the logo on fresh and frozen fish, convenience products, and on menus where restaurants support the plan.

MSC-certified fish is sold through independent fishm stores, farmers' markets, supermarkets, and delicatessens in the United States, Britain, and Australia. Fish caught at MSC-certified fisheries are also sold in Canada, New Zealand, and South East Asian countries. However, not all these countries use the logo.

Wild Fish
The last major wild food resource, the sea, is under intense threat from over-fishing. Worldwide, sea fish are now so overexploited that many once abundant stocks are now under threat of extinction. Catching wild fish has become a serious technological pursuit. Wild sea fish are hunted with the aid of radar, planes, and submarines and caught with lines or trawler nets, trapping the targeted catch and also other fish, mammals, and birds. These raids do not discriminate between adults and young fish.

Wild fish are increasingly subjected to chemical, biological, and hormonal attack from polluted fresh waters, such as rivers and lakes. Some intensive fish farms release their waste water, with its cargo of chemicals and germs, into nearby rivers and seas. Fish from these farms often escape and interbreed with wild stocks to produce hybrid mutations. Pesticides and fertilizers from agrochemical crops also flow into rivers and lakes through groundwater. The fertilizers promote algae growth, ruining the delicate balance of water ecosystems, while pesticides simply poison the inhabitants.

Wild salmon spend almost all of their lives in the sea, only returning to fresh water when it is time to spawn. They have incredible homing instincts.

Above: Wild salmon live in the sea, returning to fresh water only when it is time to spawn.

A salmon that has swum hundreds of miles away from its birthplace will return to the very creek where its life began. If the water it has to pass through has been contaminated by fish farm, agrochemical farm, or factory pollution, this ancient cycle is irrevocably disturbed.

Types of Wild Sea Fish
Wild sea fish fall into two groups: those that live at the bottom of the sea, and those that live in the middle waters or near the surface. Surface fish include common varieties, such as sardines, mackerel, anchovies, pilchards, Atlantic herring, and swordfish. Fishermen utilize many methods to catch these fish, including traps, lines, and drag nets. In Japan, fishermen sometimes lure squid using mechanical jiggers with bright lights. The squid attach themselves to the machinery, so they can be hauled onto the boats easily. Knowledgeable fishermen easily target surface species, ensuring a good percentage of the catch is the target fish. Despite this, many of these species are now fully or over fished.

Fish species from the middle waters include tuna, salmon, and herring. These fish are almost always caught with nets.

Tuna are a similar size to dolphins and often associate with them. In the past, this frequently meant that when tuna were caught, so were dolphins. The public outcry that ensued when this became common knowledge has diminished this practice. All tuna sold in the United States and Canada now has to be dolphin friendly, and most other industrialized nations offer dolphin-friendly tuna.

However, catching tuna without catching dolphins is difficult. One technique that has replaced dolphin-associated tuna fishing is to use floating aggregate devices, or FADs. These float in the sea and attract the tuna because of the cover they provide. Fishermen then net all of the fish below the FAD, including juvenile tuna and other by-catch species. Although dolphin-friendly tuna does save dolphins, it is often at the expense of other species with a less popular public image.

Probably the best way to catch tuna in terms of the ecosystem is with so-called "long lines". These fishing lines with multiple hooks are dragged behind boats and target tuna extremely efficiently. Some successful long-line tuna fisheries use this method, including one in the Maldives that supplies retailers and restaurants around the world.

Below: Wild cockles can be picked by hand.

Fish that live on the bottom of the sea are generally trawled with big nets. Cod, carp, hake, haddock, and Alaskan pollock all live near the seabed, as do flat fish, including halibut and sole. Cephalopods, such as squid and octopus, are often also trapped in the nets, but offer a valuable source of under-exploited seafood. Trawling the seabed can be extremely destructive, disturbing ancient ecosystems. The Marine Stewardship Council has approved one fishery that trawls responsibly, and more fisheries that use other sustainable harvesting methods for species at the bottom of the sea. Fisheries awarded MSC certification are sustainable, so you can be sure that buying these products will not contribute to bad fishing practices.

Shellfish

Lobsters and crabs also live at the bottom of the sea but they are only harvested in coastal waters. They are usually collected in pots, either using bait or trapdoors. Scallops and oysters, which also live in coastal waters, are traditionally trawled. Today, they are often harvested by divers. This method protects the delicate ecosystems found at the bottom of the sea, while providing top quality seafood for the caring cook. Other shellfish, such as wild cockles and mussels, are more easily harvested. They can be picked by hand from the bottom of shallower waters. However, most commercially available shellfish are currently farmed.

Intensively farmed shrimp are bad news for organic consumers. Try to buy wild shellfish. Those from Iceland are particularly acceptable as an alternative to organically farmed shrimp. Iceland is heavily reliant on its fishing industry, so it has become a benchmark country for sustainable fishing techniques. Most shrimp from Iceland are caught by trawling with nets with bigger holes than other fishing nations. The holes allow young shrimp to escape, so they can grow and breed.

MOULES MARINIÈRE

1 Chop 1 onion and 2 shallots. Put in a large pan with 2 tablespoons butter and cook over low heat until softened and translucent.

2 Add 1¼ cups white wine, a bay leaf, and a sprig of fresh thyme. Bring to a boil. Add 4½ pounds cleaned mussels, cover the pan tightly, and steam over a high heat for 2 minutes. Shake the pan vigorously and steam for 2 minutes more. Shake again and steam until all the mussels have opened. Discard any closed shells.

3 Stir in 2 tablespoons chopped fresh parsley and serve at once.

DAIRY FOODS and EGGS

Opting for organic products means obtaining the maximum nutrition from whatever dairy foods you consume, without supporting the negative aspects associated with intensive farming methods. Dairy foods are excellent sources of protein and calcium.

On an organic dairy farm, cows have regular access to open fields. Their diet is made up almost exclusively of organic grasses and grains and they are never routinely treated with the hormones that are used on nonorganic farms in some countries to boost milk production. Nor are they dosed with antibiotics except as a last resort. If you prefer not to eat any dairy foods, there are some excellent organic alternatives.

Milk

Organic milk is the only kind of milk that is guaranteed to be free of genetically modified ingredients, because many non-organic cows eat GM feed. It is available with varying amounts of cream, from skimmed to whole fat. Whole milk generally only contains about 2 percent fat, so all milk is a low-fat food. Most milk is pasteurized, homogenized, or sterilized, but it can also be found raw. Pasteurization is a heating process that helps to control bacteria levels in the milk. Homogenization distributes

Right: Goat's, cow's, sheep's, and soy milk

the fat content throughout the milk, so there is no need to shake it to mix in the cream. Sterilization extends the shelf life of sealed cartons of milk, so that they do not need to be refrigerated. All these processes are permitted under organic certification laws because they are mechanical processes that do not involve the use of chemicals.

Cow's milk is not the only organic option. Goat's milk has a distinctive, musky flavor, which many people love. It is much easier to digest than cow's milk, so individuals who cannot tolerate cow's milk often find they can drink goat's milk without suffering adverse reactions. Organic sheep's milk is sometimes on sale at the larger farmer's markets or in delicatessens. It doesn't taste as pungent as goat's milk, but contains more of the lactose that can cause dairy intolerance.

Yogurts, Creams, and Dairy Desserts

Live yogurt is a natural probiotic. This means it boosts the amount of beneficial bacteria in the intestines of those who eat it. This, in turn, aids the absorption of nutrients, such as calcium, as well as offering some protection from various disorders, including tooth decay and

heart disease. An even better way of improving the levels of good bacteria in your gut is to eat prebiotic foods, such as onions, leeks, wheat, oats, bananas, and Jerusalem artichokes.

Many of the world's largest non-organic dairy corporations now also offer organic yogurts, creams, and dairy desserts. While this ensures improved availability of organic dairy products, the quality is variable. Organic dairy products all have the benefits of humane and environmentally sustainable production, but mass-produced yogurts and dairy desserts are often watery, high in sugar, and low in flavor. Whether they are runny or thick, organic creams should always be mouthwateringly rich. The organic connoisseur will choose organic yogurts, desserts, and creams from smaller enterprises or companies who are primarily organic.

Butter

Organic butter has a much richer taste than nonorganic alternatives. Both types, however, are equally high in saturated fats, which can raise cholesterol levels in the body and contribute to heart disease. Consider organic butter a luxurious, delicious, and slightly decadent treat, great for the occasional indulgence, as when making the perfect fried egg, but something to be limited. Organic butter is far better for your health than many nonorganic margarines and spreads. These will often contain hydrogenated or trans fats, which may be far more damaging to the heart than butter.

Right: Organic butter

Cheeses

Organic cheeses are made from organic milk, so they offer all the environmental, humanitarian, and healthy eating benefits of other organic dairy products. They come in scores of different varieties, from hard types such as cheddar, Gouda, and Gruyère, through blues such as Stilton and Gorgonzola, to soft and creamy Camembert and cottage cheese. A lot of artisan cheesemakers now use organic ingredients. Buying organic cheese is a must if you want to avoid eating genetically modified rennet.

Soy Milk and Other Substitutes

Soy beans have been transformed into nutritious "milks" and dairy alternative foods for thousands of years. There are dozens of versions on the market, including the fresh product, which looks like cow's milk but is slightly thicker and has a nutty taste. More readily available is long-life soy milk, which comes in cartons and does not need to be refrigerated until it is opened. Sweetened versions can also be found, and it is possible to buy soy milk that has been fortified with extra vitamins as well as calcium.

Soy milk is low in calories and contains no cholesterol. Easy to digest, it is a valuable food, particularly for those who cannot tolerate cow's milk. Children who suffer from asthma and eczema often get relief when they switch from cow's milk to a nondairy alternative such as soy milk.

Soy cream is much thicker and richer than soy milk because it is made with a higher proportion of beans.

Soy beans are not the only ingredient that can be made into nutritious liquid. Other beans can be used in a similar way, as can some nuts and grains. Rice milk is thin and has a delicate taste. Tiger nut milk has a similar consistency and a sweet taste. Oat milk is pleasantly mild, while pale yellow pea milk is creamy. Non-dairy milks can be bought from health food stores or made at home. Try them on muesli or other organic cereals or in creamy soups. When using in tea, put nondairy milk in first and stir the tea thoroughly to prevent it from curdling. The high acidity in coffee means that curdling is almost inevitable, so avoid using nondairy milks here.

Above: Organic Stilton and Brie are widely available.

Eggs

Organic free-range eggs come from hens that have ample access to land free from chemical fertilizers and pesticides. The birds are not routinely debeaked to stop them retaliating when hemmed in by other hens, nor are they given growth promoters. Antibiotics are administered only when unavoidable. It is important to look for labels on eggs that attest to organic certification. Although the term "free range" suggests that hens spend their days outdoors, nonorganic free-range birds often have limited access to the open air. Organic eggs are the only eggs that can be guaranteed to be free from yolk colorants.

Look out for other types of eggs at farmers' markets. Duck eggs are a pretty shade of blue, goose eggs are big enough for two, and quail's eggs are small and speckled. All can be boiled, fried, scrambled, or used in cakes in the same way as hen's eggs. When soft-boiled, organic eggs are far less likely to contain the salmonella that is often found in eggs from intensive chicken production houses. Soft-boiled or lightly poached eggs have the advantage of containing fewer Cholesterol Oxidation Products (COPS), which means they can be beneficial to blood cholesterol levels.

Below: When farmed organically, quail and duck eggs are guaranteed free from yolk colorants.

54

BEANS and LEGUMES

These staples are a fantastic resource for any organic cook and provide vital protein for vegetarians and vegans. Organic red and white kidney beans, aduki beans, navy beans, flageolet beans, cannellini beans, soy beans, mung beans, black-eyed peas, and chickpeas are all available. A good source of B vitamins and many minerals, including iron, selenium, and zinc, organic beans are far better for you than the agrochemical equivalents, which are often grown in developing countries where pesticide use is extremely heavy.

Left: Aduki beans have a nutty flavor.

Soy beans are particularly good for women, because they are rich in the phytoestrogens that help to prevent osteoporosis and breast cancer, plus folic acid for preconceptual care. Chickpeas are especially high in calcium.

Cooking Beans and Legumes
Most beans and legumes, with the exception of lentils, must be soaked overnight before being cooked. Lentils can be cooked straight from the sieve after rinsing, but will also benefit from being soaked for an hour or more. Soaking makes

Left: Chickpeas have a delicious hearty taste and creamy texture.

beans and legumes easier to digest. So does cooking them with a small piece of kombu seaweed. Cooking with salt toughens beans, so only season them once they have been cooked.

Kidney beans, whether organic or not, must be cooked thoroughly to ensure any natural toxins they contain are neutralized. Boil the beans vigorously for about 15 minutes, then change the water and simmer for about 1¾ hours until they are tender.

Cooked beans and legumes taste great in soups, salad, stews, and meat-free pâtés, as well as classic Indian dishes such as dhal. A quick dhal soup can be made by boiling equal amounts of red lentils and yellow split

Above: Navy, red kidney, flageolet, and pinto beans

SPROUTING BEANS, SEEDS, GRAINS, AND LEGUMES
When beans, legumes, seeds, and grains germinate, their nutritional levels rise dramatically. B vitamins increase by almost 30 percent and vitamin C by up to 60 percent. Organic sprouts are easy to grow.

1 Wash 3 tablespoons beans, legumes, seeds, or grains thoroughly in water, then place in a large jar. Fill the jar with lukewarm water, cover with a piece of cheesecloth, and hold in place with an rubber band. Let stand in a warm place overnight.

2 Drain thoroughly the next morning and refill the jar with water. Shake gently, then drain again. Let the jar stand on its side in a warm place, away from direct sunlight. In the evening, rinse again, draining well.

3 Continue to rinse and drain twice daily until small roots and shoots have emerged. Most sprouts will be ready within a week. Sprinkle on salads, chop into spreads, or add to stir-fries or curries.

Below: White and black soy beans form the basis for quick high-protein meals.

peas, then stirring in onion and a chopped tomato, which has been fried with curry spices. For a delicately flavored salad, mix cooked flageolet beans with rocket leaves and add a drizzle of walnut oil.

Store beans and legumes in a cool, dry place. Keep packages tightly closed or transfer to sealed containers. Beans and legumes can be kept for years and still be capable of germinating, but the fresher they are the better, so buy them in small quantities and use quickly.

Soy Bean Products

Highly nutritious soy bean products, including tofu and tempeh, are ideal for keeping in the refrigerator or freezer to form the basis for quick, high-protein meals. It is vital to ensure that all the soy products you buy are organic. Many nonorganic soy products have been made from genetically modified beans, bred for resistance to extremely strong pesticides and herbicides. GM soy beans are able to grow in soil that has been drenched in these harsh chemicals, whereas beans that have not been genetically modified are destroyed by the toxicity. There is no benefit to the consumer in eating GM soy beans; the only advantage is to the farmer who is able to use stronger and stronger chemicals.

Tofu Also known as bean curd, tofu is derived from soy milk, which is curdled using a natural coagulant. The curds are drained and pressed to make tofu, in a process similar to that used when making soft cheese. Firm tofu can be sliced and fried. It is a popular ingredient in stir-fries, especially when it has been marinated in soy sauce to strengthen its somewhat bland flavor. For soups, sauces, and creamy desserts, choose silken tofu, which is smooth and light. Smoked, marinated, and deep-fried tofu are all available in health-food stores and Asian stores. Organic tofu can also be bought in long-life cartons.

TVP Many vegetarians rely on soy bean products for their protein, especially in the form of Textured Vegetable Protein, or TVP. This highly processed ingredient is widely used in organic processed foods and is also available dried. It can be useful to keep some in the pantry for making vegetarian burgers or lasagne, but

COOKING TIMES FOR PRESOAKED BEANS AND LEGUMES

The list below provides a rough guide only, because cooking times may alter according to how long the items have been stored and the quantity cooked. In most cases, the volume of water should be three times that of the chosen ingredient, except in the case of lima beans, where double the amount of water will be sufficient. Ingredients that need very long cooking times, such as chickpeas, dried field peas, and soy beans, may need up to four times the amount of water.

Beans	Time (minutes)
Aduki beans	45–60
Black-eyed peas	60
Chickpeas	180
Field beans, dried	45
Flageolet beans	50
Navy beans	60
Kidney beans	120
Lentils, brown	45
Lentils, green	30
Lentils, red	20–30
Lima beans	60
Mung beans	60
Peas, dried field	120
Peas, split	45
Soy beans	200

TVP is low on taste, lacking in texture, and offers limited nutrition. Fresh soy bean products, such as tofu and tempeh, are superior in every way.

Tempeh This Indonesian food is made by fermenting cooked soy beans with a cultured starter. It has a meatier, nuttier flavor than tofu, and the firmer texture means it can be used in pies. Slices of tempeh taste delicious fried in sunflower oil and tamari or soy sauce and served with pita bread.

Left: Tempeh freezes well, so conveniently keeps for long periods.

GRAINS

Getting to grips with organic grains is not difficult. There is a wide selection available, from wheat in all its various forms to lesser known grains, such as the highly nutritious quinoa.

Rice
Organic brown rice is one of the ultimate grains in terms of taste, nutrition, and healing potential. It is easily digestible, gently soothing the intestinal tract. It is simultaneously comforting and satisfying to eat, particularly when served with crisp and fresh stir-fried organic vegetables.

Above: Bulgur wheat

Above: Millet

Above: Quinoa

Although organic white rice is a convenient ingredient and has a much shorter cooking time, it is less nutritious because most of the minerals and vitamins are lost when the bran and germ of the grain is removed in the milling process.

Bulgur Wheat
This pale, sand-colored grain, made from dried and crushed cooked wheat berries, is nutty in flavor and comes in varying degrees of coarseness. When cooked, by soaking in double its volume of boiling water for 15–20 minutes, bulgur wheat is similar in appearance to couscous but is heavier, and has more flavor. Bulgur is usually served cold. Combined with flat-leaf parsley, mint, tomatoes, cucumber, onion, and a lemon and oil dressing, it forms the basis of the Middle Eastern salad, tabbouleh.

Millet
Another underused but essential grain, organic millet contains all the essential amino acids. It is the only alkaline grain, making it easily digestible. It is also a rich source of silicon, the substance that helps to build collagen for keeping skin, eyes, nails, and arteries healthy, vibrant, and flexible. Widely eaten in many parts of Africa, the small ground grain is cream in color, with a pleasant, neutral taste.

Quinoa
Until recently this tiny round grain was little known outside its native Bolivia, but quinoa (pronounced "keen-wah") is becoming increasingly popular, partly because it tastes delicious, but also because it is a very good source of protein, fiber, and B group vitamins. Like brown rice, quinoa tastes faintly nutty. Quinoa is useful for making stuffings, pilafs, and cereals.

Above: Brown rice is high in complex carbohydrates, with protein, fiber, and B vitamins. It is one of the ultimate grains.

COOKING QUINOA
Quinoa is a quick and easy side dish to prepare at home. When cooked, the tiny bead-shaped grains have a mild, slightly bitter taste and firm texture. It contains all eight essential amino acids and is a rich source of vital nutrients. Quinoa is cooked like rice, but the grains quadruple in size, becoming translucent with an unusual white outer ring.

1 Always wash quinoa before cooking to remove the fine, soapy, white powder that coats the grains.

2 Boil in a saucepan of water for about 20 minutes, until the khaki-colored round grains turn into pretty translucent white spirals. Serve with curries, stir-fries, or casseroles as an alternative to boiled rice.

COOKING TIMES FOR GRAINS

The list below provides a rough guide only, because cooking times may alter according to how long the items have been stored, and the quantity cooked. In most cases, the volume of water should be three times that of the chosen ingredient, except in the case of rolled oats, quinoa, and white rice, where double the amount of water will be sufficient. Ingredients that need very long cooking times, such as polenta, may need up to four times the amount of water.

Grains	Time (minutes)
Amaranth	20–25
Barley	80–90
Buckwheat	20
Cornmeal	25
Millet	30
Oats, groats	120
Oats, rolled	10
Quinoa	15
Rice, brown	40–60
Rice, white	15–20
Wheat, whole	90
Wheat, cracked	25
Wild rice	60

Oats

Organic oats are extraordinarily high in soluble fiber and are a fundamental food for heart health. A bowl of porridge or oat-rich muesli or granola is a great foundation for the day, giving greater stores of energy than high-sugar, nonorganic breakfast cereals. Organic oat-based muesli is readily available, but it is also easy to make at home. Simply add chopped organic hazelnuts, flax, sunflower, and pumpkin seeds to an oat base, then sweeten the mixture by stirring in chopped dried fruit. Store the muesli in an airtight container in a dry cupboard, and the muesli will last as long as the nuts—about three months.

Organic breakfast cereals not only retain their micronutrients but also tend to contain less refined sugar and salt than nonorganic varieties, supporting healthier energy levels and moderating moods throughout the day. For a special treat, make a classic Bircher muesli by soaking equal quantities of oats and milk or dairy-free milk overnight. Stir in an equal quantity of yogurt and honey the next morning, with a freshly grated apple and one other chopped fresh fruit.

Oats are also widely used in baking and are delicious in granola bars, added to the topping for a fruit crumble, or sprinkled on homemade breads.

Wheat Berries

These are whole wheat grains with the husks removed. They are packed with concentrated goodness and have a sweet, nutty flavor and chewy texture. Wheat berries are delicious when added to salads. They can be used to add texture to breads and stews, or combined with rice or other grains. They must be soaked overnight, then cooked in boiling water until they are tender. When germinated, the berries sprout into wheatgrass, a powerful cleanser and detoxifier.

Couscous

Although this looks like a grain, couscous is a form of pasta made by steaming and drying cracked durum wheat. When cooked, couscous is light and fluffy in texture. It is a mainstay of Middle Eastern cooking, its fairly bland flavor provides a good foil for spicy dishes. Couscous also tastes great flavored with ginger or galangal and rose water and served as a traditional accompaniment to a Moroccan tagine.

Left: Couscous

Combining Grains and Legumes

To maximize the amount of protein available from nonanimal sources, mix grains and proteins. This is good advice for anyone seeking to eat a well-balanced diet, but it is essential advice for vegans. Divide foods into three groups: grains; beans and legumes; and seeds and nuts. In any meal, choose a combination of two of these groups. Cooks do this naturally a lot of the time. Baked beans on toast is one classic British dish; while rice and dhal forms a traditional Indian combination.

WHEAT BERRIES

When cooked, wheat berries make a delicious addition to salads, and they can also be used to add texture to breads and stews.

1 Place the wheat berries in a bowl and cover with cold water. Soak overnight, rinse thoroughly and drain.

2 Place the berries in a large pan and fill with cold water. Bring to a boil, then cover and simmer for 1–2 hours, until the wheat berries are tender. Check regularly and replenish the water when necessary.

FLOUR and PASTA

Organic food companies produce many different kinds of milled grains, more so than nonorganic flour companies. In addition to wheat flour, there are flours made from buckwheat, rice, rye, and corn, as well as quinoa and spelt. Organic pastas are also common and come in every shape and color, from spaghetti to spirals. Japanese pastas, such as udon and soba, are also readily available in organic form.

These products have an important part to play in the organic kitchen, particularly for people who wish to

Right: Udon noodles are high in complex carbohydrates and will provide energy over a long period.

Below: Spelt flour and grain

eliminate wheat and other high-gluten grains, such as rye, barley, and oats, from their diet because they are allergic to gluten. Consult a qualified nutritionist if you have this allergy.

Many of us rely too heavily on wheat for carbohydrates—eating wheat-based cereals for breakfast, sandwiches for lunch, cookies or cakes for an afternoon snack, and pasta for dinner. Instead of cutting out wheat entirely, assess your average daily intake and make sure that you eat a good spread of different organic grains.

Wheat Flours

Depending on the degree of processing, wheat flour may be either whole-wheat or white. Stone-ground whole-wheat flour is the best for you because it

retains all its valuable nutrients, but white flour is often better in baking. Most pasta and noodles are made of plain durum wheat or whole-wheat flour. High in complex carbohydrates, pasta and noodles provide energy over a long period. Whole-wheat versions are richer in vitamins, minerals, and fiber, and often have a preferable texture. There is a wide choice of organic wheat noodles, including Japanese udon noodles, thin, white somen noodles, egg noodles, and ramen.

Non-wheat Flours

Spelt is one of the most ancient grains and is rich in vitamins and minerals. It is the ancestor to modern wheat, but many people with gluten intolerance are able to digest spelt flour. Flours that do not contain gluten, such as rice, soy, buckwheat, quinoa, and millet flours, have different cooking properties. Buckwheat is used to make blinis in Russia, soba noodles in Japan, and pasta in Italy. Buckwheat pancakes are popular in parts of the United States and France. Rice flour is used in sticky Asian cakes and desserts, and to thicken sauces. Opaque-white rice noodles are popular in many Southeast Asian countries.

Above: From back to front, hemp spaghetti, gluten-free corn spaghetti, and spiralina tagliatelle

BREAD and BAKED GOODS

All organic breads are better for you than the nonorganic equivalent because the grains contain more nutrients and fewer agrochemical toxins. Unless bread is organic, it is likely to have had chemical flour improvers, flour extenders, and preservatives added, as well as conditioners and flavorings, and invariably contains excess salt.

However, some organic loaves are better than others, and it is important to seek out a good supplier whose loaves freeze well, so that you can stock up if necessary. A good organic loaf will have been made in the traditional manner, with enough yeast to ensure an even, close texture, and will taste delicious.

Factory-Made Breads

Alongside some excellent organic factory-made breads, there are some inferior loaves. Factory-made organic bread is sometimes made by the flash-baking method. This uses excessive amounts of yeast to make the dough rise rapidly. These breads have a spongy texture, mediocre flavor, and are not as nutritional as organic loaves made by hand in the traditional way and allowed to rise slowly. The flash-baking method is cheaper for the manufacturer, but bread made this way is contributing to the current yeast intolerance boom.

Below: Organic white baguette, wheat-free loaf, and naturally leavened French crusty bread (at back).

Below: Carrot and raisin cake, gluten-free almond cakes, and chocolate chip hazelnut cookies.

Baking Bread

If you want to be absolutely certain of the quality of your organic loaf, bake your own. This is much easier than many people appreciate. Bread can be made by hand and baked in the oven or with the aid of an electric bread-maker, which mixes, kneads, rises, and bakes the bread in one easy hands-free operation.

Wheat is the easiest type of flour to use for conventional yeast-based breads, because it contains plenty of gluten, the sticky substance that keeps dough stretchy and helps it to rise. Use whole-wheat flour for preference for its fiber content. Quality flours also provide protein and vitamins, especially the B vitamins, and useful amounts of zinc and magnesium, which help to harmonize moods, improve the condition of the skin, and promote healing.

Making bread with other flours is more of a challenge, because the gluten content of different grains varies considerably. Rice flour, buckwheat flour, cornmeal, and oatmeal, which contain little or no gluten, must either be mixed with wheat flour in a yeast loaf, leavened with baking soda, or used to make flat breads such as rice cakes.

Cakes and Cookies

Commercially baked organic cookies and cakes are almost always superior to nonorganic ones because they contain more vitamins and fewer additives. However, some organic sweet products still include too much refined sugar, both in terms of health and taste. To ensure the cookies and cakes you buy are the best on the shelf, check the ingredients. Better still, bake your own. Experiment with the different organic flours available, add sweetness by using chopped dried fruit, or flavor with grated orange rind, organic cocoa powder, or a pinch of cinnamon or allspice.

THE ORGANIC PANTRY

A well stocked pantry is a valuable asset for any cook, but it is absolutely essential for the organic cook, who may not be able to obtain every ingredient at the last minute by simply making a quick trip to the local store.

It is worth spending a bit of time sourcing organic food. There is already a lot of it out there, and with more and more products becoming available all the time, switching to organic ingredients is relatively easy. You don't have to do it all at once; simply replace nonorganic oils, vinegars, jams, nuts, seasonings, and other items in your pantry with organic alternatives when they run out. A good organic supplier with a rapid turnover is a good place to start, and the Internet can be handy, too.

Sugars and Honeys

Organic sugars are beneficial because they do not cause the pollution to developing countries that agrochemically grown versions often do. Refined and unrefined organic versions of all standard sugars except refined white are readily available, from raw to soft brown. Unrefined organic sugars have far fewer vitamins and nutrients stripped out of them during processing than refined

Below: Molasses is a great source of iron.

Above: Rapadura is an excellent organic alternative to refined sugar.

sugars, and for this reason they have a slightly better flavor, too. However, organic sugar still has a high empty calorie value, so it should always be used sparingly for a healthy balanced diet.

Rapadura This exciting alternative to refined sugar is only available in organic form. Similar in color and texture to soft brown sugar, it has a much more interesting flavor and nutrient profile because it is made by simply sun-drying organic sugar cane juice, so all the beneficial vitamins and minerals of this natural product are retained. Rapadura is suitable for any style of cooking that calls for sugar, including jam-making and meringues. It is also known as jaggery, the Hindi name for this product.

Molasses Another excellent natural sweetener derived from sugar cane is molasses. Organic molasses has all the minerals in sugar cane in concentrated form, and is a great source of iron. The most nutritionally valuable type is thick and very dark blackstrap molasses. The powerful taste of molasses makes it a good choice for treacly cookies, cakes, puddings, and sauces.

Honey The most popular alternative to refined sugar is honey. Organic honey must come from unpolluted areas if it is to retain its purity. Most nonorganic honey comes from bees fed on liquid sugar instead of collecting pollen. It is inferior to the organic version, both in its blandness and its lack of nutrition.

There are some wonderful organic honeys, each reflecting the flavors of the flowering plants visited by the bees. From Australian manuka honey to Zimbabwean forest honey, the choices range from powerful, dark solid honeys to delicate golden liquid honeys. It is worth tasting a selection to discover your personal favorite and familiarizing yourself with each variety so you can select the ideal match when cooking. Try using honey instead of syrup or sugar in cakes, or to give a hint of sweetness to salad dressings and hot sauces.

Honey has long been highly valued for its medicinal and healing properties. Mixed with lemon juice and hot water, it has antiseptic properties and can relieve sore throats. It is also thought to be helpful in treating diarrhea and asthma.

Left: Organic farmers' markets are a good place to seek out unusual and homemade organic jams, marmalades, honeys, pickles, and preserves.

Above: Fruit syrups are natural sweeteners, which can be used in place of sugar.

Other Natural Sweeteners

There are a lot of other sweetening options for the organic cook to explore, including organic maple syrup, maple sugar, and a wide range of fruit products. **Maple Syrup and Sugar** Made by tapping the sap of the maple tree, organic maple syrup and sugar are not overprocessed, so retain their richness. Drizzled over hot pancakes, maple, with its buttery tones, is the ultimate syrup. A small amount, added to a savory batter, tantalizes the palate. Maple syrup is sweeter than sugar so less is required in cooking.
Fruit Syrups and Pastes Concentrated organic fruit syrups also make great sweeteners, whether you choose the liquid form or the solid paste. They contain none of

the pesticides found in agrochemical versions and no added sugar or preservatives. They are just as popular with children as with adults. Concentrates are made from many types of organic fruits, including apples, pears, grapes, dates, peaches, black currants, and oranges. Apple and date versions add most sweetness, so they can be used more sparingly than some other types. Their flavors are also not particularly dominant, so they will not overwhelm other ingredients. Pastes can also be used in cooking, but they will need to be dissolved in water first. On their own, fruit pastes taste delicious when spread on bread. Most organic outlets sell concentrated fruit syrups and pastes. They can be stored in a refrigerator for 2–3 months.

Pureed dried fruit, such as prunes, figs, dates, and apricots, can also be used to sweeten pies, crumbles, and cakes. To make spiced apricot puree, place some apricots in a pan with enough water to cover, add a cinnamon stick, two cloves, and a little freshly grated nutmeg, and simmer for 20 minutes, until the apricots are plump. Let coo,l then puree in a food processor until smooth. Add more water if the mixture seems a little thick.

Above: A selection of organic honeys

Above: Organic chocolate comes in dark, white, and milk varieties.

Cocoa and Chocolate

Agrochemical cocoa is the most heavily sprayed food crop, and is often unfairly traded, too. By buying organic cocoa and chocolate products, you ensure that you are not supporting agrochemical pollution in developing countries.

Organic chocolate products are usually higher in cocoa and lower in sugar than the nonorganic equivalent, and are free from hydrogenated fats, emulsifiers, and other chemical additives. Organic cocoa is naturally high in tannins and antioxidant flavonoids, plus B vitamins and iron, so this means that eating organic chocolate in moderation can do you good. It is thought to offer some protection against heart attacks.

The darker the chocolate, the higher the percentage of cocoa solids and the more intense the taste. Chocolate with 70 percent cocoa solids has a proportionally higher nutritional content.

Organic chocolate comes in a wide array of products, from speciality handmade pralines to slabs of bittersweet, milk, and white and flavored chocolates. They all keep well and can be stored in the refrigerator, so there is no need to eat all the chocolate at once.

Nuts and Seeds

Organic nuts and seeds are little powerhouses that would grow into new plants or mighty trees if sown and allowed to germinate. This makes them an incredibly rich source of nutrients. High in plant oils and protein, they also yield B complex vitamins, potassium, magnesium, calcium, phosphorus, and iron. The fat they contain is largely monounsaturated or polyunsaturated (only coconuts and brazil nuts contain saturated fat) and they are the richest vegetable source of vitamin E, which has been credited with reducing the risk of heart disease, strokes, and certain cancers.

Many people equate a healthy diet with a low-fat diet, but this is not true. It is important that we eat a balanced diet, including proteins, carbohydrates, and fats. While saturated and hydrogenated fats are undesirable, unrefined polyunsaturated fats are essential. They provide energy and help to prevent heart disease, eczema, ulcers, and arthritis when eaten as part of a healthy diet and combined with a balanced lifestyle. The best way of obtaining polyunsaturated fats is to eat nuts and seeds, because these also provide the antioxidants necessary to optimize the value of these fats.

Seeds are very good for you for many other reasons, too. Sunflower seeds are rich in many minerals, including zinc, which aids skin regeneration and helps to heal cuts and minor abrasions. The

Walnuts (above) and hazelnuts (below) are a good source of protein.

seeds also contain B vitamins and will ease fatigue, irritability, and depression. Flax seeds are gentle healers for the intestinal tract. Sesame seeds are a good source of protein, zinc, and iron, so are good for sexual health. Pumpkin seeds have similar nutrients, plus calcium and B vitamins.

Cooking With Organic Nuts And Seeds

Health reasons aside, organic nuts and seeds taste great. You can add chopped nuts and seeds to salads, savory roasts, breads, and cakes. Roasting nuts and seeds in a dry, nonstick skillet for a few

MAKING NUT BUTTER

Nut butters don't have to contain just one type of nut. Make your own wholesome nut butter using a combination of organic peanuts, hazelnuts, and cashew nuts.

1 Place ½ cup shelled nuts in a food processor or blender and process until finely ground.

2 Pour 1–2 tablespoons sunflower oil into the processor or blender and process to a coarse paste. Spread on toast or stir into stir-fries to produce a rich, creamy sauce. Store in an airtight container.

Above: *Peanuts*

Right: *Organic chestnuts are sweet and starchy.*

NUT NOTES

The perfect snack food, nuts provide plenty of nutrients, too.

• Brazil nuts are a good source of protein, with a lot of vitamin B₁ and magnesium to aid concentration and support the nervous system.

• Walnuts contain as much protein as eggs, plus potassium, zinc, and iron.

• Pecan nuts, walnuts, and hemp seeds are a source of linoleic acid, which has anti-inflammatory properties. Smokers who have kicked the habit find it soothes lungs irritated by the free radicals in cigarette smoke. These nuts and seeds are also a first line of defense against other forms of cancer, because of their high vitamin E content, plus the fact that they are the only known sources of an antioxidant group called avenanthramides. People who eat walnuts or pecans five times a week have been discovered to lower their risk of developing coronary heart disease by 35 percent.

• Pine nuts are the richest source of protein of any nut, with a deliciously buttery flavor that makes them great in salads.

• Peanuts are a good source of both iron and protein.

• Hazelnuts have a sweet flavor but are relatively low in calories.

• Chestnuts are sweet and starchy, and help to bind other ingredients, in nut roasts or stuffings, for instance.

Below: Black and white sesame seeds

minutes greatly improves the flavor. Watch them carefully and toss frequently so that they don't scorch.

Store-bought nonorganic nut butters, including peanut butter, often contain unwanted hydrogenated oil and can be loaded with sugar, so buy organic nut or seed butters. Alternatively, make your own by processing your favorite nuts and seeds through a masticating juicer or in a food processor or blender.

Tahini, made by grinding sesame seeds, is especially good. Stir tahini or nut butter into a stir-fry for an instant sauce. When used in this way, nut and seed butters become favorite seasonings. When spread on toast, they make nutritious and very tasty toppings.

Oils

Cold-pressed organic oils retain almost all the health and taste benefits of the raw nuts and seeds from which they are made. This is not the case with most agrochemical oils, which are extracted at high temperatures. In the process, the natural antioxidants, minerals, and other vitamins in the oil are destroyed. Non-organic oil is then further processed with solvents to lessen the color and tone down the taste of the final product. Cold-pressed organic oils are prized for these very characteristics.

Olive oil is a firm favorite. In terms of color and taste, it is a wonderful addition to any meal. It is a versatile food that can be eaten alone on bread instead of butter, added to salads, or used for cooking, and is the perfect partner for organic food. It is the most digestible oil, and is universally acknowledged as being highly effective in preventing heart disease and treating liver disorders. Many nut oils make delicious salad dressings when whisked with lemon juice or vinegar. Organic sunflower and safflower oils are rich in polyunsaturates that are great for heart health. Use them in dishes that require a lighter taste than olive oil, such as in oriental cooking and cake baking.

Above: Pumpkin seeds make a perfect organic snack food.

Storing Nuts, Seeds, and Oils

Buy nuts in the shell, if possible, and eat them as soon as possible after shelling. If you must store them, put them in airtight bags and keep them in a cool place or the refrigerator. Store seeds in the same way. Buy cold-pressed organic oils in small quantities, so that they can be used quickly, and store in a cool place. Never expose to heat during storage. Do not store nuts, seeds, or oils for more than a few months, or their oil may become rancid.

Above: Cold-pressed organic sunflower and safflower oils

SEASONINGS

If you are new to organic cooking, you may find you need to rethink your approach to seasonings of all kinds. Organic ingredients taste so good that to mask their flavors would be a sin. Use spices, condiments, and strong flavorings, such as vinegar, with care, choosing always the organic option.

Spices

Over sixty different kinds of spices are regularly used in cooking around the world. About twenty of these are easily available organically grown. Try to find organic spices where you can, because nonorganic ones have often been heavily sprayed with pesticides. Most of these plants are grown in developing countries where nonorganic farming practices can undermine farmers' health and the environment. Until recently, dried spices with organic certification were difficult to track down. Now they are much more readily available in good organic stores, direct from the suppliers, or through mail-order companies.

Spices are almost always used dried when their flavors are condensed. However, fresh versions of chiles and ginger are also popular. Organic dried chiles are a useful pantry ingredient. They come whole, powdered, or in flakes and tend to be hotter than fresh chiles. Especially valuable chiles include fruity, mild anchos, chipotles, and hot habaneros.

Below: Fresh organic ginger has an intense fiery flavor.

Above: Organic dried chiles are free from harmful pesticide residues.

Fry dried spices before adding them to a dish. Heat a pan with or without oil and fry or toast the spices for about 1 minute, until they release their aroma. Shake the pan often to prevent them from sticking. Most spices should be toasted whole, then crushed with a pestle in a mortar or whizzed in a coffee blender. However such spices as nutmeg and cinnamon are too large or bulky to be heated whole. Crush cinnamon bark or grate whole nutmeg just before toasting it. These spices retain more flavor when they are stored whole.

Fresh organic ginger is smaller and has a more intense flavor than the swollen and sometimes watery nonorganic spice. Ginger and galangal add a hot yet refreshing flavor to sweet and savory dishes, including marinades, stir-fries, fresh vegetables, poached fruit, and cakes and bakes.

The five spices most often used in Indian cooking are coriander, cumin, turmeric, pepper, and chile. Many other spices are used alongside this quintet, including star anise and fenugreek. Try adding nutmeg to savory dishes, such as pumpkin soup and baked fish, as well as more traditional sweet dishes, such as rice pudding. The powerful essential oils in this spice have slightly euphoric properties, so they lift the spirits. No wonder nutmeg is a popular spice in mulled wine and other festive Christmas treats. Add

caraway seeds to sauerkraut or bean stews, because they help to ease flatulence. Coriander seeds can help to cool an otherwise hot and spicy dish, as well as adding their distinctive flavor. Chili powder acts like cornstarch, thickening stews and curries, and pepper adds accent to almost everything, including strawberries.

Salt

The main flavoring used in cooking throughout the world is salt. At one time this was guaranteed to be a natural product extracted from seawater. Table salt is now almost exclusively over-refined, with magnesium carbonate

---

PREPARING FRESH GINGER

1 You don't need to peel fresh organic ginger. Using a small, sharp paring knife, simply chop to the size specified in the recipe.

2 Alternatively, grate ginger finely. Special bamboo graters can be found in many Asian stores, but an ordinary grater will do the job equally well. Freshly grated ginger can be squeezed with the fingers to release the juice, if required.

Left: Sea salt contains a variety
of minerals and salts.

Right:
Whole-grain
organic
mustard.

added to
ensure it flows
freely. Sea salt,
whether organically certified
or not, has a much broader
spectrum of taste because it contains a
variety of different minerals and salts
alongside the sodium chloride that is its
main component. Keep your salt usage
low, because using too much of this
mineral compound can lead to high
blood pressure. One benefit of using
good-quality salt is that it has a stronger
flavor, so you do not need to use as
much salt. Organically certified salts are
particularly delicious and it is most
reassuring to know that such salts are
routinely inspected by the certifier
whose logo they bear.

Right: Organic light and dark shoyu
(soy sauce) adds flavor.

are plenty of organic varieties, including
balsamic and Japanese mirin rice vinegar.
Some nonorganic vinegars are good-
quality products, with fine flavors and
good fragrances. However, many
nonorganic vinegars are horrible.
The vinegar most commonly used
bears little resemblance to a good-
quality vinegar.

At the opposite end of the
spectrum is organic cider
vinegar. This raw, unfiltered,
non-distilled, undiluted product
is aged in wooden barrels and
contains no preservatives and has
superb health benefits. It is antibacterial,
antiseptic, anti-inflammatory, and
detoxifying. It also helps to keep blood
thin, which is useful for people who eat
meat and dairy products.

Soy Sauces

Many organic cooks use organic soy
sauces, such as tamari and shoyu, to add
saltiness and depth to their meals. These
products will enhance the flavor of most
savory dishes, but they should be added
in moderation at the end of the cooking
process. High temperatures destroy the
delicate proteins and enzymes that are so
beneficial in these products.

Vinegars

Organic vinegars are made by fermenting
ingredients, such as organic apples and
grapes. Over time, these fine ingredients
will develop into zesty condiments to
be drizzled over fish or added to salad
dressings, pickles, and marinades. There

Other Condiments

Many condiments contain vinegar as a
major ingredient, including mustard,
prepared salad dressings, mayonnaise,
chutneys, pickles, and olives. The benefits
of buying organic versions of these
products are obvious, because you can
be sure that a good vinegar has been
used as a base. Other ingredients will
be organic, too, so whatever you buy
is likely to be flavorsome and of good
quality. The eggs in organic mayonnaise
will have come from free-range organic
chickens. Vegan organic mayonnaise is
also readily available, made from soy
or pea protein. The taste of some
organic full grain mustards puts regular
nonorganic mustards to shame. While
many nonorganic commercial salad
dressings threaten to drown your healthy
leaves in refined, sugary oils, organic
salad dressings have been known
to outshine a homemade mixture.
Although the best chutneys and pickles
are made in your kitchen, there are
plenty of excellent ones available in
supermarkets, farmers' markets, and
good organic stores.

Above: Cider vinegar is antibacterial.

BEVERAGES

Over the past decade or so, the demand for organic beverages has grown. From a niche market, the beverage industry has burgeoned, producing drinks that are often so delicious that even those who are not yet fully committed to the organic ideal seek them out. From table water to gin, an organic certification mark on the bottle is a sign of fine quality and sustainable ingredients.

Below, left to right: Organic biodynamic white and red wines and elderflower wine.

Wine

Organic wine is an explosion of flavors. Very often produced by small artisan vineyards, the organic grapes used in organic wines are much more diverse than those found in the majority of standard nonorganic wines. Hangovers are usually caused by sulfites, which can also provoke asthma and migraines. Levels of sulfur are much lower in organic wines, so you really can feel the difference the next day. Organic vineyards recycle their waste grape skins by

composting them, and they often plant flowering plants among the vines to attract pollinating insects and predators.

Prize-winning organic and biodynamic red and white wines are produced all over the world, including in France, Italy, Australia, and California. Red wine is full of health-promoting antioxidants, so it is good for preventing heart disease as well as relieving stress if drunk in moderation.

To find a good supplier of organic wine, contact an independent wine dealer. The Internet is an invaluable tool for finding such retailers; simply make a search for organic wine dealers and look for one in your area. Alternatively, buy the wines direct from the vineyard.

Fruit wines can also be delicious. Organic stores sell several varieties, but the best way to investigate the many delights of elderberry, elderflower, and black currant wine is to make your own. Home wine-making kits can be used with organic ingredients to produce excellent results.

Store organic wine on its side in a cool, dark place to keep the cork moist. Try adding your favorite wines to sauces and fruit salads, or organic sherry and port to cakes and other desserts.

Spirits

Wines are not the only prize-winning organic drinks. Some incredible spirits are available, including industry award winners such as Del Meguey mezcal. This organic mezcal is produced by traditional artisans in Mexico who have had the craft passed down to them through countless generations. Del Meguey produce five kinds of organic mezcal, with their top-of-the-range product achieving international status as one of the finest spirits in the world.

Organic gin and vodka have also reached a fine quality now, with Juniper Green gin and UK5 vodka made in London, England. Distilled from organic raw ingredients, you will find that these spirits have a clean, round taste, with a lot of warm flavors in the gin. You can also buy organic Scotch whiskey, plus more unusual spirits, including Grappa and Calvados.

Beer and Cider

Organic beer and lager microbreweries have sprung up and begun to flourish all over the world, from North America to Belgium and Germany. The intensity that organic hops impart to the flavor of organic beers and lagers has encouraged the general trend toward high quality traditional brews. There are dark stouts and light lagers, bronze bitters and extra strong Belgian beers. There is even a German hemp beer, Cannabia, based on an ancient Roman recipe.

Organic hard ciders are made from organic apples, and often contain much less added sulfur dioxide than nonorganic hard ciders. This makes them less likely to provoke hangovers in the morning. The largest range of organic hard cider is currently produced in England, but they are also brewed in France.

Serve hard cider cold with a hot pork dinner or ham lunch. Alternatively, add a little to the pan when roasting lamb for additional flavor and acidity.

Water

The ultimate soft drink is water. Essential for human health, it is undeniably the most thirst-quenching drink of them all. Add a squeeze of lemon juice or a sprig of fresh mint, and it becomes even more enjoyable. Although bottled water cannot be certified as organic, the label can state that it was sourced from organically farmed land. This is important if you want to avoid pesticides that may have run off agrochemical farmland into the water table beneath.

Tap water quality varies hugely between regions, depending on the geology of the area and its filtration capabilities. At best, it is pure and full of beneficial mineral,s such as calcium. At worst, it can contain pesticides, hormones, and heavy metals.

Water Filters The best way to ensure that the water you drink is as pure as possible is to invest in a good-quality water filter. There are many variations on three basic types. The most common is the carbon filter, which is good at cleaning most impurities, including fluoride. An even better version incorporates a built-in reverse osmosis system that guarantees absolute purity from all heavy metals and other pollutants. Distillers are

Above: Fresh organic lemonade

also available, but the water they produce must be supplemented carefully with minerals from foods or supplements. Choosing organic beverages is a good way of avoiding additives, but drinking pure water is even better.

Carbonated Beverages

If you want to enjoy carbonated beverages as part of an organic diet it is essential that the beverages you buy are also organic. Nonorganic colas are bad for your health. Although it is usual for both organic and nonorganic carbonated beverages to contain a high proportion of sugar, the nonorganic versions are full of artificial chemical additives that are seriously undermining. The phosphoric acid in colas is directly related to loss of calcium in bone. This can lead to osteoporosis, a disease that is now more common in the industrialized world.

Nonorganic diet beverages usually contain synthetic sweeteners such as aspartame and saccharine. These artificial additives are strictly banned in organic foods, with very good reason. Aspartame is a neurotoxin that affects the appetite control centers in the brain. As a result, serotonin levels in the brain drop, often leading to depression. Consumers of artificially sweetened drinks often have difficulty dieting.

Left to right: Organic Juniper Green gin, made in London, and German hemp beer, Cannabia.

Fruit Juice Concentrates

Not only are organic fruit juice concentrates better than nonorganic ones in terms of taste and sweetness, but they are also more nutritious. They contain no artificial colorings or flavorings, refined sugars, or artificial sweeteners. Made from real fruit juices, they taste much more like the original than the highly processed alternatives. However, many organic versions are still high in sugar, so check the ingredients, especially if you are preparing the drink for a child. Organic sugar is almost as unhealthy as nonorganic sugar, and just as destructive to teeth.

Fruit and Vegetable Juices

Commercially available organic juices vary considerably in terms of flavor, but all score over nonorganic ones because they are free of pesticide residues. It takes a lot of fruit and vegetables to make a relatively small amount of juice. If the produce contains pesticide residues, these will be concentrated when the fruit or vegetable is juiced. Drinking organic juice means that you are getting more concentrated vitamins, mineral,s and phytonutrients instead.

If you buy fruit or vegetable juices, try to ensure that they come from freshly pressed

Right: Organic fruit and vegetable juices are a fabulous source of vitamins, minerals, and phytonutrients.

Right: Vanilla spice tea leaves, fair-trade breakfast, and Japanese nagata kukicha teas

produce instead of concentrates. Minimal processing results in a more natural taste and higher nutrient content. Some juices now include natural healers and energizers, such as ginseng, chlorophyl-rich spirulina, and wheatgrass.

Juicing The best juices are freshly made, either squeezed manually from citrus fruits or processed with the aid of a juice machine, or juicer. Most juicers are based on the centrifugal system. The fresh produce is grated and strained at high speed to separate the juice from the pulp. Other juicers work by effectively "chewing" the produce. The juice that is released comes from between the plant's cell walls and is extremely high in nutrients and flavor. These machines are called masticating juicers, and although expensive, they are the best on the market. All fruits and vegetables, leafy greens, and fresh herbs can be juiced in machines.

If you do not own a juicer, make fruit juices in a food processor or blender. Peel, pit, core, or seed the fruit before blending. Juices made in this way tend to be thicker and have a higher fiber content than regular juices because the pulp has not been removed. Fruits such as melon and grapes are ideal for blended juices.

Teas, Fruit Teas, and Herb Teas

Organic teas are grown with respect for the land and the people who tend it. The teas are generally fairly traded, with communities far away from the end beverage gaining real benefits whenever a package is sold. Pesticide residues are at issue here. Although these are not high in agrochemically grown teas, the crop is generally sprayed intensively throughout its growth. This pollutes the land and

poses a serious health threat to the workers. Organic teas are full of flavor, and are available in a lot of different varieties, including loose leaves and tea bags containing either single estate varieties or blends. Flavored or spiced teas are also on sale. All these products contain vitamins and minerals, as well as powerful antioxidants that protect the heart and help to prevent cancer. When you buy organic, even the tea bags are better for the environment, because unlike nonorganic tea bags, they have to be chlorine-free.

There are hundreds of organic fruit teas, spice teas, and herbal teas available, generally with much better flavor than the nonorganic equivalents.

Fruit Teas Organic fruit teas rely on natural fruit for their flavor and color, whereas nonorganic fruit teas are often boosted with synthetic and "nature-identical" flavorings and colors. This results in overpoweringly strong instead of less subtle tastes.

Herbal Teas and Spice Teas These have direct healing benefits as well as delicate flavors. The herbs and spices they contain are often pharmacopeial grade, meaning that they are of the same quality as herbs prescribed by herbalists.

Some blends are available specifically formulated for medicinal purposes as well as flavor, including mixes to help you sleep, to aid digestion, to ward off colds, or to ease stress.

Lavender, hyssop, thym,e and marjoram infused together are taken as a remedy for cold symptons. Hops, chamomile, and lime flower are used to beat insomnia. Rosemary is said to stimulate the circulation and improve concentration, while thyme boosts the immune system and helps fight infections. Elderflower tea can ease painful sinuses and bronchial conditions.

Almost any herb and its flowers can be used to make tea, and the method is generally the same. Place several sprigs of the freshly picked herb in a cup, pour over hot, but not boiling, water, and let stand for several minutes to infuse. Strain the liquid to remove the leaves and drink it hot or cold with honey, lemon, or sugar to taste. Spices require

Above: Organic drinking chocolate powder

greater heat to extract the constituents, so they need to be placed in a saucepan of cold water, heated, and simmered for 10 to 15 minutes.

Coffee and Cocoa

Organic coffee and cocoa are grown in hot, tropical, mountainous regions, such as South and Central America, East Africa, and Indonesia. It is essential to have faith in the producer's trading practices. The cultivation of agrochemical coffee often involves heavy pesticide use, especially in developing countries. There are health and safety concerns, too, about conditions for workers on the plantations. The confidence that comes from buying organically grown, fairly traded coffee doubles the pleasure of drinking this beverage. Look out for organic instant coffee granules or powder, as well as ground coffee or whole roasted beans. Store whole or ground beans in the refrigerator so they will retain their freshness for longer.

Organic drinking chocolate is available as an instant powder. Although organic coffee and drinking chocolate powder are not the healthiest organic products, organic drinking chocolate is much better for you than the nonorganic version because it contains only natural ingredients, including antioxidant-rich organic cocoa. Intensively produced nonorganic drinking chocolate contains dried nonorganic milk, hydrogenated fats, refined sweeteners, and artificial flavorings.

Above: Buying and grinding fair-traded organic coffee beans can double the pleasure of drinking coffee.

SPRING

As the days start to get a little longer and the weather gets warmer, the fresh organic ingredients traditionally associated with this time of year—such as tender young vegetables and new season lamb—start to appear in the stores and farmers' markets.

The season's vegetables require little cooking to bring out their sweet flavor: Try asparagus with a tangy lemon sauce, or sweet young carrots and leeks, or Escalopes of Chicken with new potatoes. Brightly colored spring vegetables also look and taste good when served with pasta, or when added to soups.

Light fish dishes are a popular choice now after long, dark winter days—Salmon Fish Cakes or Fillets of Sea Bream in Filo Dough, served simply with spring vegetables, are a real treat. And this is the time of year to enjoy organic lamb, in such dishes as Lamb Stew, Herb-crusted Rack of Lamb with Puy Lentils, and Lamb Burgers. For dessert, nothing tastes better than tender spring rhubarb served with ginger ice cream, or made into a meringue pie.

CHICKEN, AVOCADO, and SCALLION SOUP

Organic avocados ripen naturally over a longer period of time than nonorganic, producing really rich-flavored fruit. Combined here with chicken and scallions, they add a creaminess to this delicious soup.

SERVES SIX

6¼ cups chicken stock
½ fresh chile, seeded
2 skinless, boneless chicken breast fillets
1 avocado
4 scallions, finely sliced
1 can (14 ounces) chickpeas, drained
sea salt and freshly ground black pepper

1 Put the chicken stock into a large pan and add the chile. Bring to a boil, add the whole chicken breast fillets, then lower the heat and simmer for about 10 minutes, or until the chicken is cooked.

COOK'S TIP
Handle chiles carefully because they can irritate the skin and eyes. It is advisable to wear rubber gloves when preparing them.

2 Remove the pan from the heat and lift out the chicken breasts with a slotted spoon. Let cool a little, then, using two forks, shred the chicken into small pieces. Set the shredded chicken aside.

3 Put the chicken stock into a food processor or blender and add the chile. Process the mixture until smooth, then return to the pan.

4 Cut the avocado in half, remove the skin and pit, then slice the flesh into ¾ inch pieces. Add it to the stock, with the scallions and chickpeas.

5 Return the shredded chicken to the pan, with salt and pepper to taste, and heat gently. When the soup is heated through, spoon into warmed bowls and serve.

PASTA and CHICKPEA SOUP

A simple, country-style soup. The shapes of the pasta and the beans complement one another well. Look out for really large pasta shells, which you can find in farmers' markets and good organic stores.

SERVES FOUR TO SIX

1 onion
2 carrots
2 celery stalks
4 tablespoons olive oil
1 can (14 ounces) chickpeas, rinsed
    and drained
1 can (7 ounces) cannellini beans,
    rinsed and drained
⅔ cup passata
    (strained tomatoes)
½ cup water
6¼ cups chicken stock
2 fresh or dried rosemary sprigs
7 ounces dried giant conchiglie
sea salt and ground black pepper
freshly grated Parmesan cheese or
    premium Italian-style vegetarian
    cheese, to serve

1 Chop the onion, carrots, and celery stalks finely, either in a food processor or by hand.

2 Heat the olive oil in a large saucepan, add the chopped vegetable mixture and cook over a low heat, stirring frequently, for 5 minutes, or until the vegetables are just beginning to soften.

3 Add the chickpeas and cannellini beans, stir well to mix, then cook for 5 minutes. Stir in the strained tomatoes and water, then cook, stirring, for 2–3 minutes.

4 Add 2 cups of the stock and one of the rosemary sprigs. Bring to a boil, cover, then simmer gently, stirring occasionally, for 1 hour.

5 Put in the remaining stock, add the pasta, and bring to a boil, stirring. Lower the heat slightly and simmer, stirring frequently, until the pasta is *al dente*: 7–8 minutes, or according to the package instructions.

6 When the pasta is cooked, taste the soup for seasoning. Remove the rosemary and serve the soup hot in warmed bowls, topped with grated cheese and a few rosemary leaves from the rosemary sprig.

COOK'S TIP
Organic tomatoes is a must for this recipe—most nonorganic tomato products contain genetically modified tomatoes.

TAPENADE with QUAIL EGGS and CRUDITÉS

*This olive-based spread or dip makes a sociable start to a meal. Serve the tapenade
with hard-boiled quail eggs or small organic hen eggs and a selection of mixed spring
vegetable crudités and let everyone help themselves.*

SERVES SIX

2 cups pitted black olives
2 large garlic cloves, peeled
1 tablespoon salted capers, rinsed
6 canned or bottled anchovy
    fillets, drained
2 ounces good-quality canned tuna
1–2 teaspoons Cognac (optional)
1 teaspoon chopped fresh thyme
2 tablespoons chopped
    fresh parsley
2–4 tablespoons extra virgin olive oil
a dash of lemon juice
2 tablespoons crème fraîche, fromage frais,
    or sour cream (optional)
12–18 quail eggs
ground black pepper

For the crudités
bunch of scallions, halved if large
bunch of radishes, trimmed
bunch of baby fennel, trimmed and halved
    if large, or 1 large fennel bulb, cut into
    thin wedges

To serve
French bread
unsalted butter or olive oil and
    sea salt to dip

1 Process the olives, garlic cloves, capers,
anchovies, and tuna in a food processor
or blender. Transfer to a mixing bowl and
stir in the Cognac, if using, the thyme,
parsley, and enough olive oil to make a
paste. Season to taste with pepper and
a dash of lemon juice. Stir in the crème
fraîche, fromage frais, or sour cream if
using, and transfer to a serving bowl.

2 Place the quail eggs in a saucepan of
cold water and bring to a boil. Cook for
only 2 minutes, then immediately drain
and plunge the eggs into iced water to
stop them from cooking any further and
to help make them easier to shell.

3 When the eggs are cold, carefully
part-shell them.

4 Serve the tapenade with the eggs
and crudités and offer French bread,
unsalted butter or oil, and sea salt to
accompany them.

COOK'S TIPS
• Crème fraîche or fromage frais softens
the distinctive flavor of the olives for a
milder tapenade.
• In Provence, where tapenade comes
from, it is traditional to serve it with
crudités of celery, fennel, and tomato.
• Tapenade is also delicious spread on
toast and served with pre-dinner drinks.

OYSTERS ROCKEFELLER

This is the perfect dish for those who prefer to eat their oysters lightly cooked. As a less-expensive alternative, for those who are not "as rich as Rockefeller", give mussels or clams the same treatment—they will also taste delicious.

SERVES SIX

3 cups coarse sea salt,
plus extra to serve
24 oysters, opened
½ cup butter or
nonhydrogenated margarine
2 shallots, finely chopped
1¼ pounds spinach leaves, finely chopped
4 tablespoons chopped fresh parsley
4 tablespoons chopped celery leaves
6 tablespoons fresh white or whole-wheat
breadcrumbs
2–4 teaspoons vodka
cayenne pepper
sea salt and ground black pepper
lemon wedges, to serve

COOK'S TIP

If you prefer a smoother stuffing, whiz it
to a paste in a food processor or blender
at the end of step 3.

1 Preheat the oven to 425°F. Make a
bed of coarse salt on two large baking
sheets. Set the oysters in the half-shell
in the bed of salt to keep them steady.
Set aside.

2 Melt the butter or margarine in a
skillet. Add the chopped shallots
and cook them over a low heat for
2–3 minutes, until they are softened.
Stir in the spinach and let it wilt.

3 Add the parsley, celery leaves, and
breadcrumbs to the skillet and fry gently
for 5 minutes. Season with salt, pepper,
and cayenne pepper.

4 Divide the stuffing among the oysters.
Drizzle a few drops of vodka over each
oyster, then bake for about 5 minutes,
until bubbling and golden brown. Serve
on a heated platter on a shallow salt bed
with lemon wedges.

LEEK and MUSSEL TARTLETS

Wild mussels are easily harvested and are simply gathered off rocks in shallow water by hand. Serve these vividly colored little tarts as a first course, with a few salad greens, such as watercress, arugula, and frisée.

3 Preheat the oven to 375°F. Roll out the dough and line six 4-inch quiche pans. Prick the bottoms and line the sides with foil. Bake for 10 minutes. Remove the foil and bake for another 5–8 minutes. Reduce the temperature to 350°F.

4 Soak the saffron in 1 tablespoon of hot water for 10 minutes. Fry the leeks in the oil in a medium-hot pan for 6–8 minutes. Add the peppers and cook for 2 minutes.

SERVES SIX

large pinch of saffron threads
2 large leeks, sliced
2 tablespoons olive oil
2 large yellow bell peppers, halved, seeded, broiled, peeled, and cut into strips
2 pounds mussels
2 large eggs
1¼ cups light cream or soy cream
2 tablespoons finely chopped fresh parsley
sea salt and ground black pepper
salad greens, to serve

For the pastry
2 cups all-purpose flour
½ cup chilled butter, diced
3–4 tablespoons chilled water

1 To make the pastry, sift the flour into a mixing bowl and add the butter. Rub the butter in with your fingertips until the mixture resembles fine breadcrumbs.

2 Sprinkle 3 tablepsoons of the water over and mix with a round-bladed knife until the mixture comes together and a soft dough is formed. Add more water if necessary. Wrap the dough in plastic wrap and chill for 30 minutes.

COOK'S TIP
Use soy cream instead of the light cream and soy margarine instead of butter for a nondairy option.

5 Bring water 1 inch deep to a boil in a large pan and add 2 teaspoons of salt. Scrub the mussels and remove the beards. Discard any mussels that stay open when tapped, then throw the rest into the pan. Cover and cook over a high heat, shaking the pan occasionally, for 3–4 minutes, or until the mussels open. Discard any unopened mussels. Shell the remainder.

6 Beat the eggs, cream, and saffron liquid together. Season with salt and pepper and whisk in the parsley. Arrange the leeks, peppers, and mussels in the shells, add the egg mixture, and bake for 20–25 minutes. Serve with salad greens.

DEEP-FRIED TOFU BALLS

Tofu is a wonderfully healthy and versatile ingredient and is flavored to perfection in this Japanese dish, known as hiryozu, *which means flying dragon's head. The tangy lime sauce provides a lovely contrast to the savory tofu balls.*

SERVES FOUR

2 packages (10¼ ounces) firm tofu
½ small carrot, peeled
¼ cup trimmed green beans
2 extra large eggs, beaten
2 tablespoons sake
2 teaspoons mirin
1 teaspoon sea salt
2 teaspoons shoyu
pinch of unrefined superfine sugar
      or rapadura
sunflower oil, for deep-frying

For the lime sauce
3 tablespoons shoyu
juice of ½ lime
1 teaspoons rice vinegar or mirin

To garnish
11 ounces daikon, peeled
2 dried red chiles, halved and seeded
4 chives, finely chopped

1 Drain the tofu and wrap in a dish towel or paper towel. Set a cutting board on top and let stand for 2 hours, or until it loses most of its liquid.

2 Cut the daikon for the garnish into 1½-inch thick slices. Make 3–4 small holes in each slice with a skewer or chopstick and insert chile pieces into the holes. Leat stand for 15 minutes, then grate the daikon and chile finely.

3 To make the tofu balls, chop the carrot finely. Cut the beans into ¼ inch lengths. Cook both vegetables for 1 minute in boiling water.

4 In a food processor, blend the tofu, eggs, sake, mirin, salt, shoyu, and sugar until smooth. Transfer to a bowl and mix in the carrot and beans.

5 Fill a wok or pan with oil 1½ inch deep, and heat to 365°F.

6 Soak a paper towel with a little vegetable oil, and lightly moisten your hands with it. Scoop 2½ tablespoons of the mixture in one hand and shape into a ball between your hands.

7 Carefully slide the ball into the oil and deep-fry until crisp and golden brown. Drain on paper towel. Repeat with the remaining mixture.

8 Arrange the tofu balls on a plate and sprinkle with chives. Put 2 tablespoons of grated daikon in each of four bowls. Mix the lime sauce ingredients in a small serving bowl. Serve the hot tofu balls with the lime sauce to be mixed with grated daikon by each guest.

ASPARAGUS with LEMON SAUCE

This is a good spring dish because the asparagus gives the immune system a kickstart to help detoxify after winter. The sauce has a light, fresh taste and brings out the best in asparagus.

SERVES FOUR AS A FIRST COURSE

1½ pounds asparagus, tough ends
   removed, and tied in a bundle
1 tablespoon cornstarch
2 teaspoons unrefined sugar or rapadura
2 egg yolks
juice of 1½ lemons
sea salt

COOK'S TIP

Use tiny asparagus spears for an elegant appetizer for a special dinner party.

1 Cook the bundle of asparagus in boiling salted water for 7–10 minutes.

2 Drain the asparagus well (reserving scant 1 cup of the cooking liquid) and arrange the spears attractively in a serving dish. Set aside.

3 Blend the cornstarch with the cooled, reserved cooking liquid and place in a small pan. Bring to a boil, stirring all the time with a wooden spoon, then cook over a gentle heat until the sauce thickens slightly. Stir in the sugar, then remove the pan from the heat and let cool slightly.

4 Beat the egg yolks thoroughly with the lemon juice and stir gradually into the cooled sauce. Cook the sauce over a very low heat, stirring all the time, until it thickens. Be careful not to overheat the sauce or it may curdle. Once the sauce has thickened, remove the pan from the heat and continue stirring for 1 minute. Season with salt or sugar if necessary. Let the sauce cool slightly.

5 Stir the cooled lemon sauce, then pour a little over the cooked asparagus. Cover and chill for at least 2 hours before serving, accompanied by the rest of the lemon sauce.

BRAISED LEEKS with CARROTS

Sweet carrots and leeks go well together and are delicious finished with a little chopped mint or chervil. This is an easy accompaniment for roast lamb for a spring Sunday lunch.

4 Add seasoning, the wine, and half the chopped herb. Heat until simmering, then cover and cook gently for 5–8 minutes, until the leeks are tender, but not collapsed.

5 Uncover the leeks and turn them in the buttery juices. Increase the heat slightly, then boil the liquid rapidly until reduced to a few tablespoons.

6 Add the carrots to the leeks and reheat them gently, then swirl in the remaining butter or oil. Adjust the seasoning, if necessary. Transfer to a warmed serving dish and serve sprinkled with the remaining chopped herb.

SERVES SIX

5 tablespoons butter or
    olive oil
1½ pounds carrots, thickly sliced
2 fresh bay leaves
5 tablespoons water
1½ pounds leeks, cut into
    2 inch lengths
½ cup white wine
2 tablespoons chopped fresh mint
    or chervil
sea salt and ground black pepper

1 Heat 2 tablespoons of the butter or 2 tablespoons of oil in a pan and cook the carrots gently for 4–5 minutes.

2 Add the bay leaves, seasoning, and the water to the pan. Bring to a boil, cover lightly, and cook for 10–15 minutes, until the carrots are tender. Uncover, then boil the cooking juices until they have evaporated, leaving the carrots moist and glazed.

3 Meanwhile, heat another 2 tablespoons of the remaining butter or 2 tablespoons of oil in a deep skillet or wide saucepan that will take the sliced leeks in a single layer. Add the leeks and fry them very gently in the melted butter over a medium to low heat for 4–5 minutes, without allowing them to turn brown.

VARIATION
Braised leeks in tarragon cream
Cook 2 pounds leeks in 3 tablespoons butter or olive oil as above. Season, add a pinch of sugar, 3 tablespoons tarragon vinegar, 6 fresh tarragon sprigs, and 4 tablespoons white wine. Cover and cook as above. Add ⅔ cup heavy cream or soy cream and allow to bubble and thicken. Season and sprinkle with chopped fresh tarragon.

PARSLEY and ARUGULA SALAD

This salad is light but full of flavor, and makes a tasty first course, ideal for a spring dinner party. Shavings of rich-tasting cheese ensure that this salad is special.

SERVES SIX AS A FIRST COURSE

1 garlic clove, halved
4 ounces good white bread, cut into
  ½-inch thick slices
3 tablespoons olive oil, plus extra for
  shallow frying
3 ounces arugula leaves
3 ounces baby spinach
scant 1 cup flat-leaf parsley, leaves only
3 tablespoons salted capers,
  rinsed and dried
1½ ounce Parmesan cheese or premium
  Italian-style vegetarian cheese,
  pared into shavings

For the dressing
1½ tablespoon black olive paste
1 garlic clove, finely chopped
1 teaspoon smooth organic mustard
5 tablespoons olive oil
2 teaspoons balsamic vinegar
ground black pepper

1 First make the dressing. Whisk the black olive paste, garlic, and mustard together in a mixing bowl. Gradually whisk in the olive oil, then the vinegar. Adjust the seasoning to taste with black pepper—the dressing should be sufficiently salty already and not need any additional salt.

2 Preheat the oven to 375°F. Rub the halved garlic clove over the bread and cut or tear the slices into bite-size croutons. Toss them in the olive oil and place on a small baking sheet. Bake in the oven for 10–15 minutes, stirring once, until golden brown. Cool on paper towels.

3 Mix the arugula, baby spinach, and flat-leaf parsley in a large salad bowl.

4 Heat a shallow layer of olive oil in a skillet. Add the capers and fry briefly until crisp. Scoop out straight away and drain on paper towels.

5 Toss the dressing and croutons into the salad and divide it among six individual bowls or plates.

6 Scatter the cheese shavings and the fried capers over the top of the salad and serve immediately.

COOK'S TIP
You can use any type of vegetable peeler to cut thin shavings from a block of Parmesan or premium Italian-style vegetarian cheese.

BEET and RED ONION SALAD

*There is a wide variety of organic beets available—this salad looks especially attractive when made
with a mixture of red and yellow. Try it with rich meats, such as roast beef or cooked ham.*

SERVES SIX

1¼ pounds small red and
    yellow beets
5 tablespoons water
4 tablespoons olive oil
scant 1 cup walnut or pecan halves
1 teaspoon unrefined superfine sugar
    or rapadura, plus a little extra
    for the dressing
2 tablespoons walnut oil
1 tablespoon balsamic vinegar
1 teaspoon soy sauce
1 teaspoon grated orange rind
½ teaspoon ground roasted
    coriander seeds
1–2 teaspoons orange juice
1 red onion, halved and very
    thinly sliced
1–2 tablespoons chopped
    fresh fennel
3 ounces watercress or
    mizuna leaves
handful of baby red chard or
    beet leaves (optional)
sea salt and ground black pepper

1 Preheat the oven to 350°F. Place
the beets in a shallow ovenproof dish
just large enough to hold them in a
single layer, and add the water. Cover
the dish tightly with a close-fitting lid
or foil and bake for 1–1½ hours,
or until the beets are just cooked
and tender.

2 Let the beets cool. Once cooled, peel
the beets, then slice them or cut them
into strips and toss with 1 tablespoon
of the olive oil. Transfer to a large bowl
and set aside.

3 Meanwhile, heat 1 tablespoon of the
olive oil in a small skillet and cook the
walnuts or pecans until they begin to
brown. Add the sugar and cook, stirring,
until the nuts begin to caramelize.
Season with ½ teaspoon of salt and a
lot of ground black pepper, then turn
the nuts out onto a plate and let cool.

4 In a pitcher or small bowl, whisk
together the remaining olive oil, the
walnut oil, vinegar, soy sauce, orange rind,
and ground roasted coriander to make
the dressing. Season with salt and pepper
to taste and add a pinch of superfine
sugar. Whisk in orange juice to taste.

5 Separate the red onion slices into
half-rings and add them to the slices or
strips of beets. Add the dressing and
toss thoroughly to mix.

6 When ready to serve, toss the salad
with the fennel, watercress or mizuna,
and red chard or beet leaves, if using.
Transfer to individual bowls or plates
and sprinkle with the caramelized nuts.
Serve immediately.

ASSORTED SEAWEED SALAD

*This salad is a fine example of the traditional Japanese idea of eating: Look after your
appetite and your health at the same time. Seaweed is a nutritious, alkaline food that
is rich in fiber. Its unusual flavors are a great complement to fish and tofu dishes.*

SERVES FOUR

⅛ ounce each dried wakame, dried arame,
    and dried hijiki seaweeds
about 4½ ounces enokitake mushrooms
2 scallions
a few ice cubes
½ cucumber, cut lengthwise
9 ounces mixed salad greens

For the marinade
1 tablespoon rice vinegar
1¼ teaspoons salt

For the dressing
4 tablespoons rice vinegar
1½ teaspoons toasted sesame oil
1 tablespoon shoyu
1 tablespoon water with a pinch
    of dashi stock granules)
1 inch piece fresh ginger,
    finely grated

1 First rehydrate the seaweeds. Soak the
dried wakame seaweed for 10 minutes
in one bowl of water and, in a separate
bowl of water, soak the dried arame and
hijiki seaweeds together for 30 minutes.

2 Trim the hard end of the enokitake
mushroom stalks, then cut the bunch in
half and separate the stems.

3 Slice the scallions into thin, 1½-inch
long strips, then soak the strips in a
bowl of cold water with a few ice
cubes added to make them curl up.
Drain. Slice the cucumber into thin,
semicircular shapes.

4 Cook the wakame and enokitake in
boiling water for 2 minutes, then add
the arame and hijiki for a few seconds.
Immediately remove from the heat.
Drain and sprinkle over the vinegar and
salt while still warm. Chill until needed.

5 Mix the dressing ingredients in a bowl.
Arrange the mixed salad greens in a
large bowl with the cucumber on top,
then add the seaweed and enokitake
mixture. Decorate the salad with scallion
curls and serve with the dressing.

MARINATED SALMON with AVOCADO SALAD

Use only the freshest of salmon for this delicious salad. The marinade of lemon juice and dashi-konbu "cooks" the salmon, which is then served with avocado, toasted almonds, and salad greens, accompanied by a miso mayonnaise.

SERVES FOUR

2 very fresh salmon tails, 9 ounces total
    weight, skinned and filleted
juice of 1 lemon
4 inches dashi-konbu seaweed, wiped with
    a damp cloth and cut into 4 strips
1 ripe avocado
4 shiso or basil leaves, stalks removed
    and cut in half lengthwise
about 4 ounces mixed leaves such as
    lamb's lettuce, frisée, or arugula
3 tablespoons sliced almonds,
    toasted in a dry skillet until
    just slightly browned

For the miso mayonnaise
6 tablespoons good-quality mayonnaise
1 tablespoon miso paste
ground black pepper

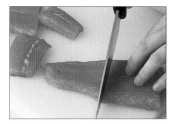

1 Cut the first salmon fillet in half diagonally at the tail end where the fillet is not wider than 1½ inches. Next, cut the wider part in half lengthwise. This means the fillet from one side is cut into three. Cut the other fillet into three pieces in the same way.

2 Put the lemon juice into a wide, shallow plastic container and add two of the dashi-konbu pieces. Lay the salmon fillets in the bottom of the container and sprinkle with the rest of the dashi-konbu. Marinate for about 15 minutes, then turn the salmon and let stand for a further 15 minutes. The salmon should change to a pink "cooked" color. Remove the salmon from the marinade and wipe with paper towels.

3 Holding a very sharp knife at an angle, cut the salmon into ¼-inch thick slices against the grain.

4 Halve the avocado and sprinkle with a little of the remaining salmon marinade. Remove the avocado pit and skin, then carefully slice to the same thickness as the salmon.

5 Mix the miso mayonnaise ingredients in a small bowl. Spread 1 teaspoon onto the back of each of the shiso or basil leaves, then mix the remainder with 1 tablespoon of the remaining marinade to loosen the mayonnaise.

6 Arrange the salad greens on four plates. Add the avocado, salmon, shiso leaves, and almonds and toss lightly. Drizzle over the remaining mayonnaise and serve immediately.

VARIATION
Alternatively, build a tower of avocado and salmon. For each serving, place one-eighth of the avocado slices in the center of a plate, slightly overlapping. Add a shiso or basil leaf, miso-side down. Then place one-eighth of the salmon on top, slightly overlapping. Repeat the process. Arrange the salad and almonds, and spoon over the mayonnaise.

GARGANELLI with SPRING VEGETABLES

Fresh, brightly colored spring vegetables both look and taste good when served with pasta.
A light sauce of dry white wine, extra virgin olive oil, and fresh herbs is used to marry the
two together for a delicious flavor.

SERVES FOUR

1 bunch asparagus, about 12 ounces
4 young carrots
1 bunch scallions
4½ ounces shelled fresh peas
3 cups dried garganelli
4 tablespoons dry white wine
6 tablespoons extra virgin olive oil
a few sprigs fresh flat-leaf parsley, mint,
    and basil, leaves stripped and chopped
sea salt and ground black pepper
freshly grated Parmesan cheese or premium
    Italian-style vegetarian cheese, to serve

1 Trim off and discard the woody part
of each asparagus stem, then cut off
the tips on the diagonal. Cut the stems
on the diagonal into 1½ inch pieces.
Cut the carrots and scallions on the
diagonal into similar-size pieces.

2 Plunge the carrots, peas, and
asparagus stems and tips into a large
pan of salted boiling water. Bring back
to a boil, then reduce the heat and
simmer for 8–10 minutes, until tender.

3 Meanwhile, cook the pasta in salted
boiling water for 10–12 minutes, or
according to the package instructions,
until just tender.

4 Drain the asparagus, carrots, and peas
and return them to the pan. Add the
white wine, olive oil, and salt and black
pepper to taste, then gently toss over a
medium to high heat until the wine has
reduced and the vegetables glisten with
the olive oil.

5 Drain the garganelli and put it into a
warmed large bowl. Add the vegetables,
scallions, and sprigs of fresh herbs and
toss well. Divide the pasta among four
warmed individual plates and serve
immediately with freshly grated cheese.

COOK'S TIP
Garganelli are rolled short pasta shapes
made with pasta dough enriched with egg.
If you can't get garganelli, use another
short shape, such as penne.

PENNE with CREAM and SMOKED SALMON

*This modern classic uses just three essential ingredients, which create a delicious
combination in a dish that is quick and easy make. Accompany with a green salad,
ciabatta bread, and sparkling wine for a simple but nutritious and tasty meal.*

SERVES FOUR

3 cups dried penne or other
    pasta tubes
4 ounces thinly sliced
    smoked salmon
2–3 fresh thyme sprigs
2 tablespoons extra virgin olive oil
⅔ cup extra-thick light cream or
    soy cream
sea salt and ground black pepper

1 Cook the pasta in a large saucepan
of lightly salted boiling water for
10 minutes, until it is just tender, or
according to the package instructions.

2 Meanwhile, using sharp kitchen
scissors, cut the smoked salmon slices
into thin strips, about ¼ inch wide. Strip
the leaves from the thyme sprigs and
rinse them thoroughly in cold water.

3 Drain the pasta and return it to the
pan. Add the oil and heat gently, then
stir in the cream with about one-quarter
of the smoked salmon and thyme leaves,
then season with pepper. Heat gently
for 3–4 minutes, stirring all the time.
Check the seasoning. Divide the pasta
among four warmed bowls, top with
the remaining salmon and thyme leaves,
and serve immediately.

VARIATION
Although white penne is the traditional pasta
to serve with this sauce, it also goes well
with fresh whole-wheat penne or ravioli
stuffed with spinach and ricotta cheese.

CHICKEN and ASPARAGUS RISOTTO

Use fairly thick asparagus in this classic springtime risotto, because fine spears tend to overcook. The thick ends of the asparagus are full of flavor and they become wonderfully tender in the time it takes for the rice to absorb the stock.

SERVES FOUR

5 tablespoons olive oil
1 leek, finely chopped
1½ cups oyster or cremini mushrooms,
    sliced
3 skinless, boneless chicken breast
    fillets, cubed
12 ounces asparagus
1¼ cups risotto rice
3¾ cups chicken stock,
    simmering
sea salt and ground black pepper
fresh Parmesan or premium
    Italian-style vegetarian cheese curls,
    to serve

1 Heat the olive oil in a saucepan. Add the finely chopped leek and cook gently until softened, but not colored. Add the sliced mushrooms and cook for 5 minutes. Remove the vegetables from the pan and set aside.

2 Increase the heat and cook the cubes of chicken until golden on all sides. Do this in batches, if necessary, and then return them all to the pan.

3 Meanwhile, discard the woody ends from the asparagus and cut the spears in half. Set the tips aside. Cut the thick ends in half and add them to the pan. Return the leek and mushroom mixture to the pan and stir in the rice.

4 Put in a ladleful of boiling stock and cook gently, stirring occasionally, until the stock is completely absorbed. Continue adding the stock a ladleful at a time, simmering until it is absorbed, the rice is tender, and the chicken is cooked.

COOK'S TIP
To thoroughly remove all the soil from organic leeks, slice in half along their length and rinse under running water.

5 Add the asparagus tips with the last ladleful of boiling stock for the final 5 minutes and continue cooking the risotto very gently until the asparagus is tender. The whole process should take about 25–30 minutes.

6 Season the risotto to taste with salt and freshly ground black pepper and spoon it into individual warm serving bowls. Top each bowl with curls of cheese and serve.

ESCALOPES of CHICKEN with VEGETABLES

This is a quick and light dish—ideal as the weather starts to warm up and easy meals become the order of the day. Flattening the chicken breasts thins and tenderizes the meat and also speeds up the cooking time.

SERVES FOUR

4 skinless, boneless chicken breast fillets,
    6 ounces each
juice of 1 lime
½ cup olive oil
1½ pounds mixed small new season
    potatoes, carrots, fennel (sliced
    if large), asparagus, and peas
sea salt and ground black pepper
sprigs of fresh flat-leaf parsley,
    to garnish

For the tomato mayonnaise
⅔ cup mayonnaise
1 tablespoon sun-dried tomato paste

1 Lay the chicken fillets between sheets of plastic wrap or parchment paper and use a rolling pin to beat them until they are evenly thin. Season the chicken and sprinkle with the lime juice.

2 Heat 3 tablespoons of the oil in a skillet or griddle and cook the chicken escalopes for 10–12 minutes on each side, turning frequently.

3 Meanwhile, put the new potatoes and carrots in a small pan with the remaining oil and season with sea salt. Cover and cook over a medium heat for 10–15 minutes, stirring frequently.

4 Add the fennel and cook for a further 5 minutes, stirring frequently. Finally, add the asparagus and peas and cook for 5 minutes more, or until all the vegetables are tender and cooked.

5 To make the tomato mayonnaise, mix together the mayonnaise and sun-dried tomato paste in a small bowl. Spoon the vegetables onto a warmed serving platter or individual plates and arrange the chicken on top. Serve the tomato mayonnaise with the chicken and vegetables. Garnish with sprigs of flat-leaf parsley.

COOK'S TIP
Any combinations of baby vegetables can be used. The weight specified is for prepared vegetables. Adjust the cooking time or the order in which they are added to the pan according to how long the chosen vegetables take to cook; for example, add root vegetables first, before quick-cooking ones, such as zucchini, snow peas, or green beans.

ROAST LEG of LAMB

Tender young organic lamb is available only in the springtime, and is often served with a sauce using the first sprigs of mint of the year and early new potatoes. If you buy organic young lamb, you can be happy in the knowledge that countryside seasons are being utilized and respected, and that the meat is fresh.

SERVES SIX

3¼ pounds leg of lamb
4 garlic cloves, sliced
2 fresh rosemary sprigs
2 tablespoons light olive oil
1¼ cups red wine
1 teaspoon honey
3 tablespoons red currant jelly
sea salt and ground black pepper
spring vegetables, to serve

For the roast potatoes
3 tablespoons olive oil
3 pounds potatoes, such as Bintje,
    peeled and cut into chunks

For the mint sauce
about ½ cup fresh mint
2 teaspoons unrefined superfine sugar
    or rapadura
1 tablespoon boiling water
2 tablespoons white wine vinegar

1 Preheat the oven to 425°F. Make small slits into the lamb all over the joint. Press a slice of garlic and a few rosemary leaves into each slit, then place the joint in a roasting pan and season well. Drizzle the oil over the lamb and roast for about 1 hour.

COOK'S TIP
To make a quick and tasty gravy from the pan juices, add about 1¼ cups red wine, stock, or water and boil, stirring occasionally, until reduced and well-flavored. Season to taste, then strain into a sauceboat to serve.

2 Meanwhile, mix the wine, honey, and red currant jelly in a small pan and heat, stirring, until the jelly melts. Bring to a boil, then reduce the heat and simmer until reduced by half. Spoon this glaze over the lamb and return it to the oven for 30–45 minutes.

3 To make the potatoes, put the oil in a roasting pan on the shelf above the meat. Boil the potatoes for 5–10 minutes, then drain them and fluff up the surface of each with a fork.

4 Add the prepared potatoes to the hot oil and baste well, then roast them for 45 minutes, or until they are crisp.

5 While the potatoes are roasting, make the mint sauce. Place the mint on a cutting board and scatter the sugar over the top. Chop the mint finely, then transfer to a bowl.

6 Add the boiling water and stir until the sugar has dissolved. Add 1 tablespoon of vinegar and taste the sauce before adding the remaining vinegar. (You may want to add slightly less or more than the suggested quantity.) Let the mint sauce stand until you are ready to serve the meal.

7 Remove the lamb from the oven, cover it loosely with foil, and set it aside in a warm place to rest for 10–15 minutes before carving. Serve with the crisp roast potatoes, mint sauce, and a selection of seasonal spring vegetables.

HERB-CRUSTED RACK of LAMB with PUY LENTILS

This lamb roast is quick and easy to prepare but looks impressive when served—it is the perfect choice when entertaining. Puy lentils are a favorite ingredient in the south of France. Their delicate flavor is the perfect complement to the rich meat.

SERVES FOUR

2 × 6-bone racks of lamb, chined
1 cup fresh white or whole-wheat
    breadcrumbs
2 large garlic cloves, crushed
6 tablespoons chopped mixed fresh herbs,
    plus extra sprigs to garnish
4 tablespoons butter, melted or
    3½ tablespoons olive oil
sea salt and ground black pepper
new potatoes, to serve

For the Puy lentils
1 red onion, chopped
2 tablespoons olive oil
1 can (14 ounces) Puy lentils, rinsed
    and drained
1 can (14 ounces) chopped tomatoes
2 tablespoons chopped flat-leaf parsley

1 Preheat the oven to 425°F. Trim any excess fat from the lamb, and season with salt and pepper.

2 Mix together the breadcrumbs, garlic, herbs, and butter or oil, and press onto the fat sides of the lamb. Place in a roasting pan and roast for 25 minutes. Cover with foil; stand for 5 minutes before carving.

3 Cook the onion in the olive oil until softened. Add the lentils and tomatoes and cook gently for 5 minutes, or until the lentils are piping hot. Stir in the parsley and season to taste.

4 Cut each rack of lamb in half and serve with the lentils and new potatoes. Garnish with herb sprigs.

LAMB BURGERS with RED ONION and TOMATO RELISH

A sharp-sweet red onion relish works well with burgers based on Middle Eastern-style lamb. Serve with pita bread and tabbouleh for an authentic taste, although baked potatoes and a crisp green salad are also good.

SERVES FOUR

3 tablespoons bulgur wheat
1¼ pounds lean ground lamb
1 small red onion, finely chopped
2 garlic cloves, finely chopped
1 green chile, seeded and finely chopped
1 teaspoon ground toasted cumin seeds
½ teaspoon ground sumac (optional)
¼ cup chopped fresh flat-leaf parsley
2 tablespoons chopped fresh mint
olive oil, for frying
sea salt and ground black pepper

For the relish
2 red bell peppers, halved and seeded
2 red onions, cut into ¼-inch
   thick slices
5–6 tablespoons extra virgin olive oil
12 ounces cherry tomatoes, chopped
½–1 fresh red or green chile, seeded
   and finely chopped (optional)
2 tablespoons chopped fresh mint
2 tablespoons chopped fresh parsley
1 tablespoon chopped fresh oregano
   or marjoram
½–1 teaspoon ground toasted
   cumin seeds
½–1 teaspoon sumac (optional)
juice of ½ lemon
unrefined superfine sugar or rapadura,
   to taste

1 Pour ⅔ cup hot water over the bulgur wheat in a mixing bowl and let stand for 15 minutes, then drain the wheat in a sieve and squeeze out the excess moisture.

2 To make the relish, broil the bell peppers, skin side up, until the skin chars and blisters. Place in a bowl, cover, and let stand for 10 minutes. Peel off the skin, dice the peppers finely, and place in a bowl.

3 Brush the onions with 1 tablespoon of oil and broil for 5 minutes on each side, until browned. Let cool.

4 Place the bulgur in a bowl and add the ground lamb, onion, garlic, chile, cumin, sumac, if using, parsley, and mint. Mix the ingredients thoroughly together by hand, then season with ½ teaspoon of salt and plenty of black pepper and mix again. Form the mixture into eight small burgers.

5 Chop the onions for the relish. Add with the tomatoes, chile to taste, herbs, and ½ teaspoon each of the cumin and sumac, if using, to the peppers. Stir in 4 tablespoons of the remaining oil and 1 tablespoon of the lemon juice. Season with salt, pepper, and sugar and let stand for 20–30 minutes.

6 Heat a heavy skillet over a high heat and grease lightly with olive oil. Cook the burgers for about 5–6 minutes on each side, or until just cooked at the center.

7 While the burgers are cooking, taste the relish and adjust the seasoning, adding more pepper, sugar, oil, chile, cumin, sumac, if using, and lemon juice to taste. Serve the burgers with the relish.

LAMB STEW with NEW POTATOES and SHALLOTS

*This fresh lemon-seasoned stew is finished with an Italian mixture of chopped garlic,
parsley, and lemon rind known as gremolata, the traditional topping for osso bucco.*

SERVES SIX

2¼ pounds boneless shoulder of lamb,
    trimmed of fat and cut into 2 inch cubes
1 garlic clove, finely chopped
finely grated rind of ½ lemon and
    juice of 1 lemon
6 tablespoons olive oil
3 tablespoons whole-wheat flour
1 large onion, sliced
5 anchovy fillets in olive oil, drained
½ teaspoon unrefined superfine sugar
    or rapadura
1¼ cups fruity white wine
2 cups lamb stock or half stock
    and half water
1 fresh bay leaf
fresh rosemary sprig
fresh parsley sprig
1¼ pounds small new potatoes
9 ounces shallots, peeled but left whole
3 tablespoons heavy cream or
    soy cream (optional)
sea salt and ground black pepper

For the gremolata
1 garlic clove, finely chopped
finely shredded rind of ½ lemon
3 tablespoons chopped fresh
    flat-leaf parsley

1 Mix the lamb with the garlic and
the rind and juice of ½ lemon in a
nonmetallic container. Season with
pepper and mix in 1 tablespoon of olive
oil, then let marinate in the refrigerator
for 12–24 hours.

2 Drain the lamb carefully, reserving
the marinade, and pat the lamb dry
with paper towels. Preheat the oven
to 350°F.

COOK'S TIP
A mezzaluna (double-handled, half-moon
shaped, curved chopping blade) makes
a very good job of chopping gremolata
ingredients. If using a food processor
or electric chopper, be careful not to
overprocess the mixture because it is
easy to ground the ingredients to a paste.

3 Heat 2 tablespoons of olive oil in a
large, heavy skillet. Season the flour with
salt and pepper and toss the drained,
dried lamb in it to coat it lightly, shaking
off any excess flour. Add the lamb to the
skillet, in small batches, and seal it on all
sides in the hot oil stirring constantly
with a wooden spoon.

4 As each batch of lamb becomes brown,
transfer it to an ovenproof pan or flameproof casserole. You may need to add an
extra 1 tablespoon of olive oil to the pan.

5 Reduce the heat, add another
1 tablespoon of oil to the pan, and cook
the sliced onion gently over a low heat,
stirring frequently, for 10 minutes, until
softened and golden but not browned.
Add the drained anchovy fillets and the
sugar, and cook, mashing the anchovies
into the onion with a wooden spoon.

6 Add the reserved marinade,
increase the heat a little, and cook for
1–2 minutes, then pour in the white wine
and lamb stock or stock and water, and
bring to a boil. Simmer the sauce gently
for about 5 minutes, then pour the sauce
over the lamb in the pan or casserole.

7 Tie the bay leaf, rosemary, and parsley
together to make a bouquet garni and
add to the lamb. Season the stew, then
cover tightly and cook in the oven for
1 hour. Add the potatoes to the stew
and stir well, then return the stew to the
oven and cook for a further 20 minutes.

8 Meanwhile, to make the gremolata,
chop the garlic, lemon rind, and parsley
together finely. Place in a dish, then
cover and set aside.

9 Heat the remaining olive oil in a skillet
and brown the shallots on all sides,
then stir them into the lamb stew.
Cover and cook the stew for a further
30–40 minutes, until the lamb is tender.
Transfer the lamb and vegetables to a
warmed serving dish and keep hot.
Discard the bunch of herbs.

10 Boil the remaining cooking juices to
reduce, then add the heavy cream or
soy cream, if using, and simmer for
2–3 minutes. Adjust the seasoning,
adding a little lemon juice to taste if
desired. Pour this sauce over the lamb,
scatter the gremolata mixture over the
top, and serve immediately.

SALMON FISH CAKES

The secret of a good fish cake is to make it with freshly prepared fish and potatoes,
homemade breadcrumbs, and plenty of fresh herbs, such as dill and parsley or tarragon.
Serve simply with arugula leaves and lemon wedges.

SERVES FOUR

1 pound cooked salmon fillet
1 pound freshly cooked potatoes,
   mashed
2 tablespoons butter, melted, or
   olive oil
2 teaspoons whole-grain mustard
1 tablespoon each chopped fresh dill and
   chopped fresh parsley or tarragon
grated rind and juice of ½ lemon
2 tablespoons whole-wheat flour
1 egg, lightly beaten
2 cups dried breadcrumbs
4 tablespoons sunflower oil
sea salt and ground black pepper
arugula leaves and chives, to garnish
lemon wedges, to serve

1 Flake the cooked salmon, discarding
any skin and bones. Put it in a bowl with
the mashed potato, melted butter or oil,
and whole-grain mustard, and mix well.
Stir in the herbs and the lemon rind and
juice. Season to taste with plenty of sea
salt and ground black pepper.

2 Divide the mixture into eight portions
and shape each into a ball, then flatten
into a thick disk. Dip the fish cakes
first in flour, then in egg, and finally in
breadcrumbs, making sure that they
are evenly coated with crumbs.

3 Heat the oil in a skillet until it is very
hot. Fry the fish cakes in batches until
golden brown and crisp all over. As each
batch is ready, drain on paper towels
and keep hot. Garnish with arugula and
chives and serve with lemon wedges.

COOK'S TIP

Any fresh white or hot-smoked fish is
suitable. Always buy organically farmed
fish, or sustainably caught wild fish.

FILLETS of SEA BREAM in FILO DOUGH

Any firm fish fillets can be used for this dish—bass, grouper and red mullet or snapper are particularly good—and, as the number of organic seawater fish farms grows, an increasing variety of breeds is becoming available. Each parcel is a meal in itself and can be prepared several hours in advance.

3 Thinly slice the potatoes lengthwise. Brush a baking sheet with a little of the oil. Lay a sheet of filo dough on the sheet, brush it with oil, then lay a second sheet diagonally over the first. Repeat with two more pastry sheets. Arrange a quarter of the sliced potatoes in the centre, season and add a quarter of the shredded sorrel. Lay a bream fillet on top, skin-side up. Season.

4 Loosely fold the filo dough up and over to make a neat parcel. Make three more parcels; place on the baking sheet. Brush with half the melted butter or oil. Bake for about 20 minutes, until the filo is puffed up and golden brown.

SERVES FOUR

8 small waxy salad potatoes,
    preferably red-skinned
7 ounces sorrel, stalks removed
2 tablespoons olive oil
16 filo dough sheets, thawed
    if frozen
4 sea bream fillets, about 6 ounces each,
    scaled but not skinned
4 tablespoons butter, melted or
    olive oil
½ cup fish stock
1 cup whipping cream or soy cream
sea salt and ground black pepper
finely diced red bell pepper and
    salad greens, to garnish

VARIATION

Use small spinach leaves or baby chard in place of the sorrel.

1 Preheat the oven to 400°F. Cook the potatoes in a saucepan of lightly salted boiling water for about 20 minutes, or until just tender. Drain and let cool.

2 Set about half the sorrel leaves aside. Shred the remaining leaves by piling up six or eight at a time, rolling them up like a fat cigar and slicing them.

5 Meanwhile, make the sorrel sauce. Heat the remaining butter or oil in a pan, add the reserved sorrel, and cook gently for 3 minutes, stirring, until it wilts. Stir in the stock and cream. Heat almost to a boiling point, stirring so that the sorrel breaks down. Season to taste and keep hot until the fish parcels are ready. Serve garnished with red pepper and salad greens. Pass around the sauce separately.

SEARED SCALLOPS with CHIVE SAUCE on LEEK and CARROT RICE

Scallops are one of the most delicious shellfish. Organically farmed scallops feed on naturally occurring plankton and are a healthy food whose cultivation has a low environmental impact.

SERVES FOUR

12–16 shelled scallops
3 tablespoons olive oil
⅓ cup wild rice
5 tablespoons butter or
    olive oil
4 carrots, cut into long thin strips
2 leeks, cut into thick, diagonal slices
1 small onion, finely chopped
⅔ cup long grain rice
1 fresh bay leaf
scant 1 cup white wine
scant 2 cups fish stock
4 tablespoons heavy cream or
    soy cream
a little lemon juice
1½ tablespoons chopped fresh chives
2 tablespoons chervil sprigs
sea salt and ground black pepper

1 Lightly season the shelled scallops, brush with 1 tablespoon of the olive oil and set aside.

2 Cook the wild rice in a saucepan in plenty of boiling water for about 30 minutes, or according to the package instructions, until tender, then drain.

3 Heat half the butter or oil in a small skillet and cook the carrot strips fairly gently for 4–5 minutes. Add the leek slices and fry for another 2 minutes. Season with sea salt and black pepper and add 2–3 tablespoons of water, then cover and cook the vegetables for a few minutes more. Uncover the pan and cook until the liquid has reduced. Set aside off the heat.

4 Melt half the remaining butter with 1 tablespoon of the remaining oil in a heavy pan. Add the onion and fry for 3–4 minutes, until softened but not browned.

5 Add the long grain rice and bay leaf to the pan and cook, stirring constantly, until the rice looks translucent and the grains are coated with oil.

6 Put in half the wine and half the stock. Season to taste with salt and bring to a boil. Stir, then cover and cook very gently for 15 minutes, or until the liquid is absorbed and the rice is cooked and tender.

7 Reheat the carrots and leeks gently, then stir them into the long grain rice with the wild rice. Taste and adjust the seasoning, if necessary.

8 Meanwhile, put the remaining wine and stock into a small saucepan and boil it rapidly until reduced by half.

COOK'S TIP
Choose fresh instead of frozen scallops because the frozen ones tend to exude water on cooking. Have the pan very hot because scallops need only the briefest cooking at high heat—just until they turn opaque and brown on each side.

VARIATION
Use organic brown rice instead of the white long grain rice—it has a longer cooking time so check the package for instructions.

9 Heat a heavy skillet over a high heat. Add the remaining butter or oil. Add the scallops, and lightly sear them for 1–2 minutes on each side, then set aside and keep warm.

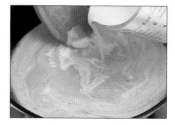

10 Put the reduced stock and wine into the pan and heat until bubbling, then add the cream and boil until thickened. Season with lemon juice, sea salt, and plenty of ground black pepper. Stir in the chopped chives and seared scallops.

11 Stir the chervil sprigs into the mixed rice and vegetables and pile it onto individual serving plates. Arrange the scallops on top and spoon the sauce over the rice. Serve immediately.

FROZEN CLEMENTINES

These pretty, sorbet-filled fruit store well in the freezer, so make them in advance and
they will be perfect for an impromptu dinner party. Organic citrus fruit has a matte skin—
evidence that they have not been coated with shiny antifungal wax.

MAKES TWELVE

16 large clementines or small oranges
scant 1 cup unrefined superfine sugar
   or rapadura
7 tablespoons water
juice of 2 lemons
a little fresh orange juice (if necessary)
fresh mint leaves, to decorate

1 Carefully slice the tops off 12 of the clementines to make lids. Place the lids on a baking sheet. Loosen the clementine flesh with a sharp knife, then carefully scoop it out into a mixing bowl, keeping the shells intact. Scrape out as much of the membrane from the shells as possible. Place the shells on the baking tray and place the tray in the freezer.

2 Put the sugar and water in a heavy saucepan and heat gently, stirring until the unrefined superfine sugar or rapadura dissolves. Boil for 3 minutes without stirring,, then let the syrup cool. Stir in the lemon juice.

3 Grate the rind from the remaining four clementines. Squeeze the fruit and add the juice and rind to the lemon syrup.

4 Process the clementine flesh in a food processor or blender, then press it through a sieve placed over a bowl to extract as much juice as possible. Add this to the syrup. You need about 3¾ cups of liquid. Make up to the required amount with fresh orange juice if necessary.

5 If making by hand, put the mixture into a shallow plastic container and freeze for 3–4 hours, beating twice as the sorbet thickens to break up the ice crystals. If using an ice-cream maker, churn the mixture until it holds its shape.

6 Gently pack the citrus sorbet into the clementine shells, mounding them up slightly in the center. Position the lids on top and return the fruit to the freezer for several hours, or until the sorbet is frozen solid.

7 Transfer the frozen clementines to the refrigerator about 30 minutes before serving to allow the sorbet to soften a little. Serve on individual plates and decorate with fresh mint leaves.

RHUBARB and GINGER ICE CREAM

The tangy combination of gently poached rhubarb and chopped ginger is blended with mascarpone to create this pretty blush-pink ice cream. Look for tender slim stalks of forced rhubarb in spring—it has a delicate pink color and a delicious flavor.

SERVES FOUR TO SIX

5 pieces of preserved ginger
1 pound trimmed rhubarb, sliced
generous ½ cup unrefined superfine sugar
   or rapadura
2 tablespoons water
⅔ cup mascarpone cheese
⅔ cup whipping cream or
   soy cream
wafer baskets, to serve (optional)

1 Using a sharp knife, roughly chop the preserved ginger and set it aside. Put the rhubarb slices into a saucepan and add the sugar and water. Bring to a boil, then cover and simmer for about 5 minutes, until the rhubarb is just tender and still bright pink.

2 Put the mixture into a food processor or blender, process until smooth, then let cool. Chill if time permits.

3 If making by hand, in a bowl, mix together the mascarpone, cream, and ginger with the rhubarb puree. Put the mixture into a plastic container and freeze for 6 hours, or until firm, beating the mixture once or twice during the freezing time to break up the ice crystals.

COOK'S TIP

Rapadura is an alternative to refined sugar. It is made by sun-drying organic sugar cane juice and has a similar color and texture to soft brown sugar, but has more flavor and is more nutritious.

4 If using an ice-cream maker, churn the puree for 15–20 minutes, until it is thick. Put the mascarpone into a bowl, soften it with a wooden spoon, then beat in the cream. Add the ginger, then churn in the ice cream maker until firm. Serve scoops of the ice cream in bowls or wafer baskets.

BANANA and APRICOT CARAMEL TRIFLE

Organic bananas are an excellent source of potassium and very good for the digestion—making this an irresistible dessert for a special occasion. Ginger cake makes an ideal base, adding sharpness to the creamy flavors.

SERVES SIX TO EIGHT

1¼ cups milk or soy milk
1 vanilla bean, or 4–5 drops
    vanilla extract
3 tablespoons unrefined superfine sugar
    or rapadura
4 teaspoons cornstarch
3 egg yolks
4 tablespoons apricot jam
6–8 ounce ginger cake,
    cubed
3 bananas, sliced, with one reserved
    for topping
generous ½ cup granulated sugar
    or rapadura
1¼ cups heavy cream or
    soy cream
a few drops of lemon juice

1 Put the milk into a small saucepan. Carefully split the vanilla bean (if using) down the middle and scrape the tiny seeds into the pan.

2 Add the vanilla bean, or vanilla extract, to the milk and bring just to a boil, then remove the pan from the heat and set aside. When the milk has cooled slightly, remove the vanilla bean.

VARIATION

For an adult-only version of this trifle, substitute a plainer sponge cake for the ginger cake and moisten the sponge with a little apricot brandy and a small glass of sweet dessert wine in step 6.

3 Whisk together the sugar, cornstarch, and eggs until pale and creamy. Whisk in the milk and return the mixture to the pan. Heat to simmering point, stirring all the time, and cook gently over a low heat until the custard coats the back of a wooden spoon thickly.

4 Let cool, covered tightly with plastic wrap. Ensure the plastic wrap is pressed against the surface of the custard to prevent a skin from forming.

5 Put the apricot jam and 4 tablespoons of water in a saucepan and heat gently for 2–3 minutes, stirring.

COOK'S TIP

Use whatever type of cake you prefer in the bottom of the trifle. Leftover Madeira cake, with its tangy citrus flavor, makes a perfect choice. Choose a jam with flavors that complement those of your chosen cake: strawberry jam and raspberry jam are good with lemon cake, or try peach jam with a chocolate sponge.

6 Put the cubed cake in a deep serving bowl or dish and pour on the apricot jam. Cover with sliced bananas, then the custard. Chill for 1–2 hours.

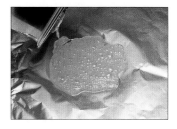

7 Melt the sugar in a small saucepan with 4 tablespoons of water and, when it has dissolved, cook until it is just turning golden. Immediately pour onto a sheet of foil and let harden, then break the caramel into pieces.

8 Whip the cream until it forms soft peaks and spread it evenly over the custard. Chill the trifle for 2–3 hours, then top with the remaining sliced banana, dipped into lemon juice, and the cracked caramel pieces.

CITRUS and CARAMEL CUSTARDS

Make these Spanish-style custards with organic milk because it is the only type of milk guaranteed to be free of GMOs and excess added antibiotics and hormones. Wonderfully smooth, the custards are delicately scented with tangy citrus flavors and aromatic cinnamon.

2 Preheat the oven to 325°F. Whisk the egg yolks, cornstarch, and sugar together. Remove the rinds and cinnamon from the hot milk and cream and discard. Whisk the hot milk and cream into the egg yolk mixture.

3 Add the grated citrus rind to the custard mixture and stir through. Put into four individual dishes, each 5 inches in diameter. Place in a roasting pan and pour warm water into the pan to reach three-quarters of the way up the sides. Bake for 25 minutes, or until the custards are just set. Remove the dishes from the water; let cool, then chill.

4 Preheat the broiler to high. Sprinkle the custards liberally with confectioner's sugar and place under the broiler until the tops turn golden brown and caramelize.

SERVES FOUR

scant 2 cups milk or soy milk
⅔ cup light cream
   or soy cream
1 cinnamon stick, broken in half
thinly pared rind of ½ lemon
thinly pared rind of ½ orange
4 egg yolks
1 teaspoon cornstarch
3 tablespoons unrefined superfine sugar
   or rapadura
grated rind of ½ lemon
grated rind of ½ orange
unrefined confectioner's sugar,
   to dust

1 Place the milk and cream in a saucepan. Add the cinnamon stick halves and the strips of pared lemon and orange rind. Bring to a boil, then reduce the heat and simmer for 10 minutes.

COOK'S TIPS
• Prepare the grated rind first, then cut a few strips of rind from the ungrated side using a swivel-bladed vegetable peeler.
• You can use a special cook's blowtorch or salamander to caramelize the tops instead of broiling them.

RICOTTA CHEESECAKE

This Sicilian-style cheesecake makes good use of ricotta's firm texture. Here, the cheese is enriched with eggs and cream and enlivened with the unwaxed grated rind of organic orange and lemon, producing an irresistible, tangy dessert cheesecake filling.

SERVES EIGHT

2 cups ricotta cheese
½ cup heavy cream or
    soy cream
2 eggs
1 egg yolk
6 tablespoons unrefined superfine sugar
    or rapadura
finely grated rind of 1 orange and 1 lemon,
    plus extra to decorate

For the pastry
1½ cups all-purpose flour
3 tablespoons unrefined superfine sugar
    or rapadura
½ cup chilled butter, diced
1 egg yolk

1 To make the pastry, sift the flour and sugar onto a cold work surface. Make a well in the center and add the butter and egg yolk. Work the flour into the butter and egg yolk.

2 Gather the dough together, reserve one-quarter of it, and press the rest into a 9-inch fluted quiche pan with a removable bottom, and chill.

3 Preheat the oven to 375°F. Put the cheese, cream, eggs and egg yolk, sugar, and citrus rinds in a large bowl and beat well.

4 Prick the bottom of the pastry shell, then line with foil and fill with dried beans. Bake for 15 minutes, transfer to a wire rack, remove the foil and beans, and let the pastry cool in the pan.

5 Spoon the cheese and cream filling into the pastry shell and level the surface. Roll out the reserved dough and cut into long, even strips. Arrange the strips on the top of the filling in a lattice pattern, sticking them in place with water.

6 Bake the tart for 30–35 minutes, until golden and set. Transfer to a wire rack and let cool, then carefully remove the side of the pan. Use a metal spatula to transfer the cheesecake to a serving plate. Decorate with citrus rind before serving.

VARIATIONS
• Add ⅓ cup dark chocolate chips to the filling in step 3.
• Scatter 3 ounces golden raisins into the pastry shell before adding the filling.

RHUBARB MERINGUE PIE

The sharp tang of tender forced rhubarb with its sweet meringue topping will really tantalize the taste buds. This pudding is delicious hot or cold with cream or vanilla ice cream.

SERVES SIX

1¾ cups all-purpose flour, plus extra
    for flouring
¼ cup ground walnuts
½ cup chilled butter or nonhydrogenated
    magarine, diced
generous 1½ cups unrefined superfine
    sugar or rapadura
4 egg yolks
1½ pounds rhubarb, cut into small pieces
grated rind and juice of 3 oranges
5 tablespoons cornstarch
3 egg whites
whipped cream or soy cream, to serve

1 Sift the flour into a bowl and add the ground walnuts. Rub in the butter until the mixture resembles fine breadcrumbs. Stir in 2 tablespoons of the sugar with 1 egg yolk beaten with 1 tablespoon of water. Mix to a firm dough. Turn out on to a floured surface and knead. Wrap in a plastic bag and chill for 30 minutes.

2 Preheat the oven to 375°F. Roll out the pastry on a floured surface and use to line a 9-inch fluted quiche pan. Prick the bottom with a fork. Line with foil and fill with dried beans. Bake for 15 minutes.

3 Put the rhubarb, 6 tablespoons of the remaining sugar, and the orange rind in a pan. Cover and cook gently until the rhubarb is tender.

4 Remove the foil and beans from the pastry shell, then brush with a little of the remaining egg yolk. Bake for 10–15 minutes, until the pastry is crisp.

5 Blend together the cornstarch and the orange juice in a small bowl. Remove from the heat, stir the cornstarch mixture into the cooked rhubarb, then bring back to a boil, stirring constantly until thickened. Cook for a further 1–2 minutes. Let the mixture cool slightly, then beat in the remaining egg yolks. Put into the cooked pastry shell, spreading it evenly.

6 Whisk the egg whites in a large mixing bowl until they form soft peaks, then gradually whisk in the remaining sugar, 1 tablespoon at a time, whisking well after each addition.

7 Spoon the meringue over the filling to cover completely. Bake for 25 minutes, until golden. Serve warm, or let cool for about 30 minutes and serve with whipped cream.

TUSCAN CITRUS SPONGE

This tangy cake comes from the little Tuscan town of Pitigliano. It is a light and airy whisked sponge made with matzo and potato flours instead of traditional wheat flour.

SERVES SIX TO EIGHT

12 eggs, separated
1½ cups unrefined superfine sugar
   or rapadura
½ cup fresh orange juice
grated rind of 1 orange
grated rind of 1 lemon
½ cup potato flour, sifted
¾ cup fine matzo meal or matzo meal
   flour, sifted
unrefined confectioner's sugar,
   for dusting
orange juice and segments of orange,
   to serve

1 Preheat the oven to 325°F. Whisk the egg yolks until pale and frothy, then whisk in the sugar, orange juice, orange rind, and lemon rind.

2 Fold the sifted flours or flour and meal into the egg and sugar mixture. In a clean bowl, whisk the egg whites until stiff, then fold into the egg yolk mixture.

VARIATION
Omit the lemon and replace the orange with two blood oranges for a really fresh fruity flavor.

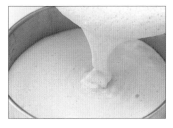

3 Put the cake mixture into a deep, ungreased 10-inch cake pan and bake for about 1 hour, or until a toothpick inserted in the center comes out clean. Let cool in the pan.

4 When cold, turn out the cake and invert onto a serving plate. Dust with a little confectioner's sugar and serve in wedges with orange segments, moistened with a little fresh orange juice.

COOK'S TIPS
• When testing to see if the cake is cooked, if you don't have a toothpick at hand, use a strand of raw dried spaghetti instead—it will work just as well.
• If you cannot find organic matzo meal, try fine cornmeal instead.

RUSSIAN POPPY SEED CAKE

This plain and simple cake is based on my mother's recipe. Flavored with lemon and vanilla, and studded with tiny black organic poppy seeds, it has a nutty, distinctive taste that is truly delicious.

SERVES ABOUT EIGHT

generous 1 cup self-rising flour
1 teaspoon baking powder
2 eggs
generous 1 cup unrefined superfine
   sugar or rapadura
1–2 teaspoons vanilla extract
scant 1½ cups poppy seeds, ground
1 tablespoon grated lemon rind
½ cup milk or soy milk
generous ½ cup unsalted butter or
   nonhydrogenated margarine, melted and
   cooled
2 tablespoons sunflower oil
unrefined confectioners' sugar, sifted, for
   dusting
whipped cream or soy cream,
   to serve

1 Preheat the oven to 350°F. Grease a deep 9-inch round springform cake pan. Sift together the flour and baking powder.

2 Using an electric mixer, beat together the eggs, sugar, and vanilla extract for 4–5 minutes, until pale and fluffy. Stir in the poppy seeds and the lemon rind.

VARIATION
To make a poppy seed tart, put the cake mixture into a par-cooked pastry shell, then bake for 30 minutes, or until the filling is firm and risen.

3 Gently fold the sifted ingredients into the egg and poppy seed mixture, in three batches, alternating with the milk, then fold in the melted butter or margarine and sunflower oil.

4 Put the mixture into the pan; bake for 40 minutes, until firm. Cool in the pan for 15 minutes, invert onto a wire rack, and let stand until cold. Dust with confectioner's sugar; serve with cream.

DOUBLE-GINGER CAKE

Preserved ginger and organic fresh ginger, which is smaller and has a more intense flavor
than the nonorganic variety, are used in this tasty quick bread.

SERVES EIGHT TO TEN

3 eggs
generous 1 cup unrefined superfine
    sugar or rapadura
1 cup sunflower oil
1 teaspoon vanilla extract
1 tablespoon syrup from a jar of
    preserved ginger
8 ounces zucchini, grated
1-inch piece fresh ginger, peeled
    and finely grated
3 cups unbleached, all-purpose
    flour
1 teaspoon baking powder
1 teaspoon ground cinnamon
2 pieces preserved ginger, drained
    and finely chopped
1 tablespoons unrefined raw sugar
    or rapadura
butter, to serve (optional)

4 Mix together the chopped preserved ginger and raw sugar in a small bowl, then sprinkle the mixture evenly over the surface of the zucchini mixture.

5 Bake for 1 hour, or until a skewer comes out clean when inserted into the center. Let the cake cool in the pan for 20 minutes, then turn out onto a wire rack and let cool completely. Serve in slices with butter, if you desire.

3 Lightly grease a 2-pound loaf pan and put in the zucchini mixture, making sure it fills the corners. Smooth and level the top.

1 Preheat the oven to 375°F. Beat together the eggs and sugar until light and fluffy. Slowly beat in the oil until the mixture forms a batter. Mix in the vanilla extract and ginger syrup, then stir in the grated zucchini and fresh ginger.

2 Sift together the flour and baking powder into a large bowl. Add the cinnamon and mix well, then stir the dried ingredients into the zucchini mixture.

COOK'S TIP
There is no need to peel fresh organic ginger. Special bamboo graters can be found in many Asian stores, but an ordinary grater will do the job, too.

SUMMER

The abundance of fresh produce at this time of year makes summer a wonderful time for any cook. With hot, sunny days and long, balmy evenings for picnics and barbecues, summer eating is a sheer delight. Chilled dishes are easy to prepare in advance: Choose the classic Vichyssoise or the popular Japanese dish, Cold Somen Noodles. Or take your pick from the wide selection of colorful salads, including Tabbouleh and Country Pasta Salad, to make the most of the dazzling array of organic fruits and vegetables available now. If you fancy cooking outside, try barbecueing Marinated Beef with Onion Rings, and accompany them with organic bread and a green salad for a simple meal. With a wide selection of mouthwatering juicy fruits in season, summer desserts really are special. Try a refreshing Watermelon Granita or, if you want something really indulgent, Coffee Crepes with Peaches and Cream, or Blueberry Frangipane Flan. Summer is also the beginning of the preserving season and you just can't beat homemade strawberry jam served with freshly baked scones and cream—delicious!

VICHYSSOISE

This classic, chilled summer soup is based on the flavorful combination of leeks and potatoes, made luxuriously velvety by adding dairy or soy cream.

SERVES FOUR TO SIX

4 tablespoons unsalted butter or
    3½ tablespoons olive oil
1 pound leeks, white parts only,
    sliced
3 large shallots, sliced
9 ounce starchy potatoes, peeled
    and cut into chunks
4 cups light chicken stock
    or water
1¼ cups heavy cream or soy cream
a little lemon juice (optional)
sea salt and ground black pepper
fresh chives, to garnish

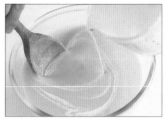

1 Heat the butter or oil in a heavy pan. Add the leeks and shallots and cook gently, covered, for 15–20 minutes, stirring once or twice, until soft but not browned.

2 Add the potato chunks to the pan and cook, uncovered, for a few minutes, stirring occasionally.

3 Stir in the light chicken stock or water, 1 teaspoon of sea salt and ground pepper to taste. Bring to a boil, then reduce the heat and partly cover the pan. Simmer for 15 minutes, or until the potatoes are soft.

4 Cool, then process the soup until smooth in a food processor or blender. Put the soup into a bowl and stir in the cream. Season to taste.

5 Chill the soup for at least 4 hours, or until very cold. Taste the chilled soup for seasoning and add a squeeze of lemon juice, if required. Put the soup into bowls and garnish with chives.

COLD SOMEN NOODLES

At the height of summer, cold somen noodles served immersed in ice cold water
and accompanied by sauces and relishes make a refreshing and exotic meal.

SERVES FOUR

11 ounces dried somen or soba noodles

For the dipping sauce
7 tablespoons mirin
½ teaspoon sea salt
7 tablespoons shoyu
¾ ounce kezuri-bushi
1⅔ cups water

For the relishes
2 scallions, trimmed and
    finely chopped
1 inch fresh ginger, peeled and
    finely grated
2 shiso or basil leaves, finely
    chopped (optional)
2 tablespoons toasted sesame seeds

For the garnishes
4-inch piece cucumber
1 teaspoon sea salt
ice cubes or a block of ice
ice-cold water
4 ounces cooked, peeled shrimp
orchid flowers or nasturtium flowers
    and leaves (optional)

1 To make the dipping sauce, put the mirin in a saucepan and bring to a boil to evaporate the alcohol. Add the salt and shoyu and shake the pan gently to mix. Add the kezuri-bushi and mix with the liquid. Add the water to the pan and bring to a boil. Cook over a vigorous heat for 3 minutes without stirring. Remove from the heat and strain through a cheesecloth bag. Let cool, then chill for at least an hour.

2 Prepare the cucumber garnish. If the cucumber is bigger than 1½ inches in diameter, cut in half and scoop out the seeds, then slice thinly. For a smaller cucumber, first cut into 2-inch lengths, then use a vegetable peeler to remove the seeds and make a hole in the center. Slice thinly. Sprinkle with the salt and let stand in a sieve for 20 minutes, then rinse in cold water and drain.

3 Bring at least 6¼ cups water to a boil in a large saucepan. Meanwhile, untie the bundle of somen. Have ⅓ cup cold water at hand. Somen only take 2 minutes to cook. Put the somen in the rapidly boiling water. When it foams again, pour the glass of water in. When the water boils again, the somen are ready. Drain into a colander. Rinse under cold running water, and rub the somen with your hands to remove the starch. Drain well.

4 Put some ice cubes or a block of ice in the center of a chilled, large glass bowl and add the somen. Gently pour on enough ice-cold water to cover the somen, then arrange cucumber slices, shrimp, and flowers, if using, on top.

5 Prepare all the relishes separately in small dishes or small sake cups.

6 Divide approximately one-third of the dipping sauce among four small cups. Put the remaining sauce in a pitcher or sauceboat.

7 Serve the noodles cold with the relishes. The guests are invited to put any combination of relishes into their dipping-sauce cup. Hold the cup over the somen bowl, pick up a mouthful of somen, then dip them into the sauce and eat. Add more dipping sauce from the jug and more relishes as required.

PROVENÇAL AIOLI with SMOKED HADDOCK

This substantial salad is a meal on its own and perfect for summer entertaining. Choose organic vegetables and vary them according to what is in season as the summer progresses.

SERVES SIX

2¼ pounds smoked haddock
bouquet garni
18 small new potatoes, scrubbed
1 large or 2 small fresh mint sprigs, torn
8 ounces green beans, trimmed
8 ounces broccoli florets
6 eggs, hard-boiled
12 baby carrots, with leaves if possible,
   scrubbed
1 large red bell pepper, seeded and cut
   into strips
2 fennel bulbs, cut into strips
18 red or yellow cherry tomatoes
sea salt
6 large whole cooked shrimp
   in the shell, to garnish
   (optional)

For the aioli
2½ cups homemade or good-quality,
   store-bought mayonnaise
2 fat garlic cloves (or more if you
   prefer), crushed
cayenne pepper

1 Put the smoked haddock into a sauté pan and pour in enough water to barely cover the fish. Add the bouquet garni. Bring the water to a boil, then cover and poach very gently for about 10 minutes until the fish flakes easily when tested with the tip of a sharp knife. Drain the fish, discard the bouquet garni, and set aside until required.

2 Cook the potatoes with the mint in a saucepan of lightly salted boiling water until just tender. Drain and set aside.

3 Cook the beans and broccoli in separate pans of lightly salted boiling water for about 5 minutes. They should still be crisp. Refresh the vegetables under cold water and drain again, then set aside.

4 Remove the skin from the haddock and break the flesh into large flakes. Shell the eggs and halve them lengthwise.

5 Pile the haddock in the middle of a large serving platter and arrange the eggs and all the vegetables around the edges or randomly. Garnish with the shrimp if you are using them.

6 To make the aioli, put the mayonnaise in a bowl and stir in the crushed garlic and cayenne pepper to taste. Serve in individual bowls or one large bowl to hand around.

SKEWERED CHICKEN

Organic chicken has a superb flavor and these fabulous little skewers make great finger food. Cook on the barbecue or broiler and serve sizzling hot.

SERVES FOUR

8 chicken thighs with skin, boned
8 large, thick scallions, trimmed
oil, for greasing
lemon wedges, to serve

For the yakitori sauce
4 tablespoons sake
5 tablespoons shoyu
1 tablespoon mirin
1 tablespoon unrefined superfine sugar
   or rapadura

1 First, make the *yakitori* sauce. Mix all the ingredients together in a small saucepan. Bring to a boil, then reduce the heat and simmer for 10 minutes.

2 Cut the chicken thighs into 1-inch cubes. Cut the scallions into 1-inch long sticks.

3 To cook the chicken on a barbecue, soak eight bamboo skewers overnight in water. This prevents the skewers from burning during cooking. Prepare the barbecue. Thread about four pieces of chicken and three scallion pieces onto each of the skewers. Place the *yakitori* sauce in a small bowl and have a brush ready.

4 Cook the skewered chicken on the barbecue. Keep the skewer handles away from the fire, turning them frequently. Brush the chicken with sauce. Return to the coals and repeat this process twice more until the chicken is well cooked.

5 Alternatively, to broil, preheat the broiler to high. Oil the wire rack and spread out the chicken cubes on it. Broil both sides of the chicken until the juices drip, then dip the pieces in the sauce and put back on the rack. Broil for 30 seconds on each side, repeating the dipping process twice more.

6 Set aside and keep warm. Gently broil the scallions until soft and slightly brown outside. Do not dip. Thread the chicken and scallion pieces onto skewers as above.

7 Arrange the skewered chicken and scallions on a serving platter and serve accompanied by lemon wedges.

ZUCCHINI FRITTERS with PISTOU

A wide variety of different organic zucchini is available, ranging in color from pale yellow to deep green. The pistou sauce, made with fresh basil, provides a lovely contrast in flavor, but you could substitute other sauces, such as a tomato and garlic one or a herb dressing.

SERVES FOUR

1 pound zucchini, grated
⅔ cup all-purpose or whole-
　wheat flour
1 egg, separated
1 tablespoon olive oil
oil for shallow frying
sea salt and ground black pepper

For the pistou sauce
½ cup basil leaves
4 garlic cloves, crushed
1 cup finely grated Parmesan
　cheese or premium Italian-style
　vegetarian cheese
finely grated rind of 1 lemon
⅔ cup olive oil

1 To make the pistou sauce, crush the basil leaves and garlic in a mortar with a pestle to make a fine paste. Transfer the paste to a bowl and stir in the grated cheese and lemon rind. Gradually blend in the oil, a little at a time, until combined, then transfer to a serving dish.

2 To make the fritters, put the grated zucchini in a sieve over a bowl and sprinkle with plenty of salt. Let stand for 1 hour then rinse thoroughly. Dry well on paper towels.

3 Sift the flour into a bowl and make a well in the center, then add the egg yolk and oil. Measure 5 tablespoons of water and add a little to the bowl.

4 Whisk the egg yolk and oil, gradually incorporating the flour and water to make a smooth batter. Season and set aside for 30 minutes.

5 Stir the grated, rinsed zucchini into the batter. Whisk the egg white until stiff, then fold into the batter.

6 Heat ½ inch of oil in a skillet. Add tablespoons of batter to the oil and fry for about 2 minutes, until golden brown and crispy. Remove from the skillet, using a slotted spoon. Place the fritters on paper towels and keep warm while frying the rest. Serve the hot fritters with the pistou sauce.

BROILED EGGPLANT PARCELS

This is a great organic recipe—little Italian bundles of tomatoes, mozzarella cheese, and basil, wrapped in slices of eggplant. The parcels are naturally low in saturated fat, sugar, and salt but are indulgent and delicious, too.

SERVES FOUR

2 large, long eggplants
1 package (8 ounces) mozzarella cheese
2 plum tomatoes
16 large basil leaves
2 tablespoons olive oil
sea salt and ground black pepper

For the dressing
4 tablespoons olive oil
1 teaspoon balsamic vinegar
1 teaspoon sun-dried tomato paste
1 teaspoon lemon juice

For the garnish
2 tablespoons toasted pine nuts
torn basil leaves

1 Remove the stalks from the eggplants and then cut the eggplants lengthwise into thin, even slices—the aim is to get 16 slices in total (each about ¼ inches thick), disregarding the first and last slices.

2 Bring a large saucepan of water to a boil and cook the eggplant slices for 2 minutes. Drain, then dry on paper towels.

3 Cut the mozzarella cheese into eight slices. Cut each tomato into eight slices, not counting the first and last slices.

4 Take two eggplant slices and place on a flameproof tray, in a cross. Place a slice of tomato in the center, season lightly, add a basil leaf, then add a slice of mozzarella, another basil leaf, a slice of tomato, and more seasoning.

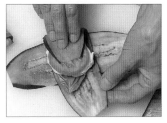

5 Fold the ends of the eggplant slices around the mozzarella and tomato filling to make a parcel. Repeat with the rest of the ingredients to make eight parcels. Chill the parcels for 20 minutes.

6 To make the tomato dressing, whisk together all the ingredients and season to taste with salt and pepper.

7 Preheat the broiler. Brush the parcels with oil and cook for 5 minutes on each side. Serve hot, with the dressing, sprinkled with pine nuts and basil.

TABBOULEH

This is a wonderfully refreshing, tangy salad of soaked bulgur wheat and masses of fresh organic mint and parsley. Increase the amount of fresh herbs for a greener salad.

SERVES FOUR TO SIX

1½ cups bulgur wheat
1 large bunch scallions, thinly sliced
1 cucumber, finely chopped or diced
3 tomatoes, chopped
¼–½ teaspoon ground cumin
1 large bunch fresh flat-leaf
    parsley, chopped
1 large bunch fresh mint, chopped
juice of 2 lemons, or to taste
4 tablespoons extra virgin olive oil
romaine lettuce leaves
olives, lemon wedges, tomato wedges,
    cucumber slices, and mint sprigs,
    to garnish (optional)
plain yogurt, to serve (optional)

1 Pick over the bulgur wheat to remove any dirt. Place it in a bowl, cover with cold water, and let soak for about 30 minutes. Put the bulgur wheat into a sieve and drain well, shaking to remove any excess water, then return it to the bowl.

2 Add the scallions to the bulgur wheat, then mix and squeeze together with your hands to combine.

3 Add the cucumber, tomatoes, cumin, parsley, mint, lemon juice, and oil to the bulgur wheat and toss well.

4 Heap the tabbouleh onto a bed of lettuce leaves and garnish with olives, lemon wedges, tomato, cucumber, and mint sprigs, if you desire. Serve with a bowl of plain yogurt, if you desire.

VARIATION
Use couscous soaked in boiling water in place of the bulgur wheat and use fresh cilantro instead of parsley.

TOMATO and MOZZARELLA SALAD

Sweet naturally ripened organic tomatoes and fresh basil capture the essence of summer in this simple salad. Choose plum or beefsteak tomatoes for this dish.

SERVES FOUR

5 ripe tomatoes
2 packages (8 ounces) mozzarella cheese,
    drained and sliced
1 small red onion, chopped

For the dressing
½ small garlic clove, peeled
½ cup fresh basil leaves
2 tablespoons chopped fresh flat-
    leaf parsley
1½ tablespoons small salted capers, rinsed
½ teaspoon mustard
5–6 tablespoons extra virgin olive oil
1–2 teaspoons balsamic vinegar
ground black pepper

For the garnish
fresh basil leaves
fresh parsley sprigs

1 First make the dressing. Put the garlic, basil, parsley, half the capers, and the mustard in a food processor or blender and process briefly to chop. Then, with the motor running, gradually pour in the olive oil through the feeder tube to make a smooth puree with a dressing consistency. Add the balsamic vinegar to taste and season with plenty of ground black pepper.

2 Slice the tomatoes. Arrange the tomato and mozzarella slices on a plate. Scatter the onion over and season with a little ground black pepper.

3 Drizzle the dressing over the salad, then scatter a few basil leaves, parsley sprigs, and the remaining capers on top as a garnish. Let stand for 10–15 minutes before serving.

SUMMER SALAD

Ripe organic tomatoes, mozzarella, and olives make a good base for a fresh and tangy pasta salad that is perfect for a light summer lunch.

SERVES FOUR

3 cups dried penne
1 package (5 ounces) mozzarella,
   drained and diced
3 ripe tomatoes, diced
10 pitted black olives, sliced
10 pitted green olives, sliced
1 scallion, thinly sliced on
   the diagonal
1 handful fresh basil leaves

For the dressing

6 tablespoons extra virgin olive oil
1 tablespoon balsamic vinegar or
   lemon juice
sea salt and ground black pepper

COOK'S TIP
Mozzarella made from buffalo milk
has more flavor than the type made
with cow's milk. Look for *mozzarella de
buffalo* in your organic store.

1 Cook the pasta for 10–12 minutes,
or according to the package instructions.
Put it into a colander and rinse briefly
under cold running water, then shake
the colander to remove as much water
as possible and leave to drain.

VARIATION
Make the salad more substantial by adding
sliced peppers, flaked tuna, anchovy fillets,
or diced ham. Always choose sustainably
caught tuna and anchovies.

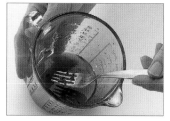

2 Make the dressing. Whisk the olive
oil and balsamic vinegar or lemon juice
in a pitcher with a little salt and pepper
to taste.

3 Place the pasta, mozzarella, tomatoes,
olives, and scallion in a large bowl, pour
the dressing over, and toss together well.
Taste for seasoning before serving,
sprinkled with basil leaves.

COUNTRY PASTA SALAD

*Colorful, tasty, and nutritious, this is the ideal pasta salad for a summer picnic. A variety
of organic pasta is available—any medium-size shapes are suitable for this salad.*

SERVES SIX

2¾ cups dried fusilli
5 ounces fine green beans,
   trimmed and cut into
   2-inch lengths
1 potato (about 5 ounces), diced
7 ounces cherry tomatoes, halved
2 scallions, finely chopped
scant 1¼ cups Parmesan cheese
   or premium Italian-style vegetarian
   cheese, coarsely shaved
6–8 pitted black olives, cut into rings
1–2 tablespoons capers, to taste

For the dressing
6 tablespoons extra virgin olive oil
1 tablespoon balsamic vinegar
1 tablespoon chopped fresh
   flat-leaf parsley
sea salt and ground black pepper

1 Cook the pasta according to the
package instructions. Drain it into a
colander, rinse under cold running water
until cold, then shake the colander to
remove as much water as possible.
Let drain and dry.

2 Cook the beans and diced potato in a
pan of boiling water for 5–6 minutes, or
steam for 8–10 minutes. Drain and let cool.

3 To make the dressing, put all the
ingredients in a large bowl with a little
sea salt and ground black pepper to
taste and whisk well to mix.

4 Add the tomatoes, scallions,
Parmesan, olive rings, and capers to
the dressing then stir in the cold pasta,
beans, and potato. Toss well to mix.
Cover and let stand for 30 minutes.
Taste for seasoning before serving.

VARIATIONS
Use other pasta shapes, such as penne
or conchigli, instead of fusilli. Try whole-
wheat pasta shapes for a nuttier taste.
Other summer vegetables—steamed
zucchini or snow peas, or roasted red
bell peppers—all taste wonderful in
this salad.

THAI BEEF SALAD

Meat does not need to dominate a meal, as this light Thai salad shows. Especially when cooking with good-quality organic meat, a little adds a lot of flavor.

SERVES FOUR

1½ pounds tenderloin or top round
    beef steak
2 tablespoons olive oil
2 small mild red chiles, seeded and sliced
3¼ cups shiitake mushrooms,
    finely sliced

For the dressing
3 scallions, finely chopped
2 garlic cloves, finely chopped
juice of 1 lime
1–2 tablespoons fish or oyster sauce,
    to taste
1 tablespoon unrefined soft light brown
    sugar or rapadura
2 tablespoons chopped fresh cilantro

To serve
1 romaine lettuce, torn into strips
6 ounces cherry tomatoes, halved
2-inch piece cucumber, peeled, halved
    and thinly sliced
3 tablespoons toasted sesame seeds

1 Preheat the broiler until hot, then cook the steak for 2–4 minutes on each side, depending on how well done you like steak. (In Thailand, the beef is traditionally served rare.) Let the beef stand to cool for at least 15 minutes.

2 Use a very sharp knife to slice the meat as thinly as possible and place the slices in a bowl.

VARIATION
If you can find them, yellow chiles make a colorful addition to this dish. Substitute one for one of the red chiles.

3 Heat the olive oil in a small skillet. Add the seeded and sliced red chiles and the sliced mushrooms and cook for 5 minutes, stirring occasionally. Turn off the heat and add the broiled steak slices to the skillet, then stir well to coat the beef slices in the cooked chile and mushroom mixture.

4 Stir all the ingredients for the dressing together, then pour it over the meat mixture and toss gently.

5 Arrange the salad ingredients on a serving plate. Spoon the warm steak mixture in the center and sprinkle the sesame seeds over. Serve at once.

FRESH TUNA SALAD NIÇOISE

This classic colorful salad is transformed into something really special by using fresh tuna. When buying tuna make sure it is line-caught tuna that is certified as sustainably caught by the Marine Stewardship Council (MSC).

SERVES FOUR

4 tuna steaks, about 5 ounces each
2 tablespoons olive oil
8 ounces fine green beans, trimmed
1 small romaine lettuce or
    2 little Boston lettuce
4 new potatoes, boiled
4 ripe tomatoes, or 12 cherry tomatoes
2 red bell peppers, seeded and cut
    into thin strips
4 hard-boiled eggs, sliced
8 drained anchovy fillets in oil,
    halved lengthwise (optional)
16 large black olives
sea salt and ground black pepper
12 fresh basil leaves, to garnish

For the dressing
1 tablespoon red wine vinegar
6 tablespoons olive oil
1 fat garlic clove, crushed

1 Brush the tuna on both sides with a little olive oil and season. Heat a ridged grill pan or the broiler until very hot, then grill or broil the tuna steaks for 1–2 minutes on each side; the flesh should be pink and juicy in the middle.

2 Cook the beans in a pan of lightly salted boiling water for 4–5 minutes, or until crisp-tender. Drain, refresh under cold water and drain again.

COOK'S TIP
To intensify the flavor of the peppers, broil them until the skins are charred, place in a bowl, and cover with paper towels. Let stand for 10–15 minutes, then rub off the skins.

3 Separate the lettuce leaves and rinse them thoroughly under cold running water and dry them on paper towels. Arrange them on four individual serving plates. Slice the cooked potatoes and tomatoes, if large (leave cherry tomatoes whole or halve them) and divide them among the plates. Arrange the beans and red bell pepper strips over the potatoes and tomatoes.

4 Shell the hard-boiled eggs and cut them into thick slices. Place a few slices of egg on each plate with the anchovy fillets, if using, and olives.

5 To make the dressing, whisk together the vinegar, olive oil, and garlic and season to taste. Drizzle over the salads, arrange the tuna steaks on top, scatter over the basil, and serve.

SPICED VEGETABLE COUSCOUS

This tasty vegetarian main course is easy to make and can be prepared with any number of seasonal organic vegetables, such as spinach, peas, fava beans, or corn.

SERVES SIX

3 tablespoons olive oil
1 large onion, finely chopped
2 garlic cloves, crushed
1 tablespoons tomato paste
½ teaspoon ground turmeric
½ teaspoon cayenne pepper
1 teaspoon ground coriander
1 teaspoon ground cumin
1½ cups cauliflower florets
8 ounces baby carrots, trimmed
1 red bell pepper, seeded and diced
8 ounces zucchini, sliced
1 can (14 ounces) chickpeas, drained
   and rinsed
4 beefsteak tomatoes, skinned
   and sliced
3 tablespoons chopped fresh cilantro
sea salt and ground black pepper
fresh cilantro sprigs, to garnish

For the couscous
½ tsp sea salt
2⅔ cups couscous
4 tablespoons cup butter or
   3½ tbsp sunflower oil

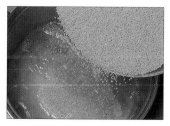

1 Heat 2 tablespoons oil in a large pan, add the onion and garlic, and cook until soft and translucent. Stir in the tomato paste, turmeric, cayenne, coriander, and cumin. Cook, stirring, for 2 minutes.

2 Add the cauliflower, baby carrots, and bell pepper with enough water to come halfway up the vegetables. Bring to a boil, then lower the heat, cover, and simmer for 10 minutes.

3 Add the zucchini, chickpeas and tomatoes to the pan and cook for 10 minutes. Stir in the fresh cilantro and season. Keep hot.

4 To cook the couscous, bring about 2 cups water to a boil in a large pan. Add the remaining olive oil and the salt. Remove from the heat and add the couscous, stirring. Allow to swell for 2 minutes.

5 Add the butter or sunflower oil, and heat through gently, stirring to separate the grains.

6 Turn the couscous out onto a warm serving dish, and spoon the cooked vegetables on top, pouring over any liquid. Garnish with fresh cilantro sprigs and serve immediately.

VEGETABLE PIZZA

You really can't go too far wrong with this classic mixture of Mediterranean broiled vegetables on homemade pizza dough. It is filling and healthy, and is a favorite with children.

3 Place the pizza dough on a sheet of baking parchment on a baking sheet and roll or gently press it out to form a 25cm/10in round, making the edges slightly thicker than the centre.

4 Lightly brush the pizza dough with any remaining oil, then spread the chopped plum tomatoes evenly over the dough.

SERVES SIX

1 zucchini, sliced
2 baby eggplant or 1 small
   eggplant, sliced
2 tablespoons olive oil
1 yellow bell pepper, seeded and sliced
1 cup cornmeal
½ cup potato flour
½ cup soy flour
1 teaspoon baking powder
½ teaspoon sea salt
¼ cup nonhydrogenated margarine
7 tablespoons milk
4 plum tomatoes, skinned and chopped
2 tablespoons chopped fresh basil
4 ounces mozzarella cheese, sliced
sea salt and ground black pepper
fresh basil sprigs, to garnish

1 Preheat the broiler. Brush the zucchinni and eggplant slices with a little oil and place on a wire rack with the pepper slices. Cook under the broiler until lightly browned, turning once.

2 Meanwhile, preheat the oven to 400°F. Place the cornmeal, potato flour, soy flour, baking powder, and salt in a mixing bowl and stir to mix. Lightly rub in the margarine until the mixture resembles coarse breadcrumbs, then stir in enough of the milk to make a soft but not sticky dough.

VARIATION
Top the pizza with 4 ounces sliced goat's cheese instead of the mozzarella for a creamy alternative.

5 Sprinkle with the chopped basil and season with salt and pepper. Arrange the broiled vegetables over the tomatoes and top with the cheese.

6 Bake for 25–30 minutes, until crisp and golden brown. Garnish the pizza with fresh basil sprigs and serve immediately, cut into slices.

COOK'S TIP
This recipe uses a combination of different types of flours to give an interesting flavor and texture to the base. If you prefer, use 2 cups of all-purpose flour or a combination of half all-purpose and half whole-wheat flours.

OLIVE OIL ROASTED CHICKEN
with SUMMER VEGETABLES

This is a delicious alternative to a traditional roast chicken. Organic chicken can be much tastier and more tender than intensively reared poultry, especially if the birds are raised biodynamically.

SERVES FOUR

4–4½ pounds roasting chicken
⅔ cup extra virgin olive oil
½ lemon
few sprigs of fresh thyme
1 pound small new potatoes
1 eggplant, cut into 1-inch cubes
1 red bell pepper, seeded and
   quartered
1 fennel bulb, trimmed and quartered
8 large garlic cloves, unpeeled
coarse sea salt and ground black pepper

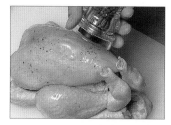

1 Preheat the oven to 400°F. Rub the chicken all over with olive oil and season with pepper. Place the lemon half inside the bird, with a sprig or two of thyme. Put the chicken breast side down in a large roasting pan. Roast for about 30 minutes.

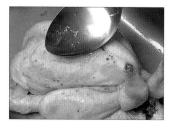

2 Remove the chicken from the oven and season with salt. Turn the chicken right side up, and baste. Surround the bird with the potatoes, roll them in the pan juices, and return to the oven.

3 After 30 minutes, add the eggplant, red bell pepper, fennel, and garlic cloves to the pan. Drizzle with the remaining oil, and season with salt and pepper. Add any remaining thyme to the vegetables. Return to the oven and cook for about 40 minutes more, basting and turning the vegetables occasionally.

4 To find out if the chicken is cooked, push the tip of a sharp knife between the thigh and breast. If the juices run clear, it is done. The vegetables should be tender and just beginning to brown. Serve the chicken and vegetables from the pan, or transfer the vegetables to a serving dish, joint the chicken, and place it on top. Serve the skimmed juices in a sauceboat.

VARIATION
Serve rosemary potato wedges with the chicken. Heat 4 tablespoons olive oil for 10 minutes in a roasting pan in an oven preheated to 400°F. Cut the potatoes into wedges and add to the oil. Sprinkle over 2 teaspoons dried rosemary. Season and bake for 50–60 minutes.

GRIDDLED CHICKEN with TOMATO SALSA

This simple meal is a great way to enjoy the flavour, color, and health benefits
of organic ingredients. For the best result, marinate the chicken overnight.

SERVES FOUR

4 boneless, skinless chicken breast fillets,
    about 6 ounces each
2 tablespoons fresh lemon juice
2 tablespoons olive oil
2 teaspoons ground cumin
2 teaspoons dried oregano
1 tablespoon coarse black pepper

For the salsa
1 green chile
1 pound plum tomatoes, seeded
    and chopped
3 scallions, chopped
1 tablespoon chopped fresh parsley
2 tablespoons chopped
    fresh cilantro
2 tablespoons fresh lemon juice
3 tablespoons olive oil

1 With a meat mallet, pound the
chicken between two sheets of plastic
wrap until thin.

2 In a shallow dish, combine the lemon
juice, oil, cumin, oregano, and pepper.
Add the chicken and turn to coat. Cover
and let marinate for at least 2 hours, or
in the refrigerator overnight.

3 To make the salsa, char the chile skin
either over a gas flame or under the
broiler. Let cool for 5 minutes. Carefully
rub off the charred skin, being careful to
wash your hands afterward. For a less
hot flavor, discard the seeds.

4 Chop the chile very finely and place
in a bowl. Add the seeded and chopped
tomatoes, the chopped scallions,
chopped fresh parsley and cilantro,
lemon juice, and olive oil and mix well.
Set aside until ready to serve.

5 Remove the chicken from the
marinade. Heat a ridged grill pan.
Add the chicken fillets and cook on one
side until browned, for about 3 minutes.
Turn over and cook for a further 4
minutes. Serve with the chile salsa.

COOK'S TIP
The hottest part of the chile is the white
membrane that connects the seeds to
the flesh. By charring the flesh, the
natural sweetness is released and the
heat is moderated.

MARINATED BEEF with ONION RINGS

Mexican chiles combine well with garlic in this marinade for broiled steak. Organic beef is
tastier and has a better balance of cholesterol than the nonorganic kind.

SERVES FOUR

¾ ounces large mild dried red chiles
    (such as mulato or pasilla)
2 garlic cloves, plain or smoked,
    finely chopped
I teaspoon ground toasted cumin seeds
I teaspoon dried oregano
4 tablespoons olive oil
4 beef steaks, top round or rib-eye,
    6–8 ounces each
sea salt and ground black pepper

For the onion rings
2 onions, sliced into rings
I cup milk or soy milk
¾ cup coarse cornmeal
½ teaspoon dried red chili flakes
I teaspoon ground toasted cumin seeds
I teaspoon dried oregano
sunflower or safflower oil,
    for deep-frying

I Cut the stalks from the dried red
chiles and discard the seeds. Toast
the chiles in a dry skillet over a high
heat, stirring constantly, for 2–4 minutes,
until they give off their aroma. Place the
chiles in a bowl, cover with warm water,
and let them to for 20–30 minutes.
Drain the chiles and reserve the
soaking water.

2 Process the soaked, drained chiles to
a paste with the finely chopped garlic,
toasted cumin seeds, oregano, and oil in
a food processor. Add a little of the
soaking water, if needed. Season with
ground black pepper.

3 Wash and dry the steaks, place them
in a nonmetallic container, rub the chile
paste all over them, and let marinate in
the refrigerator for up to 12 hours.

4 To make the onion rings, soak the
onion slices in the milk for 30 minutes.
Mix the cornmeal, chili flakes, cumin, and
oregano, and season with salt and pepper.

5 Heat the oil for deep-frying in a deep
pan to 325–350°F, or until a cube of
day-old bread turns brown in about
a minute.

6 Drain the onion rings and dip each
one into the cornmeal mixture, coating
it thoroughly. Fry for 2–4 minutes, until
browned and crisp. Do not overcrowd
the pan, but cook in batches. Lift the
onion rings out of the pan with a slotted
spoon and drain on paper towels.

7 Heat a barbecue or cast-iron grill pan.
Season the steaks with salt and cook for
about 4 minutes on each side for a
medium result; reduce or increase this
time according to how rare or well done
you prefer steak. Serve the steaks with
the onion rings.

MOROCCAN FISH TAGINE with COUSCOUS

Fish is a staple food for the organic cook, with its balance of amino acids and oils. Always ensure that it is either organically farmed or sustainably caught in the wild.

SERVES EIGHT

3 pounds firm fish fillets, such
    as monkfish, skinned and cut
    into 2-inch cubes
4 tablespoons olive oil
4 onions, chopped
1 large eggplant, cut into ½-inch cubes
2 zucchini, cut into ½-inch cubes
1 can (14 ounces) chopped tomatoes
1⅔ cups passata (strained
    tomatoes)
scant 1 cup fish stock
1 preserved lemon, chopped
scant 1 cup olives
4 tablespoons chopped fresh cilantro
sea salt and ground black pepper
couscous, to serve
cilantro sprigs, to garnish

For the harissa
3 large fresh red chiles, seeded
    and chopped
3 garlic cloves, peeled
1 tablespoon ground coriander
2 tablespoons ground cumin
1 tablespoon ground cinnamon
grated rind of 1 lemon
2 tablespoons sunflower oil

1 To make the harissa, whiz everything in a food processor to a smooth paste.

2 Put the fish in a wide bowl and add 2 tablespoons of the harissa. Toss to coat, cover, and chill for at least 1 hour.

3 Heat half the oil in a shallow pan. Cook the onions for about 10 minutes. Stir in the remaining harissa; cook for 5 minutes, stirring occasionally.

4 Heat the remaining olive oil in a separate pan. Add the eggplant cubes and fry for 10 minutes, or until they are golden brown. Add the cubed zucchini and fry the vegetables for a further 2 minutes, stirring occasionally.

5 Put the eggplant mixture into the shallow pan and combine with the onions, then stir in the chopped tomatoes, the passata, and fish stock. Bring to a boil, then lower the heat and simmer the mixture for about 20 minutes.

6 Stir the fish cubes and preserved lemon into the pan. Add the olives and stir gently. Cover and simmer over a low heat for about 15–20 minutes, until the fish is just cooked through. Season to taste. Stir in the chopped cilantro. Serve with couscous and garnish with cilantro sprigs.

COOK'S TIP
To make the fish go further, you can add 1¼ cups cooked chickpeas to the tagine.

HAKE AU POIVRE with BELL PEPPER RELISH

Use South African hake instead of hake from European waters, where stocks are low due to overfishing. If not available, try line-caught tuna or haddock from Icelandic waters.

3 Make the relish. Cut the red bell peppers in half lengthwise, remove the core and seeds, and cut the flesh into ½-inch wide strips. Heat the olive oil in a wok or a shallow pan that has a lid. Add the peppers and stir them for about 5 minutes, or until they are slightly softened. Stir in the chopped garlic, tomatoes, and the anchovies, then cover the pan and simmer the mixture very gently for about 20 minutes, until the peppers are very soft.

4 Put the contents of the pan into a food processor and whiz to a coarse puree. Transfer to a bowl and season to taste. Stir in the capers, balsamic vinegar, and basil. Keep the relish hot.

SERVES FOUR

2–3 tablespoons mixed peppercorns (black, white, pink, and green)
4 hake steaks, about 6 ounces each
2 tablespoons olive oil
sea salt and ground black pepper

For the relish
2 red bell peppers
1 tablespoon olive oil
2 garlic cloves, chopped
4 ripe tomatoes, peeled, seeded, and quartered
4 drained canned anchovy fillets, roughly chopped
1 teaspoon capers
1 tablespoon balsamic vinegar, plus a little extra to serve
12 fresh basil leaves, shredded, plus a few extra to garnish

1 Put the peppercorns in a mortar and crush them coarsely with a pestle. Alternatively, put them in a plastic bag and crush them with a rolling pin.

2 Season the hake fillets lightly with salt, then coat them evenly on both sides with the crushed peppercorns. Set the coated fish steaks aside while you make the red pepper relish.

5 Heat the olive oil in a shallow pan, add the hake steaks, and fry them in batches, if necessary, for 5 minutes on each side, turning them once or twice, until they are just cooked through.

6 Place the fish on individual plates and spoon a little red pepper relish onto each plate. Garnish with basil leaves and a little extra balsamic vinegar. Serve the rest of the relish separately.

WATERMELON GRANITA

Pastel pink flakes of ice, subtly blended with the citrus freshness of lime and the delicate,
refreshing flavor of organic watermelon, make this granita a treat for the eye and the tastebuds.

2 Bring the sugar and water to a boil in a small saucepan, stirring constantly until the sugar has dissolved. Pour the syrup into a bowl. Allow the syrup to cool, then chill until needed.

3 Strain the puree through a sieve into a large plastic container. Discard the melon seeds. Pour in the chilled syrup and lime rind and juice, and mix well.

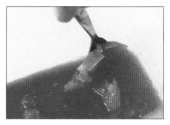

4 Cover and freeze for 2 hours, until the granita mixture around the sides of the container is mushy. Mash the ice finely with a fork and return to the freezer.

5 Freeze for a further 2 hours, mashing the mixture every 30 minutes, until the granita has a slushy consistency. Scoop it into individual dishes and serve with the wedges of lime.

SERVES SIX

1 whole watermelon,
    about 4–4½ pounds
³/₄ cup unrefined superfine sugar
    or rapadura
²/₃ cup water
finely grated rind and juice
    of 2 limes
lime wedges, to decorate

COOK'S TIP

If you are using another melon, such as cantaloup, you may not need as much lime juice. Add half in step 3, then taste the mixture and adjust as necessary.

1 Cut the watermelon into quarters. Discard most of the seeds, scoop the flesh into a food processor, and process briefly until smooth. Alternatively, use a blender and process the watermelon quarters in small batches.

VARIATION

To serve this granita cocktail-style, dip the rim of each glass serving dish in a little water, then dip it into unrefined superfine sugar. Spoon in the granita, pour over a little Tequila, and decorate with lime wedges.

FROZEN MELON

Freezing sorbet in hollowed out fruit, which is then cut into icy wedges, is an excellent idea. The refreshing flavor makes this dessert irresistible on a hot summer's day.

SERVES SIX

¼ cup unrefined superfine sugar
  or rapadura
2 tablespoons clear honey
1 tablespoon lemon juice
4 tablespoons water
1 medium cantaloupe melon,
  about 2¼ pounds
crushed ice, cucumber slices, and borage
  flowers, to decorate

1 Put the sugar, honey, lemon juice, and water in a heavy saucepan, and heat gently until the sugar dissolves. Bring to a boil, and boil for 1 minute, without stirring, to make a syrup. Let cool.

2 Cut the cantaloupe melon in half and discard the seeds. Carefully scoop out the flesh using a metal spoon or melon baller and place in a food processor, being careful to keep the halved shells intact.

3 Blend the melon flesh until very smooth, then transfer to a mixing bowl. Stir in the cooled sugar syrup and chill until very cold. Invert the melon shells and let them drain on paper towels for a few minutes, then transfer them to the freezer while making the sorbet.

4 If making by hand, put the mixture into a container and freeze for 3–4 hours, beating well twice with a fork, a whisk, or in a food processor to break up the ice crystals and produce a smooth texture. If using an ice-cream maker, churn the melon mixture in the ice-cream maker until the sorbet holds its shape.

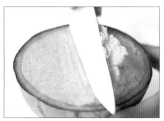

5 Pack the sorbet into the melon shells and level the surface with a knife. Use a tablespoon to scoop out the center of each filled melon shell to simulate the seed cavity. Freeze the prepared fruit overnight until firm.

6 To serve, use a large knife to cut each melon half into three wedges. Serve on a bed of ice on a large platter or individual serving plates, and decorate with the cucumber slices and borage flowers.

COOK'S TIP
If the melon sorbet is too firm to cut when taken straight from the freezer, let it soften in the refrigerator for 10–20 minutes. Be careful when slicing the frozen melon shell into wedges. A serrated kitchen knife is easier to work with.

CHOCOLATE MERINGUES with MIXED FRUIT COMPOTE

Mini-chocolate meringues are sandwiched with crème fraîche and served with a compote of mixed fresh berries to make this impressive dessert.

SERVES SIX

7 tablespoons unsweetened red
    grape juice
7 tablespoons unsweetened apple juice
2 tablespoons clear honey
4 cups mixed fresh berries, such
    as raspberries, blackberries, red
    currants, and black currants

For the meringues
3 egg whites
¾ cup unrefined superfine sugar
    or rapadura
3 ounces good-quality dark chocolate,
    finely grated
scant 1 cup crème fraîche or sour cream

1 Preheat the oven to 225°F. Grease and line two large baking sheets with parchment paper, cutting the paper to fit.

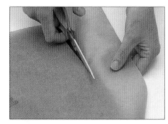

2 To make the meringues, whisk the egg whites in a large mixing bowl until stiff. Gradually whisk in half the sugar, then fold in the remaining sugar, using a metal spoon. Gently fold in the grated dark chocolate.

3 Carefully spoon the meringue mixture into a large pastry bag with a large star nozzle attached. Pipe small round whirls of the mixture onto the prepared baking sheets.

4 Bake the meringues for 2½–3 hours, until they are firm and crisp. Remove from the oven. Carefully peel the meringues off the paper, then transfer them to a wire rack to cool.

5 Meanwhile, make the compote. Heat the fruit juices in a small saucepan with the honey until almost boiling.

COOK'S TIP
Organic chocolate has a slightly higher proportion of cocoa and less sugar than nonorganic equivalents. And, because organic cocoa is naturally high in tannins and antioxidant flavonoids as well as B vitamins and iron, organic chocolate consumed in moderation is actually good for you. Look for chocolate that has 70 percent cocoa solids for the best flavor and higher nutritional content.

6 Place the mixed fresh berries in a large bowl and pour over the hot fruit juice and honey mixture. Stir gently to mix, then set aside and let cool. Once cool, cover the bowl with plastic wrap and chill until required.

7 When ready to serve, gently sandwich the cold meringues together with the crème fraîche or sour cream and arrange them on a serving plate or dish.

8 Serve the meringues immediately on individual plates with the mixed fruit compote to accompany.

VARIATION
Packs of frozen mixed berries are available and can be used in place of fresh in this recipe. Allow the berries to defrost thoroughly in a sieve over a mixing bowl, then use as in step 6.

FRAGRANT FRUIT SALAD

Organic summer fruit make a delicious seasonal fruit salad. Any combination of fruits can be used, although this exotic choice is particularly suitable for a dinner party.

SERVES SIX

scant ¾ cup unrefined sugar or rapadura
thinly pared rind and juice of 1 lime
4 tablespoons brandy
1 teaspoon instant coffee granules or
     powder dissolved in 2 tablespoons
     boiling water
1 small pineapple
1 papaya
2 pomegranates
1 medium mango
2 passion fruits or kiwis
fine strips of lime peel, to decorate

COOK'S TIP
Allow the salad to stand at room temperature for an hour before serving so the flavors can blend.

1 Put the sugar and lime rind in a small pan with ⅔ cup water. Heat gently until the sugar dissolves, then bring to a boil and simmer for 5 minutes. Let cool, then strain into a large serving bowl, discarding the lime rind. Stir in the lime juice, brandy, and dissolved coffee.

2 Using a sharp knife, cut the plume and stalk ends from the pineapple. Peel and cut the flesh into bite-size pieces. Add to the bowl. Discard the central core.

3 Halve the papaya and scoop out the seeds. Cut away the skin, then slice the papaya. Halve the pomegranates and scoop out the seeds. Add to the bowl.

4 Cut the mango lengthwise into three pieces, along each side of the pit. Peel the skin off the flesh. Cut into chunks and add to the bowl.

5 Halve the passion fruits and scoop out the flesh using a teaspoon or peel and chop the kiwis. Add to the bowl and serve, decorated with lime peel.

SUMMER BERRIES in WARM SABAYON GLAZE

This luxurious combination of fresh summer berries under a light and fluffy alcoholic sauce is lightly broiled to form a crisp, caramelized topping.

SERVES FOUR

4 cups mixed summer berries, such as
 rasperries, blackberries, blueberries,
 red currants, or black currants
4 egg yolks
¼ cup unrefined superfine sugar
 or rapadura
½ cup white dessert wine, plus extra
 to serve (optional)
a little unrefined confectioner's sugar,
 sifted, and mint leaves, to decorate
 (optional)

COOK'S TIP

If you want to omit the alcohol, use a
pure fruit juice instead, such as grape,
mango, or apricot.

1 Arrange the fruits in four flameproof dishes. Preheat the broiler.

2 Whisk the egg yolks in a large bowl with the sugar and wine. Place the bowl over a saucepan of hot water and whisk constantly until thick, fluffy, and pale.

3 Put equal quantities of the sabayon sauce into each dish. Place under the broiler for 1–2 minutes, until just turning brown. Sprinkle with confectioner's sugar and scatter with mint leaves just before serving, if you want. Add an extra splash of wine to the dishes, if you want.

COFFEE CRÊPES with PEACHES and CREAM

Juicy golden organic peaches and cream conjure up the sweet taste of summer. Here they are delicious as the filling for these light coffee-flavored buckwheat crêpes.

SERVES SIX

⅔ cup all-purpose flour
¼ cup buckwheat flour
1 egg, beaten
scant 1 cup milk or soy milk
1 tablespoon butter, melted
scant ½ cup brewed coffee,
   cooled
sunflower oil, for frying

For the filling
6 ripe peaches
1¼ cups heavy cream
1 tablespoon brandy
1 cup crème fraîche or
   sour cream
generous ¼ cup unrefined superfine
   sugar or rapadura
2 tablespoons unrefined confectioner's
   sugar, for dusting (optional)

1 Sift the flours into a mixing bowl. Make a well in the middle and add the beaten egg, half the milk, and the melted butter. Gradually mix in the flour, beating until the mixture is smooth, then beat in the remaining milk and the coffee.

2 Heat a drizzle of sunflower oil in a 6–8-inch crêpe pan. Put in just enough batter to cover the bottom of the pan thinly, swirling the pan to spread the mixture evenly. Cook for 2–3 minutes, until the underneath is golden brown, then flip the crêpe over using a metal spatula and cook the other side.

3 Slide the crêpe out of the pan onto a plate. Continue making crêpes until all the mixture is used, stacking and interleaving them with parchment paper.

4 To make the filling, halve the peaches and carefully remove the pits. Cut the peaches into thick slices. Whip the cream and brandy together until soft peaks form. Beat the crème fraîche with the sugar until smooth. Beat 2 tablespoons of the cream into the crème fraîche, then fold in the remainder.

5 Place six of the crêpes on individual serving plates. Spoon a little of the brandy cream onto one half of each crêpe and top with peach slices. Gently fold the crêpe over and dust with a little sifted confectioner's sugar, if you want. Serve immediately.

BLUEBERRY FRANGIPANE FLAN

A tangy lemon pastry case is filled with a nutty sweet almond filling dotted with ripe
blueberries. Their wonderful color and taste are a seasonal favorite.

SERVES SIX

2 tablespoons ground coffee
3 tablespoons milk or soy milk
4 tablespoons unsalted butter
¼ cup unrefined superfine sugar
    or rapadura
I egg
I cup ground almonds
I tbsp all-purpose flour, sifted
2 cups blueberries
2 tablespoons jam
I tablespoons brandy
crème fraîche or sour cream,
    to serve

For the pastry
I½ cups all-purpose flour
½ cup unsalted butter or
    nonhydrogenated margarine
2 tablespoons unrefined superfine sugar
    or rapadura
finely grated rind of ½ lemon
I tablespoon chilled water

I Preheat the oven to 375°F. To make
the pastry, sift the flour into a bowl,
then rub in the butter. Stir in the sugar
and lemon rind, then add the water
and mix to a firm dough. Wrap the
dough in plastic wrap and chill for
20 minutes.

2 Roll out the pastry on a lightly floured
work surface and use to line a 9-inch
loose-bottomed quiche pan. Line the
pastry with parchment paper and
dried beans and bake for 10 minutes.
Remove the paper and beans and
bake for a further 10 minutes. Remove
from the oven.

3 Meanwhile, to make the filling, put the
ground coffee in a bowl. Bring the milk
almost to a boil, then pour over the
coffee and let infuse for 4 minutes.
Cream the butter and sugar until pale.
Beat in the egg, then add the almonds
and flour. Strain in the coffee-flavored
milk through a fine sieve and fold in.

4 Spoon the coffee mixture into the
pastry shell and spread evenly. Scatter
the blueberries over the top and push
them down slightly into the mixture.
Bake for 30 minutes, until firm, covering
with foil after 20 minutes.

5 Remove the tart from the oven and
allow to cool slightly. Heat the jam and
brandy in a small saucepan until melted.
Brush over the flan and remove from
the tin. Serve warm with crème fraîche
or sour cream.

APRICOT and ALMOND TART

This rich tart relies on a simple but perfect combination of apricots and almond filling.
Fresh apricots are only available during the summer months so make the most of them.

SERVES SIX

½ cup butter or nonhydrogenated
 margarine
scant ½ cup unrefined superfine sugar
 or rapadura
1 egg, beaten
⅓ cup ground rice
½ cup ground almonds
few drops of almond extract
1 pound fresh apricots, halved and pitted
sifted unrefined confectioners' sugar,
 for dusting (optional)
apricot slices and fresh mint sprigs,
 to decorate (optional)

For the pastry
1 cup brown rice flour
1 cup cornmeal
½ cup butter or nonhydrogenated
 margarine
2 tablespoons unrefined uperfine sugar
 or rapadura
1 egg yolk

1 To make the pastry, place the rice
flour and cornmeal in a large mixing
bowl and stir to mix. Lightly rub in
the butter or margarine with your
fingertips until the mixture resembles
fine breadcrumbs.

VARIATIONS
For a change, use ground hazelnuts and
vanilla extract in place of the ground
almonds and almond extract. Pears,
peaches, or nectarines can be used in
this recipe instead of the apricots. Or
use a combination of the three fruits
to make a mixed fruit tart.

2 Add the sugar, stir in the egg yolk and
add enough chilled water to make a
smooth, soft but not sticky dough.
Wrap the dough in plastic wrap and
chill for 30 minutes.

3 Preheat the oven to 350°F. Line a
9½-inch loose-bottomed quiche pan
with the dough by pressing it gently over
the bottom and up the sides of the pan,
making sure that there are no holes in
the dough. Trim the edge of the pastry
with a sharp knife.

4 To make the almond filling, place the
butter or margarine and sugar in a
mixing bowl and cream together, using
a wooden spoon, until the mixture is
light and fluffy.

5 Gradually add the beaten egg to the
mixture, beating well after each addition.
Fold in the ground rice and almonds and
the almond essence and mix well to
incorporate them.

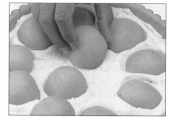

6 Spoon the almond mixture into the
pastry shell, spreading it evenly with
the back of a spoon, then arrange the
apricot halves cut side down on top.

7 Place the tart on a baking sheet
and bake for 40–45 minutes, until
the filling and pastry are cooked and
lightly browned. Serve warm or cold,
dusted with confectioner's sugar and
decorated with apricots and sprigs of
mint, if you want.

COOK'S TIP
Organic apricots are often smaller and
are more intensely colored than nonorganic fruit. They have a sweeter, juicier
flavor, too. Organic apricots, like organic
peaches and figs, help regulate the body's
digestive system. Try substituting organic
peaches and figs in this recipe.

BLUEBERRY MUFFINS

Light and fruity, these popular muffins are delicious at any time of day. Serve them warm
for breakfast or brunch, or as a afternoon treat.

MAKES TWELVE

generous 1½ cups all-purpose flour
¼ cup unrefined sugar or rapadura
2 teaspoons baking powder
2 eggs
4 tablespoons butter or
   nonhydrogenated margarine,
   melted
¾ cup milk or soy milk
1 teaspoon vanilla extract
1 teaspoon grated lemon rind
1½ cups fresh blueberries

1 Preheat the oven to 400°F. Lightly grease a 12-cup muffin pan or arrange 12 paper muffin cases on a baking tray.

2 Sift the all-purpose flour, unrefined sugar, and baking powder into a large mixing bowl.

3 In another bowl, whisk the eggs until blended. Add the melted butter, milk, vanilla extract, and grated lemon rind to the whisked eggs, and stir thoroughly to combine.

4 Make a well in the dry ingredients and pour in the egg mixture. With a large metal spoon, stir until the flour is just moistened, but not smooth.

5 Add the blueberries to the muffin mixture and gently fold in, being careful not to crush the berries.

6 Spoon the batter into the muffin pan or paper cases, leaving enough room for the muffins to rise.

7 Bake for 20–25 minutes, until the tops spring back when touched lightly. Let the muffins cool in the pan, if using, for about 5 minutes before turning out onto a wire rack to cool a little before serving.

VARIATION
Muffins are delicious with all kinds of different fruit. Replace the blueberries with the same weight of bilberries, black currants, pitted cherries or raspberries.

COOK'S TIP
If you want to serve these muffins for breakfast, prepare the dry ingredients the night before to save time.

STRAWBERRY JAM and SCONES

There is not much that can beat freshly made English-style scones with good-quality jam.
Making your own is easy and their flavor will be outstanding.

MAKES ABOUT 3 POUNDS JAM
AND 10–12 SCONES

For the strawberry jam
9 cups small strawberries
4½ cups unrefined granulated sugar
juice of 2 lemons

For the scones
2 cups all-purpose flour
1 tablespoon baking powder
4 tablespoons butter or nonhydrogenated
    margarine, diced
1 egg, beaten, plus extra to glaze
5 tablespoons milk or soy milk
heavy cream, to serve

1 Layer the strawberries and sugar in a large bowl. Cover and let stand overnight.

2 The next day, put the strawberries and their juice into a large heavy pan. Add the lemon juice. Bring to a boil, stirring until the sugar has dissolved.

3 Boil steadily for 10–15 minutes. Spoon a small amount onto a chilled saucer. Chill for 3 minutes, then push the jam with your finger; if wrinkles form, it is ready. Cool for 10 minutes.

4 Put the strawberry jam into warm, sterilized jars, filling them right to the top. Cover the jam with a disk of waxed paper, waxed side down; seal the jar with a damp cellophane film cut into a circle and secure with a rubber band while the jam is still hot. Label when the jars are cold. The jam can be stored in a cool dark place, and it should keep for up to 1 year.

5 To make the scones, preheat the oven to 425°F. Butter a baking sheet. Sift the flour and baking powder together, then rub in the butter or margarine. Make a well in the center of the flour mixture, add the egg and milk, and mix to a soft dough, using a fork or a round-bladed knife.

6 Turn out the scone dough onto a floured surface, and knead very lightly until smooth. Roll out the dough to about a ¾-inch thickness and cut into 10 or 12 circles using a 2-inch plain or fluted cutter dipped in flour.

7 Transfer to the baking sheet, brush the tops with egg, then bake for about 8 minutes, until risen and golden. Cool slightly on a wire rack then serve with the jam and heavy cream.

FALL

As the nights begin to start earlier, warming dishes become popular—make the most of hearty organic vegetables. such as parsnips, squashes, and sweet potatoes. Try Roasted Garlic Squash Soup with roasted tomato salsa, Orange Candied Sweet Potatoes, or Potatoes and Parsnips Baked with Garlic and Cream. Delicious fish dishes to try now include Sole with Wild Mushrooms or Potato-topped Fish Pie—served simply with roasted root vegetables. Fall orchards and hedges provide a wonderful array of fresh fruits— organic apples, plums, and pears are full of flavor and are popular in both sweet and savory dishes. Try Duck Sausages with Spicy Plum Sauce, or Spicy Venison Casserole with cranberries and orange. Sticky Pear Pudding is a delicious sweet treat, while individual Hot Blackberry and Apple Soufflés are just right for a dinner party.
Freshly baked cakes are especially satisfying at this time of year— try Parsnip Cake with Orange Frosting. And if you have a glut of apples, then there is no better way to use them than in Country Apple Cake—served warm straight from the oven for a real taste of fall.

CLAM, MUSHROOM, and POTATO CHOWDER

Members of the same family as mussels, scallops, and oysters, clams have a sweet flavor and firm texture, which make a delicious combination with wild mushrooms in this filling soup.

SERVES 4

48 clams, scrubbed
¼ cup unsalted butter or
    nonhydrogenated margarine
1 large onion, chopped
1 celery stalk, sliced
1 carrot, sliced
3¾ cups assorted wild and
    cultivated mushrooms
8 ounces starchy potatoes (such as
    russet), thickly sliced
5 cups boiling light chicken or
    vegetable stock
1 thyme sprig
4 parsley stalks
sea salt and ground
    black pepper
thyme sprigs, to garnish

1 Place the clams in a large, heavy pan, discarding any that are open. Add ½ inch of water to the pan, then cover and bring to a boil. Cook the clams over a medium heat for 6–8 minutes, shaking the pan occasionally, until the clams open (discard any clams that do not open).

2 Drain the clams over a bowl and remove most of the shells, leaving some in the shells as a garnish. Strain the cooking juices into the bowl, add all the clams and set aside.

3 Add the butter, onion, celery, and carrot to the pan and cook gently until just softened but not colored. Add the wild and cultivated mushrooms and cook for 3–4 minutes, until their juices begin to appear. Add the potato slices, the clams and their juices, the stock, thyme, and parsley stalks.

4 Bring to a boil, then reduce the heat, cover, and simmer for 25 minutes. Season to taste, ladle into soup bowls, and garnish with thyme sprigs.

ROASTED GARLIC and SQUASH SOUP

This is a wonderful, richly flavored dish. A spoonful of hot and spicy tomato salsa gives bite to this sweet-tasting butternut squash and garlic soup.

SERVES FOUR TO FIVE

2 garlic bulbs, outer papery
    skin removed
5 tablespoons olive oil
a few fresh thyme sprigs
1 large butternut squash, halved
    and seeded
2 onions, chopped
1 teaspoon ground coriander
5 cups vegetable or chicken stock
2–3 tablespoons chopped fresh oregano
    or marjoram
sea salt and ground black pepper

For the salsa
4 large ripe tomatoes, halved and seeded
1 red bell pepper, halved and seeded
1 large fresh red chile, halved
    and seeded
2–3 tablespoons extra virgin olive oil
1 tablespoon balsamic vinegar

3 Heat the remaining oil in a large, heavy pan and cook the onions and ground coriander gently for about 10 minutes, or until softened.

4 Skin the pepper and chile and process in a food processor or blender with the tomatoes and 2 tablespoons of olive oil. Stir in the vinegar and seasoning to taste. Add the remaining oil if you think the salsa needs it.

5 Squeeze the roasted garlic out of its papery skin into the onions. Scoop the squash out of its skin and add it to the pan. Add the vegetable or chicken stock, ½ teaspoons of salt and plenty of black pepper. Bring to a boil and simmer for 10 minutes.

6 Stir in half the chopped fresh oregano or marjoram and let the soup cool slightly, then process it in batches if necessary, in a food processor or blender until smooth. Alternatively, press the soup through a fine sieve.

7 Reheat the soup in a clean pan without allowing it to boil, then taste for seasoning before ladling it into individual warmed bowls. Top each with a spoonful of the tomato salsa and sprinkle over the remaining chopped fresh oregano or marjoram. Serve immediately.

1 Preheat the oven to 425°F. Place the garlic bulbs on a piece of foil and pour over half the olive oil. Add the thyme sprigs, then fold the foil around the garlic bulbs to enclose them completely. Place the foil parcel on a baking sheet with the butternut squash and brush the squash with 1 tablespoon of the remaining olive oil. Add the halved and seeded tomatoes, red bell pepper, and fresh chile for the salsa.

2 Roast the vegetables for 25 minutes, then remove the tomatoes, bell pepper, and chile. Reduce the temperature to 375°F and cook the squash and garlic for 20–25 minutes more, or until the squash is tender.

ROAST GARLIC with GOAT CHEESE PÂTÉ

The combination of sweet, mellow roasted garlic and goat cheese is a classic one. The pâté
is flavored with walnuts and herbs and is particularly good made with the new season's
walnuts, sometimes known as "wet" walnuts, which are available in the early fall.

SERVES FOUR

4 large garlic bulbs
4 fresh rosemary sprigs
8 fresh thyme sprigs
4 tablespoons olive oil
sea salt and ground black pepper
thyme sprigs, to garnish
4–8 slices sourdough bread and
    walnuts, to serve

For the pâté

scant 1 cup soft goat cheese
5ml/1 tsp finely chopped fresh thyme
1 tablespoon chopped fresh parsley
⅓ cup walnuts, chopped
1 tablespoon walnut oil (optional)
fresh thyme, to garnish

1 Preheat the oven to 350°. Strip the papery skin from the garlic bulbs. Place them in an ovenproof dish large enough to hold them snugly. Tuck in the fresh rosemary sprigs and fresh thyme sprigs, drizzle the olive oil over, and season with a little sea salt and plenty of ground black pepper.

2 Cover the garlic tightly with foil and bake in the oven for 50–60 minutes, opening the parcel and basting once halfway through the cooking time. Set aside and let cool.

3 Preheat the broiler. To make the pâté, cream the cheese with the thyme, parsley, and chopped walnuts. Beat in 1 tablespoon of the cooking oil from the garlic, and season to taste with plenty of ground black pepper. Transfer the pâté to a serving bowl and chill until ready to serve.

4 Brush the sourdough bread slices on one side with the remaining cooking oil from the garlic bulbs, then broil until lightly toasted.

5 Divide the pâté among four individual plates. Drizzle the walnut oil, if using, over the goat cheese pâté and grind some black pepper over it. Place some garlic on each plate and serve with the pâté and some toasted bread. Garnish the pâté with a little fresh thyme and serve a few freshly shelled walnuts with each portion.

SLOW-COOKED SHIITAKE with SHOYU

Shiitake mushrooms cooked slowly are so rich and filling, that some people call them "vegetarian steak." This Japanese dish, known as Fukumé-ni, can last a few weeks in the refrigerator, and is a useful and flavorful addition to other dishes.

SERVES FOUR

20 dried shiitake mushrooms
3 tablespoons sunflower or safflower oil
2 tablespoons shoyu
1 tablespoon toasted sesame oil

VARIATION
You can make a delicious rice dish using the slow-cooked shiitake to serve with broiled fish or chicken. Cut the slow-cooked shiitake into thin strips. Mix with 5¼ cups cooked brown rice and 1 tablespoon finely chopped chives. Serve in individual rice bowls and sprinkle with toasted sesame seeds.

1 Start soaking the dried shiitake the day before. Put them in a large bowl almost full of water. Cover the shiitake with a plate or lid to stop them from floating to the surface of the water. Let soak overnight.

2 Measure ½ cup of liquid from the bowl. Drain the shiitake into a sieve. Remove and discard the stalks.

3 Heat the oil in a wok or a large skillet. Stir-fry the shiitake over a high heat for 5 minutes, stirring continuously.

4 Reduce the heat to the lowest setting, then add the measured liquid and the shoyu. Cook the mushrooms until there is almost no moisture left, stirring frequently. Add the toasted sesame oil and remove from the heat.

5 Let cool, then slice and arrange the shiitake on a large plate.

RED ONION and MUSHROOM TARTLETS with GOAT CHEESE

Crisp and savory, these attractive little tarts are delicious served with a few mixed salad greens drizzled with a garlic-infused French dressing.

SERVES SIX

4 tablespoons olive oil
2 tablespoons butter or
  nonhydrogenated margarine
4 red onions, thinly sliced
1 teaspoon unrefined soft,
  light brown sugar
1 tablespoon balsamic vinegar
1 tablespoon soy sauce
3 cups white mushrooms, sliced
1 garlic clove, finely chopped
½ teaspoon chopped fresh tarragon
2 tablespoons chopped fresh parsley
9 ounces goat cheese log (chèvre)
sea salt and ground black pepper
mixed salad greens, to serve

For the pastry
1¾ cups all-purpose flour
pinch of cayenne pepper
scant ½ cup butter or
  nonhydrogenated margarine
½ cup freshly grated Parmesan cheese or
  premium vegetarian cheese
3–4 tablespoons iced water

1 To make the pastry, sift the flour and cayenne into a bowl, add the butter, and rub in with the fingertips.

2 Stir in the grated cheese, then bind the pastry with the iced water. Press the pastry into a ball, then wrap it in plastic wrap and chill.

3 Heat 1 tablespoon of the oil and half the butter in a heavy skillet, then add the onions. Cover and cook gently for 15 minutes, stirring occasionally.

4 Uncover the pan, increase the heat slightly, and sprinkle in the sugar. Cook, stirring frequently, until the onions begin to caramelize and brown. Add the balsamic vinegar and soy sauce and cook briskly until the liquid evaporates. Season to taste then set aside.

5 Heat another 2 tablespoons of the oil and the remaining butter or margarine in a pan, then add the sliced mushrooms and chopped garlic and cook fairly briskly for 5–6 minutes, or until the mushrooms are browned and cooked.

6 Set a few cooked mushrooms and onion rings aside, then stir the rest of the mushrooms into the onions with the fresh tarragon and parsley. Adjust the seasoning to taste. Preheat the oven to 375°F.

COOK'S TIP

Flaky pie dough is traditionally made with all-purpose flour. For a healthier, higher fiber dough, use half all-purpose flour and half whole-wheat flour. This creates a nutty, slightly textured result.

7 Roll out the dough and use to line six 4-inch quiche pans. Use a fork to prick the bottom of the pastry shells and line the sides with strips of foil. Bake for 10 minutes, remove the foil, and bake for another 5–7 minutes, or until the pastry is lightly browned and cooked. Remove the tartlets from the oven and increase the temperature to 400°F.

8 Remove the pastry shells from the pan and arrange them on a baking sheet. Divide the onion mixture equally among the pastry shells. Cut the goat cheese into six equal slices; place one slice on each tartlet. Distribute the reserved mushrooms and onion rings; drizzle with the remaining oil and season with pepper.

9 Return the tartlets to the oven and bake for 5–8 minutes, or until the goat cheese is just beginning to turn brown. Serve with mixed salad greens.

VARIATION

For a milder flavor, sliced mozzarella cheese can be used to top the tartlets instead of the goat cheese.

FLORETS POLONAISE

Simple steamed organic vegetables become something special with this pretty egg topping.
They make a perfect dinner party side dish or are great with a light weekday meal.

SERVES SIX

1¼ pounds mixed vegetables,
    such as cauliflower, broccoli,
    and Romanesca cauliflower
4 tablespoons butter or extra virgin
    olive oil
finely grated rind of ½ lemon
1 large garlic clove, crushed
½ cup fresh breadcrumbs, lightly baked
    or broiled until crisp
2 eggs, hard-boiled
sea salt and ground black pepper

VARIATION
Use whole-wheat breadcrumbs instead of
the white crumbs. They will provide a
nuttier flavor and crunchier texture.

1 Trim the vegetables and break into equal-size florets. Place the florets in a steamer over a pan of boiling water and steam for 5–7 minutes, until just tender.

2 Toss the steamed vegetables in butter or oil and transfer to a serving dish.

3 While the vegetables are cooking, mix together the lemon rind, garlic, seasoning, and breadcrumbs. Finely chop the eggs and mix together with the remaining ingredients. Sprinkle the chopped egg mixture over the cooked vegetables and serve at once.

ORANGE CANDIED SWEET POTATOES

*Organic sweet potatoes are free of the fungicides sprayed on nonorganic tubers and
are an excellent source of vitamins, including cancer-preventing betacarotene.*

SERVES EIGHT

2 pounds sweet potatoes
1 cup orange juice
¼ cup maple syrup
1 teaspoon freshly grated ginger
1½ teaspoons ground cinnamon
1¼ teaspoons ground cardamom
½ teaspoon salt
ground black pepper
ground cinnamon and orange segments,
    to garnish

COOK'S TIP

This popular American dish is delicious
served with roast turkey at Thanksgiving
and Christmas. Serve with extra orange
segments to make it really special.

1 Preheat the oven to 350°F. Peel and
dice the potatoes, then steam them
for 5 minutes.

2 Meanwhile, stir the remaining
ingredients together. Spread out
onto a nonstick shallow baking pan.

3 Scatter the potatoes over the baking
pan. Cook for 1 hour, stirring every
15 minutes, until they are tender and
well coated in the spicy syrup.

4 Serve garnished with orange segments
and ground cinnamon.

GARLIC CHIVE RICE with MUSHROOMS

A wide range of organic mushrooms is readily available. They combine well with rice and garlic chives to make a tasty accompaniment for vegetarian dishes, fish, or chicken.

SERVES FOUR

generous 1¾ cups
   long grain rice
4 tablespoons peanut oil
1 small onion, finely chopped
2 green chiles, seeded and finely chopped
½ cup garlic chives, chopped
½ cup fresh cilantro
2½ cups vegetable or mushroom stock
½ teaspoon sea salt
9 ounces mixed mushrooms, thickly sliced
scant ⅓ cup cashew nuts, fried in
   1 tablespoon olive oil until
   golden brown
ground black pepper

1 Wash and drain the rice. Heat half the oil in a saucepan and cook the onion and chiles over a gentle heat, stirring occasionally, for 10–12 minutes, until soft.

2 Set half the garlic chives aside. Cut the stalks off the cilantro and set the leaves aside. Puree the remaining chives and the coriander stalks with the stock in a food processor or blender.

VARIATION

For a higher-fibre alternative make this dish with brown rice. Increase the cooking time in step 3 to 25–30 minutes or follow the packet instructions.

3 Add the rice to the onions and fry over a low heat, stirring frequently, for 4–5 minutes. Put in the stock mixture, then stir in the salt and a good grinding of black pepper. Bring to a boil, then stir and reduce the heat to very low. Cover tightly with a lid and cook for 15–20 minutes, or until the rice has absorbed all the liquid.

4 Remove the pan from the heat and lay a clean, folded dish towel over the pan, under the lid, and press on the lid to wedge it firmly in place. Let the rice stand for a further 10 minutes, allowing the towel to absorb the steam while the rice becomes completely tender.

5 Meanwhile, heat the remaining oil in a skillet and cook the mushrooms for 5–6 minutes, until tender and browned. Add the remaining garlic chives and cook for another 1–2 minutes.

6 Stir the cooked mushroom and chive mixture and chopped cilantro leaves into the rice. Adjust the seasoning to taste, then transfer to a warmed serving dish and serve immediately, scattered with the fried cashew nuts.

ROASTED SHALLOT and SQUASH SALAD

*This is especially good served with a grain or starchy salad, based on rice or couscous,
for example. Serve with plenty of handmade organic bread to mop up the juices.*

SERVES FOUR TO SIX

5 tablespoons olive oil
1 tablespoon balsamic vinegar, plus a little
    extra, if you like
1 tablespoon sweet soy sauce
12 ounces shallots, peeled but left whole
3 fresh red chiles
1 butternut squash, peeled, seeded,
    and cut into chunks
1 teaspoon finely chopped fresh thyme
scant ½ cup flat-leaf parsley
1 small garlic clove, finely chopped
¾ cup walnuts, chopped
5 ounces feta cheese
sea salt and ground black pepper

1 Preheat the oven to 400°F. Beat the
olive oil, balsamic vinegar, and soy sauce
together in a large bowl, then season
with a little salt and plenty of freshly
ground black pepper.

2 Toss the shallots and two of the chiles
in the oil mixture and put into a large
roasting pan or ovenproof dish. Roast for
15 minutes, stirring once or twice.

3 Add the butternut squash chunks
and roast for a further 30–35 minutes,
stirring once, until the squash is tender
and browned. Remove from the oven,
stir in the chopped fresh thyme, and set
the vegetables aside to cool.

4 Chop the parsley and garlic together
and mix with the walnuts. Seed and
finely chop the remaining chile.

5 Stir the parsley, garlic, and walnut
mixture into the vegetables. Add
chopped chile to taste and adjust the
seasoning, adding a little extra balsamic
vinegar, if you desire. Crumble the feta
and add to the salad. Transfer to a
serving dish and serve immediately.

POTATOES and PARSNIPS BAKED with GARLIC and CREAM

As the potatoes and parsnips cook, they gradually absorb the garlic-flavored cream, while the cheese browns to a crispy finish.

SERVES FOUR TO SIX

3 large potatoes, about
   1½ pounds
12 ounces small–medium parsnips
scant 1 cup light cream
   or soy cream
7 tablespoons milk or soy milk
2 garlic cloves, crushed
butter or olive oil, for greasing
about 1 teaspoon freshly grated
   nutmeg
¾ cup coarsely grated
   cheddar cheese
sea salt and ground black pepper

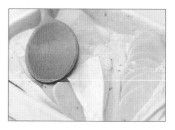

3 Lightly grease a 10-inch long, shallow rectangular earthenware baking dish with butter or oil. Preheat the oven to 350°F.

5 Put the garlic-flavored cream and milk mixture into the dish and then press the sliced potatoes and parsnips down into the liquid. The liquid should come to just underneath the top layer of vegetables. Cover the dish with a piece of lightly buttered foil or parchment paper and bake for 45 minutes.

1 Peel the potatoes and parsnips and cut them into thin slices using a sharp knife. Place them in a steamer and cook for 5 minutes. Let cool slightly.

4 Arrange the thinly sliced potatoes and parsnips in layers in the greased earthenware dish, sprinkling each layer of vegetables with a little freshly grated nutmeg and a little salt and plenty of ground black pepper.

6 Remove the dish from the oven and remove the foil or paper from the dish. Sprinkle the grated cheddar cheese over the vegetables in an even layer.

7 Return the dish to the oven and bake uncovered for a further 20–30 minutes, or until the potatoes and parsnips are tender and the topping is golden brown.

2 Meanwhile, put the cream and milk into a heavy saucepan, add the crushed garlic, and bring to a boil over a medium heat. Remove the pan from the heat and let stand at room temperature for about 10 minutes to allow the flavor of the garlic to infuse into the cream and milk mixture.

VARIATIONS

• Use sweet potatoes in place of some or all of the ordinary potatoes—choose orange-fleshed ones for a pretty color contrast with the parsnips. Other root vegetables, such as Jerusalem artichokes, carrots, rutabaga, or turnips would also work well.
• Other hard cheeses would be equally good in this recipe, such as Gruyère—or go for the even more strongly flavored Parmesan, premium Italian-style vegetarian cheese, or Pecorino.

COOK'S TIPS

• If you have one, use a mandolin or a food processor fitted with a slicing blade to slice the potatoes and parsnips thinly and evenly for this gratin.
• At the end of the cooking time, to test if the vegetables are tender, insert a sharp knife through the middle of the potatoes and parsnips. The knife should slide in easily and the vegetables feel soft.

TOFU and VEGETABLE THAI CURRY

Nonorgani soy products, including tofu, are often made from genetically modified beans that are resistant to pesticides. By using organic tofu in this fragrant curry, you benefit from its great texture and superior nutritional value while helping to protect the earth.

SERVES FOUR

6 ounces tofu, drained
3 tablespoons dark soy sauce
1 tablespoon sesame oil
1 teaspoon chili sauce
1-inch piece fresh ginger,
    finely grated
8 ounces cauliflower
8 ounces broccoli
2 tablespoons sunflower oil
1 onion, sliced
1⅔ cups coconut milk
⅔ cup water
1 red bell pepper, seeded and chopped
6 ounces green beans, halved
1½ cups shiitake or white mushrooms,
    halved
shredded scallions, to garnish
boiled brown rice or noodles,
    to serve

For the curry paste
2 chiles, seeded and chopped
1 lemon grass stalk, chopped
1-inch piece fresh galangal or
    fresh ginger, chopped
2 kaffir lime leaves
2 teaspoons ground coriander
a few sprigs fresh cilantro, including
    the stalks

1 Cut the drained tofu into 1-inch cubes and place in an ovenproof dish. Mix together the soy sauce, sesame oil, chili sauce, and ginger and pour over the tofu. Toss gently to coat all the cubes evenly, then let stand to marinate for at least 2 hours, or overnight if possible, turning and basting the tofu occasionally.

2 To make the curry paste, place the chopped chiles, lemon grass, galangal, kaffir lime leaves, ground coriander, and cilantro in a food processor, and process for a few seconds, until well blended. Add 3 tablespoons of water and process to a thick paste.

3 Preheat the oven to 375°F. Using a large sharp knife, cut the cauliflower and broccoli into small florets and cut any stalks into thin slices.

4 Heat the sunflower oil in a skillet, add the sliced onion, and gently fry for about 8 minutes, or until soft and lightly browned. Stir in the prepared curry paste and the coconut milk.

5 Add the water and bring to a boil, then stir in the red pepper, green beans, cauliflower, and broccoli. Transfer to an earthenware casserole or Chinese sand pot. Cover and place in the oven.

6 Stir the tofu and marinade, then place the dish in the top of the oven and cook for 30 minutes. After 30 minutes, stir the tofu and marinade into the curry with the mushrooms.

7 Reduce the oven temperature to 350°F and cook for about 15 minutes more, or until the vegetables are tender. Garnish with scallions and serve with boiled rice or noodles.

COOK'S TIP
Organic tofu, or beancurd, is made from organic soy beans and is sold in blocks. It is a creamy white color and has a solid gel-like texture. Tofu has a bland flavor and its absorbent nature allows it to take on the flavors of marinades or any other food that it is cooked with.

SPAGHETTI with EGGS and BACON

Organic ingredients really enhance the flavors of simple, classic dishes, such as this Italian favorite, which makes a great last-minute dinner.

SERVES FOUR

2 tablespoons olive oil
1 small onion, finely chopped
1 large garlic clove, crushed
8 pancetta or rindless, smoked
    fatty bacon strips, cut into
    ½-inch pieces
12 ounces fresh or dried spaghetti
4 eggs
6–8 tablespoons reduced-fat
    crème fraîche
4 tablespoons freshly grated Parmesan
    cheese or premium Italian-style
    vegetarian cheese, plus extra
    to serve
sea salt and ground black pepper

1 Heat the oil in a large saucepan, add the onion and garlic, and fry gently for about 5 minutes until softened.

2 Add the pancetta or bacon to the pan and cook for 10 minutes, stirring.

3 Meanwhile, cook the spaghetti in a large saucepan of salted boiling water for 10 minutes, or according to the package instructions, until *al dente*.

4 Put the eggs, crème fraîche, and grated Parmesan in a bowl. Stir in plenty of black pepper, then beat together well.

5 Drain the pasta thoroughly, put it into the pan with the pancetta or bacon, and toss well to mix.

6 Turn off the heat under the pan, then immediately add the egg mixture and toss thoroughly so that it cooks lightly and coats the pasta.

7 Season to taste, then divide the spaghetti among four warmed bowls and sprinkle with freshly ground black pepper. Serve immediately, with extra grated cheese handed separately.

COOK'S TIP
If crème fraîche is difficult to find, you can replace it with heavy cream, sour cream, or soy cream.

CHICKEN with CASHEW NUTS

This popular Chinese dish is quick and easy to make and can be enjoyed at its best by using good-quality organic products that are full of flavor.

SERVES FOUR

12 ounces skinless chicken
   breast fillets
pinch of ground white pepper
1 tablespoon dry sherry
1¼ cups chicken stock
1 tablespoon sunflower oil
1 garlic clove, finely chopped
1 small carrot, cut into cubes
½ cucumber, about 3 ounces,
   cut into ½-inch cubes
½ cup drained, canned bamboo
   shoots, cut into ½-inch cubes
   (optional)
1 teaspoon cornstarch
1 tablespoon soy sauce
¼ cup dry-roasted cashew nuts
½ teaspoon sesame oil
noodles, to serve

1 Cut the chicken into ¾-inch cubes. Place the cubes in a bowl, stir in the white pepper and sherry, cover, and marinate for 15 minutes.

2 Bring the stock to a boil in a large pan. Add the chicken and cook, stirring, for 3 minutes. Drain, reserving 6 tablespoons of the stock; set aside.

3 Heat the sunflower oil in a large nonstick skillet until it is very hot, add the finely chopped garlic, and stir-fry for a few seconds. Add the cubed carrot, cucumbe,r and bamboo shoots, if using, and continue to stir-fry the vegetables over a medium heat for 2 minutes.

4 Stir in the chicken and reserved stock. Mix the cornstarch with the soy sauce and add the mixture to the pan. Cook, stirring, until the sauce thickens slightly. Finally, add the cashew nuts and sesame oil. Toss to mix thoroughly, then serve with noodles.

MOUSSAKA

This is a traditional eastern Mediterranean dish, popular in both Greece and Turkey. Layers of minced mutton, eggplant, tomatoes, and onions are topped with a creamy yogurt and cheese sauce in this delicious, authentic recipe.

SERVES FOUR

1 pound eggplants
⅔ cup olive oil
1 large onion, chopped
2–3 garlic cloves, finely chopped
1½ pounds lean ground mutton
1 tablespoon all-purpose flour
1 can (14 ounces) chopped tomatoes
2 tablespoons chopped mixed
    fresh herbs, such as parsley,
    marjoram, and oregano
sea salt and ground black pepper

For the topping
1¼ cups plain yogurt
2 eggs
1 ounce feta cheese, crumbled
⅓ cup freshly grated Parmesan
    cheese or premium Italian-style
    vegetarian cheese

1 Slice the eggplants and layer them in a colander, sprinkling with salt. Cover the slices with a plate and a weight, then let drain for about 30 minutes.

2 Drain the eggplant, rinse well, then pat dry with paper towels.

3 Heat 3 tablespoons of the oil in a large, heavy pan. Fry the onion and garlic until softened, but not colored. Add the mutton and cook over a high heat, stirring often, until browned.

4 Stir in the flour until mixed, then stir in the tomatoes, herbs, and seasoning. Bring to a boil, reduce the heat, and simmer gently for 20 minutes.

5 Meanwhile, heat a little of the remaining olive oil in a large skillet. Add as many eggplant slices as can be laid in the pan in a single layer. Cook until golden on both sides, then remove from the pan. Heat more oil and continue frying the eggplant slices in batches, adding olive oil as necessary.

COOK'S TIP
Many kinds of organic eggplant do not taste bitter; therefore, it is not usually necessary to salt them before cooking. However, if they are to be fried, as in this recipe, salting and drying them reduces the amount of fat that they absorb and helps them to brown during cooking.

6 Preheat the oven to 350°F. Arrange half the eggplant slices in a large, shallow ovenproof dish.

7 Top the eggplant slices with about half of the meat and tomato mixture, then add the remaining eggplant slices. Spread the remaining meat mixture over the eggplant.

8 To make the topping, beat together the yogurt and eggs, then mix in the feta and Parmesan or Italian-style cheeses. Pour the mixture over the meat and spread it evenly.

9 Transfer the moussaka to the oven and bake for 35–40 minutes, or until golden and bubbling.

VARIATION
Use large zucchini in place of the eggplant, if you want, and cut them diagonally into fairly thick slices. There is no need to salt the zucchini before frying them.

DUCK SAUSAGES with SPICY PLUM SAUCE

A variety of organic sausages is available direct from farmers and small butchers, and any pork or game sausages would work in this dish. Rich duck sausages are best baked in their own juices.

SERVES FOUR

8–12 duck sausages

For the sweet potato mash
3¼ pounds sweet potatoes, cut
   into chunks
2 tablespoons butter or
   olive oil
4 tablespoons milk
sea salt and ground black pepper

For the plum sauce
2 tablespoons olive oil
1 small onion, chopped
1 small red chile, seeded and chopped
1 pound plums, pitted and chopped
2 tablespoons red wine vinegar
3 tablespoons clear honey

1 Preheat the oven to 375°F. Arrange the duck sausages in a single layer in a large, shallow ovenproof dish. Bake the sausages, uncovered, in the oven for 25–30 minutes, turning the sausages two or three times during cooking to ensure that they brown and cook evenly.

2 Meanwhile, put the sweet potatoes in a pan and add water to cover. Bring to a boil, then reduce the heat and simmer for 20 minutes, or until tender.

3 Drain and mash the potatoes, then place the pan over a low heat. Stir frequently for about 5 minutes to dry out the mashed potato. Beat in the butter or oil and milk; season to taste.

4 Make the plum sauce. Heat the oil in a small pan and fry the onion and chile gently for 5 minutes. Stir in the plums, vinegar, and honey, then simmer gently for 10 minutes.

5 Serve the freshly cooked sausages with the sweet potato mash and plum sauce.

SPICY VENISON CASSEROLE

Being high in flavor but low in saturated fat, organic venison is a good choice for healthy,
yet rich, casseroles. Cranberries and orange bring a delicious fruitiness to this spicy recipe.

SERVES FOUR

1 tablespoon olive oil
1 onion, chopped
2 celery stalks, sliced
2 teaspoons ground allspice
1 tablespoon all-purpose or
    whole-wheat flour
1½ pounds stewing venison,
    cubed
8 ounces fresh or frozen cranberries
grated rind and juice of 1 orange
3¾ cups beef or venison stock
sea salt and ground black pepper

1 Heat the oil in a flameproof casserole.
Add the onion and celery and fry for
about 5 minutes, or until softened.

2 Meanwhile, mix the ground allspice
with the flour and either spread the
mixture out on a large plate or place
in a large plastic bag. Toss a few pieces
of venison at a time (to prevent them
from becoming soggy) in the flour
mixture until they are all lightly coated.
Spread the floured venison out on a
large plate until ready to cook.

3 When the onion and celery are
just softened, remove them from the
casserole, using a slotted spoon, and set
aside. Add the venison pieces to the
casserole in batches and cook until well
browned and sealed on all sides.

COOK'S TIP

Freshly made homemade stock is always
best, but if you lack the time, look for
cartons or containers of fresh stock in
the chilled food cabinets of organic stores.

4 Add the cranberries and the orange
rind and juice to the casserole along
with the stock and stir well. Return the
vegetables and the browned venison to
the casserole and heat until simmering.
Cover tightly and reduce the heat.

5 Simmer for about 45 minutes, or until
the venison is tender, stirring occasionally.
Season the venison casserole to taste
with a little salt and plenty of ground
black pepper before serving.

VARIATIONS

Farmed organic venison is increasingly
easy to find and is available from many
good butchers and organic meat delivery
companies. It makes a rich and flavorful
stew, but lean pork or braising beef
could be used in place of the venison, if
you prefer. You could also replace the
cranberries with pitted and halved prunes
and, for extra flavor, use either ale or
stout instead of about half the stock.

STUFFED ROAST LOIN of PORK with APPLE SAUCE

The secret of a good roast with apple sauce is simple, good-quality ingredients, such as organic pork and traditionally made hard cider.

SERVES SIX

1 tablespoon light olive oil
2 leeks, chopped
⅔ cup dried apricots, chopped
scant 1 cup dried dates, pitted
    and chopped
1½ cups fresh white or whole-
    wheat breadcrumbs
2 eggs, beaten
1 tablespoon fresh thyme leaves
3¼ pounds boned loin of pork
sea salt and ground black pepper

For the apple sauce
1 pound cooking apples
2 tablespoon cider or water
2 tablespoons butter or
    olive oil

1 Preheat the oven to 425°F. Heat the oil in a large pan and cook the leeks until softened. Stir in the apricots, dates, breadcrumbs, eggs, and thyme, and season with salt and pepper.

2 Lay the pork skin side up, and use a sharp knife to score the rind diagonally.

3 Turn the meat over and cut down the center of the joint to within ½ inch of the rind and fat, then work from the middle outward toward one side, cutting most of the meat off the rind but keeping a ½-inch layer of meat on top of the rind. Cut to within 1 inch of the side of the joint. Repeat on the other side of the joint.

4 Spoon half the stuffing over the joint, then fold the meat over it.

5 Tie the joint back into its original shape, then place in a roasting pan and rub the skin with salt. Roast the pork for 40 minutes, then reduce the oven temperature to 375°F and cook for a further 1½ hours, or until the meat is tender and cooked through.

6 Meanwhile, shape the remaining stuffing into walnut-size balls. Arrange on a tray, cover with plastic wrap, and chill until 20 minutes before the pork is cooked. Then add the stuffing balls to the roasting pan and baste them with the cooking juices from the meat.

7 When cooked, cover the meat closely with foil and let stand in a warm place for 10 minutes before carving.

8 To make the apple sauce, peel, core, and chop the apples, then place in a small saucepan with the cider or water and cook for 5–10 minutes, stirring occasionally, or until very soft. Beat well or process in a food processor or blender to make smooth apple sauce. Beat in the butter or oil. Reheat the apple sauce just before serving, if necessary.

9 Carve the joint into thick slices. If the crackling is very hard, you may find that it is easier to slice the crackling off the joint first, before carving the meat, then cut the crackling into serving pieces, using poultry shears or a heavy, sharp chef's knife or cleaver. Serve the stuffed loin of pork with the crackling, stuffing balls, apple sauce, and a selection of seasonal fall vegetables.

COOK'S TIP
The resting time before carving is very important, so don't be tempted to skip it.

SALMON and RICE GRATIN

This all-in-one light meal is ideal for informal fall entertaining because it can be made in advance and reheated for about half an hour before being served with a tossed salad.

4 Remove the pan from the heat and, without lifting the lid, allow the rice to stand, undisturbed, for 5 minutes.

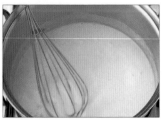

5 Meanwhile, make the sauce. Mix the milk, flour, and butter or margarine in a pan. Bring to a boil over a low heat, whisking constantly until the sauce is smooth and thick. Stir in the curry paste with salt and pepper to taste. Simmer for 2 minutes.

SERVES SIX

1½ pounds fresh salmon fillet, skinned
1 bay leaf
a few parsley stalks
4 cups water
2 cups basmati rice, soaked
    and drained
2–3 tablespoons chopped fresh parsley,
    plus extra to garnish
1½ cups grated cheddar cheese
3 hard-boiled eggs, chopped
sea salt and ground black pepper

For the sauce
4 cups milk or soy milk
⅓ cup all-purpose flour
3 tablespoons butter or
    nonhydrogenated margarine
1 teaspoon mild curry paste

1 Put the salmon fillet in a wide, shallow pan. Add the bay leaf and parsley stalks, with a little salt and plenty of black pepper. Pour in the water and bring to a simmering point. Poach the fish for about 12 minutes, until just tender.

2 Lift the salmon fillet out of the pan using a slotted spoon, then strain the cooking liquid into a large pan. Let the fish cool, then remove any visible bones and flake the flesh gently into bite-size pieces with a fork.

3 Add the soaked and drained rice to the pan containing the fish-poaching liquid. Bring the liquid to a boil, then lower the heat, cover tightly with a lid, and simmer gently for 10 minutes without lifting the lid.

6 Preheat the broiler. Remove the sauce from the heat and stir in the chopped parsley and rice, with half the cheese. Using a large metal spoon, fold in the flaked fish and eggs. Spoon into a shallow gratin dish and sprinkle with the rest of the cheese. Cook under the broiler until the topping is golden brown and bubbling. Serve in individual dishes, garnished with chopped parsley.

VARIATIONS
You can substitute organically farmed shrimp for the salmon, and you can use other hard cheeses, such as Gruyère, instead of the cheddar cheese if you prefer not to use it.

POTATO-TOPPED FISH PIE

This traditional Scottish dish should be prepared from wild fish caught sustainably.
Always ensure you buy wild fish bearing the MSC logo.

SERVES FOUR

1½ pounds white fish fillets
1¼ cups milk or soy milk
½ lemon, sliced
1 bay leaf
1 fresh thyme sprig
4–5 black peppercorns
4 tablespoons butter or
  nonhydrogenated margarine
¼ cup all-purpose flour
2 tablespoons chopped fresh parsley
1 teaspoon anchovy extract
2 cups shiitake or cremini mushrooms,
  sliced
sea salt, ground black pepper and
  cayenne pepper

For the topping
1 pound potatoes, cooked and
  mashed with milk or soy milk
4 tablespoons butter or
  nonhydrogenated margarine
2 tomatoes, sliced
¼ cup grated cheddar cheese

1 Put the fish skin side down in a shallow pan. Add the milk, lemon slices, bay leaf, thyme, and peppercorns. Bring to a boil, then lower the heat and poach gently for about 5 minutes, until just cooked. Strain off and reserve the milk. Remove the fish skin and flake the flesh, discarding any bones.

2 Melt half the butter in a small pan, stir in the flour, and cook gently for 1 minute. Add the reserved milk and boil, whisking, until smooth and creamy. Stir in the parsley and anchovy extract and season to taste.

3 Heat the remaining butter in a skillet, add the sliced mushrooms, and sauté until tender. Season and add to the flaked fish. Mix the sauce into the fish and stir gently to combine. Transfer the mixture to an ovenproof casserole.

4 Preheat the oven to 400°F. Beat the mashed potato with the butter until very creamy. Season, then spread the topping evenly over the fish. Fork up the surface and arrange the sliced tomatoes around the edge. Sprinkle the exposed topping with the grated cheese.

5 Bake for 20–25 minutes, until the topping is browned. If you prefer, finish the browning under a hot broiler.

VARIATION
Instead of using plain mashed potatoes, try a mixture of mashed potato and mashed rutabaga or sweet potato.

MACKEREL with SPICY DHAL

Oily fish, such as mackerel, are nutritious and great for your nervous system. They are complemented by a tart or sour accompaniment, such as these delicious tamarind-flavored lentils or split peas. Serve with chopped fresh tomatoes, onion salad, and flat bread.

SERVES FOUR

generous 1 cup red lentils, or yellow
    split peas (soaked overnight)
4 cups water
2 tablespoons sunflower oil
½ teaspoon each mustard seeds,
    cumin seeds, fennel seeds, and
    fenugreek or cardamom seeds
1 teaspoon ground turmeric
3–4 dried red chiles, crumbled
2 tablespoons tamarind paste
2 tablespoons chopped fresh cilantro
4 mackerels
ground black pepper
fresh red chile slices and finely
    chopped cilantro, to garnish
flat bread and tomatoes,
    to serve

1 Rinse the lentils or split peas, drain them thoroughly, and put them in a pan. Pour in the water and bring to a boil. Lower the heat, partially cover the pan, and simmer the lentils or split peas for 30–40 minutes, stirring occasionally, until they are tender and mushy.

2 Heat the oil in a wok or shallow pan. Add the mustard seeds, then cover and cook for a few seconds until they pop. Remove the lid, add the rest of the seeds with the turmeric and chiles, and fry for a few more seconds.

3 Stir in the lentils or split peas and the tamarind paste and mix well. Bring to a boil, then simmer for 10 minutes until thick. Stir in the coriander.

4 Clean the fish, then heat a ridged grill pan or the broiler until very hot. Make six diagonal slashes on either side of each fish and remove the head. Season, then cook for 5–7 minutes on each side. Serve, garnished with red chile and chopped cilantro, accompanied by the dhal, flat bread, and tomatoes.

SOLE with WILD MUSHROOMS

If possible, use organic chanterelles for this dish; their glowing orange color combines
really wonderfully with the intensely golden sauce. Otherwise, use any pale-colored or
oyster mushrooms that you can find instead.

SERVES FOUR

4 sole fillets (about 4 ounces
    each), skinned
4 tablespoons butter or
    nonhydrogenated margarine
generous 2 cups fish stock
2 cups chanterelles or
    oyster mushrooms
a large pinch of saffron threads
⅔ cup heavy cream or
    soy cream
1 egg yolk
sea salt and ground white pepper
flat-leaf parsley sprigs,
    to garnish
boiled new potatoes and
    steamed broccoli florets,
    to serve

1 Preheat the oven to 400°F. Cut the sole fillets in half lengthwise and place them on a board with the skinned side uppermost. Season, then roll them up. Use a little of the butter to grease a baking dish just large enough to hold all the sole fillets in a single layer. Arrange the rolls in it, then pour over the fish stock. Cover tightly with foil and bake for 12–15 minutes, until cooked through.

2 Meanwhile, pick off any bits of debris from the chanterelles and wipe the mushrooms with a damp cloth. Halve or quarter any large ones. Heat the remaining butter in a skillet until foaming and sauté the mushrooms for 3–4 minutes, until just tender. Season with salt and pepper and keep hot.

3 Lift the cooked sole fillets out of the cooking liquid and place them on a heated serving dish. Keep hot. Strain the liquid into a small pan, add the saffron, set over a very high heat, and boil until reduced to about 1 cup. Stir in the cream and let the sauce bubble gently for a few seconds.

4 Lightly beat the egg yolk in a small bowl, pour on a little of the hot sauce, and stir well. Stir the mixture into the remaining sauce in the pan and cook over a very low heat for 1–2 minutes, until slightly thickened. Season to taste. Stir the chanterelles into the sauce and pour it over the sole fillets. Garnish with parsley sprigs and serve at once. Boiled new potatoes and steamed broccoli florets make the perfect accompaniment.

HONEY BAKED FIGS with HAZELNUT ICE CREAM

Organic figs have a deliciously intense flavor. They are smaller than nonorganic fruit because they are not forced to absorb water during growing, so you may need three per person.

SERVES FOUR

1 lemon grass stalk, finely chopped
1 cinnamon stick, roughly broken
4 tablespoons clear honey
scant 1 cup water
8 large or 12 small figs

For the hazelnut ice cream
scant 2 cups heavy cream
   or soy cream
1/4 cup unrefined superfine sugar
   or rapadura
3 egg yolks
1/4 teaspoon vanilla extract
3/4 cup hazelnuts

1 To make the ice cream, place the cream in a pan and heat slowly until almost boiling. Place the sugar and egg yolks in a bowl and whisk until creamy.

2 Pour a little cream onto the egg yolk mixture and stir. Put into the pan and mix with the rest of the cream. Cook over a low heat, stirring constantly, until the mixture lightly coats the back of the spoon—do not let it boil. Put into a bowl, stir in the vanilla, and let cool.

3 Preheat the oven to 350°F. Place the hazelnuts on a baking sheet and roast for 10–12 minutes, or until they are golden brown. Let the nuts cool, then place them in a food processor or blender and process until they are coarsely ground.

4 Transfer the ice-cream mixture to a metal or plastic freezer container and freeze for 2 hours, or until the mixture feels firm around the edge. Remove the container from the freezer and whisk the ice cream to break down the ice crystals. Stir in the ground hazelnuts and freeze the mixture again until half-frozen. Whisk again, then freeze until firm.

COOK'S TIPS
• If you prefer, instead of whisking the semi-frozen ice cream, put it into a food processor and process until smooth.
• There are several different types of organic figs available and they can all be used in this recipe. Choose from green-skinned figs that have an amber-colored flesh, dark purple-skinned fruit with a deep red flesh ,or green/yellow-skinned figs with a pinkish-colored flesh.

5 Place the lemon grass, cinnamon stick, honey, and water in a small pan and heat slowly until boiling. Simmer the mixture for 5 minutes, then let the syrup stand for 15 minutes.

6 Preheat the oven to 400°F. Meanwhile, carefully cut the figs into quarters, leaving them intact at the bottoms. Place the figs in an ovenproof baking dish and pour over the honey-flavored syrup.

7 Cover the dish tightly with foil and bake the figs for about 15 minutes, or until tender.

8 Remove the ice cream from the freezer about 10 minutes before serving to soften slightly. Transfer the figs to serving plates. Strain a little of the cooking liquid over the figs, then serve with a scoop of hazelnut ice cream.

VARIATION
This recipe also works well with halved, pitted organic nectarines or peaches—cook as from step 6 and serve with the homemade ice cream.

STICKY PEAR PUDDING

Pears are at their best in fall and, combined with other organic ingredients, such as cloves, coffee, and maple syrup, they form the basis of this indulgent dessert.

SERVES SIX

2 tablespoons ground coffee
1 tablespoon near-boiling water
4 ripe pears
juice of ½ orange
½ cup toasted hazelnuts
½ cup butter or nonhydrogenated
    margarine, softened
generous ½ cup unrefined superfine
    sugar or rapadura, plus an extra
    1 tablespoon for baking
2 eggs, beaten
½ cup self-rising flour, sifted
pinch of ground cloves
8 whole cloves (optional)
3 tablespoons maple syrup
fine strips of orange rind,
    to decorate

For the orange cream
1¼ cups whipping cream
1 tablespoon unrefined confectioners'
    sugar, sifted
finely grated rind of ½ orange

1 Preheat the oven to 350°F. Lightly grease a 8-inch loose-bottomed shallow cake pan. Put the ground coffee in a small bowl and pour the near-boiling water over. Let infuse for 4 minutes, then strain through a fine sieve.

2 Peel, halve, and core the pears. Thinly slice across the pear halves part of the way through. Brush the pears with orange juice. Grind the hazelnuts in a coffee grinder until fine.

3 Beat the butter and the superfine sugar together until very light and fluffy. Gradually beat in the eggs, then fold in the flour, ground cloves, hazelnuts, and coffee.

4 Spoon the mixture into the prepared cake pan, then level the surface with a spatula.

5 Pat the pears dry on paper towels, then arrange them carefully in the sponge mixture, flat side down.

6 Lightly press two whole cloves, if using, into each pear half. Brush the pears with 1 tablespoon maple syrup.

7 Sprinkle 1 tbsp superfine sugar over the pears. Bake for 45–50 minutes, or until firm and well-risen.

8 While the sponge is cooking, make the orange cream. Whip the cream, confectioner's sugar, and orange rind until soft peaks form. Spoon into a serving dish and chill until needed.

9 Allow the sponge to cool for about 10 minutes in the pan, then remove and place on a serving plate. Lightly brush with the remaining maple syrup before decorating with orange rind and serving warm with the orange cream.

COOK'S TIP
Organic pears are a good source of soluble fiber and are great at lowering cholesterol and easing constipation. Buy slightly underripe fruit and let them ripen on a sunny windowsill for a few days—overripe pears go off quickly.

VARIATION
You can use apple and cinnamon in this dessert instead of pears and cloves, with a lemon cream in place of orange cream.

CUSTARD TART with PLUMS

*When this tart is made with really ripe, organic sweet plums, it makes a wonderful
hot or cold weekend dessert. Serve it with thick cream, ice cream or yogurt.*

2 Flour a deep 7-inch square or
8-inch round loose-bottomed tart
pan. Roll out the dough and use to
line the pan. This dough is soft at this
stage, so don't worry if you have to
push it into shape. Chill for another
10–20 minutes.

3 Preheat the oven to 400°F. Line the
pastry shell with parchment paper and
fill with dried beans, then bake for
15 minutes. Remove the paper and
dried beans, reduce the oven
temperature to 350°F, and bake
for a further 5–10 minutes, until
the bottom is dry.

SERVES FOUR TO SIX

1½ cups all-purpose flour,
   sifted
pinch of salt
3 tablespoons unrefined superfine sugar
   or rapadura
½ cup unsalted butter or
   nonhydrogenated margarine
2 eggs, plus 2 egg yolks
12 ounces ripe plums
1¼ cups milk or soy milk
few drops of vanilla extract
toasted sliced almonds and sifted,
   unrefined confectioner's sugar,
   to decorate

1 Place the flour, salt, 1 tablespoon of
the sugar, the butter, and one of the eggs
in a food processor or blender and
process until thoroughly combined. Pour
out the mixture onto a clean, lightly
floured surface and bring it together into
a ball. Wrap the dough in plastic wrap
and chill for 10 minutes to rest.

VARIATIONS
• This tart is equally delicious made with
organic apricots, peaches, or nectarines.
• Make a nutty dough: Replace 1 teaspoon
of the flour with ground almonds.

4 Halve and pit the plums, and arrange
them neatly in the pastry shell. Whisk
together the remaining egg and egg yolks
with the sugar, the milk, and vanilla
extract and pour over the fruit.

5 Return the tart to the oven and bake
for 25–30 minutes, or until the custard
is just firm to the touch. Remove the
tart from the oven and let cool. Sprinkle
with sliced almonds and dredge with
confectioner's sugar before serving with
cream, ice cream, or plain yogurt.

BUTTERNUT SQUASH and MAPLE PIE

This American-style pie has a rich pastry shell and a creamy filling, sweetened with maple syrup and flavored with fresh organic ginger and a dash of brandy.

SERVES TEN

1 small butternut squash
4 tablespoons water
1-inch piece of fresh ginger, peeled
　and grated
beaten egg, to glaze
½ cup heavy cream or soy cream, plus
　extra to serve
6 tablespoons maple syrup
3 tablespoons unrefined light brown sugar
　or rapadura
3 eggs, lightly beaten
2 tablespoons brandy
¼ teaspoon grated nutmeg

For the pastry
1½ cups all-purpose flour
½ cup butter or nonhydrogenated
　margarine, diced
2 teaspoons unrefined superfine sugar
　or rapadura
1 egg, lightly beaten

1 To make the dough, sift the flour into a mixing bowl. Rub in the butter or margarine until the mixture resembles fine breadcrumbs. Add the sugar and the egg. Mix to a dough. Wrap in plastic wrap. Chill for 30 minutes.

2 Cut the butternut squash in half, then peel and scoop out the seeds. Cut the flesh into cubes and put in a pan with the water. Cover and cook gently for 15 minutes. Remove the lid, stir in the ginger, and cook for a further 5 minutes, until all the liquid has evaporated and the squash is tender. Cool slightly, then puree in a food processor until smooth.

3 Roll out the dough and use to line a 9-inch tart pan. Gather up the trimmings, re-roll them thinly, then cut them into maple-leaf shapes. Brush the edge of the pastry shell with beaten egg and attach the maple leaf shapes at regular intervals to make a decorative rim. Cover with plastic wrap and chill for 30 minutes.

4 Put a heavy baking sheet in the oven and preheat to 400°F. Prick the pastry shell with a fork, line with foil, and fill with dried beans. Bake on the hot baking sheet for 12 minutes.

5 Remove the foil and beans and bake the pastry shell for a further 5 minutes. Brush the bottom of the pastry shell with beaten egg and return to the oven for about 3 minutes. Reduce the oven temperature to 350°F.

6 Mix scant 1 cup of the butternut puree with the cream, syrup, sugar, eggs, brandy, and grated nutmeg. (Discard any remaining puree.) Put into the pastry shell. Bake for about 30 minutes, or until the filling is lightly set. Cool slightly, then serve with cream.

BAKED APPLE DUMPLINGS

A wonderful way to make the most of apples in season. The sharpness of the fruit contrasts perfectly with the maple syrup drizzled over this delightful pastry parcel.

SERVES EIGHT

8 firm cooking apples, peeled
1 egg white
⅔ cup unrefined superfine sugar
    or rapadura
3 tablespoons heavy cream
    or soy cream, plus extra
    whipped cream, to serve
½ teaspoon vanilla extract
1 cup maple syrup

For the pastry
4½ cups all-purpose flour
1½ cups butter or nonhydrogenated
    margarine, diced

1 To make the pastry, sift the flour into a large bowl. Rub in the butter until the mixture resembles fine breadcrumbs.

2 Sprinkle over ¾ cup of water and mix until the dough holds together, adding more water if necessary. Gather into a ball. Wrap in plastic wrap and chill for 10 minutes. Preheat the oven to 425°F.

3 Cutting from the stem end, core the apples without cutting through the bottom. Roll out the dough thinly. Cut squares almost large enough to enclose the apples; brush with egg white and set an apple in the center of each.

4 Cut circles of pastry to cover the tops of the cored apples. Reserve the pastry trimmings. Combine the unrefined sugar, cream, and vanilla extract in a small bowl. Spoon one-eighth of the mixture into the hollow of each apple.

5 Place a pastry circle on top of each apple, then bring up the sides of the pastry square to enclose it, pleating the larger piece of pastry to make a snug fit around the apple. Moisten the joints with cold water where they overlap, and press down so they stick in place.

6 Make apple stalks and leaves from the pastry trimmings and use to decorate the dumplings. Set them in a large greased baking dish, at least ¾ inches apart. Bake for 30 minutes, then reduce the oven temperature to 350°F and continue baking for 20 minutes more, or until the pastry is golden brown and the apples are tender.

7 Transfer the dumplings to a serving dish. Mix the maple syrup with the juices in the baking dish and drizzle over the dumplings. Serve the dumplings hot with whipped cream.

HOT BLACKBERRY and APPLE SOUFFLÉS

*The deliciously tart fall flavours of blackberry and apple complement each other perfectly
to make a light, mouthwatering hot dessert.*

MAKES SIX

butter or nonhydrogenated margarine,
    for greasing
¾ cup unrefined superfine sugar or
    rapadura, plus extra for dusting
3 cups blackberries
I large cooking apple, peeled and finely diced
grated rind and juice of I orange
3 egg whites
unrefined confectioner's sugar,
    for dusting

I Preheat the oven to 400°F.
Generously grease six ⅔ cup individual
soufflé dishes with butter and dust
with superfine sugar, shaking out the
excess sugar.

2 Put a baking sheet in the oven to heat.
Cook the blackberries, diced apple, and
orange rind and juice in a saucepan for
about 10 minutes, or until the apple has
pulped down well. Press through a sieve
into a bowl. Stir in ¼ cup of the
superfine sugar. Set aside to cool.

3 Put a spoonful of the fruit puree into
each prepared soufflé dish and spread
evenly. Set the dishes aside.

4 Place the egg whites in a grease-free
bowl and whisk until they form stiff
peaks. Very gradually whisk in the
remaining superfine sugar to make a stiff,
glossy meringue mixture.

5 Fold in the remaining fruit puree and
spoon the flavored meringue into the
prepared dishes. Level the tops with a
palette knife, and run a table knife
around the edge of each dish.

6 Place the dishes on the hot baking
sheet and bake for 10–15 minutes, until
the soufflés have risen well and are lightly
browned. Dust confectioner's sugar onn
the tops and serve immediately.

COOK'S TIP
Running a table knife around the inside
edge of the soufflé dishes before baking
helps the soufflés to rise evenly without
sticking to the rim of the dish.

PLUM CHARLOTTES with FOAMY CALVADOS SAUCE

A variety of different types of organic plums are available at this time of year—from tangy yellow greengages to sweet and juicy Santa Rosas.

SERVES FOUR

½ cup butter or nonhydrogenated
    margarine, melted
¼ cup raw sugar or rapadura
1 pound ripe plums, pitted
    and thickly sliced
2 tablespoons unrefined superfine sugar
    or rapadura
2 tablespoons water
¼ teaspoon ground cinnamon
¼ cup ground almonds
8–10 large slices of white or
    whole-wheat bread

For the Calvados sauce
3 egg yolks
3 tablespoons unrefined superfine sugar
    or rapadura
2 tablespoons Calvados

1 Preheat the oven to 375°F. Line the bottom of four individual 4-inch-diameter deep, earthenware ramekin dishes with parchment paper. Brush evenly and thoroughly with a little of the melted butter or margarine, then sprinkle each dish with a little of the raw sugar, rotating the dish in your hands to coat each dish evenly.

VARIATIONS
• Slices of peeled pear or eating apples can be used in this recipe instead of the pitted, sliced plums.
• If you cannot find organic Calvados, any organic fruit-based liquor will work in this dish.

2 Place the pitted plum slices in a pan with the superfine sugar, water, and ground cinnamon and cook gently for 5 minutes, or until the plums have softened slightly. Let the plums cool, then stir in the ground almonds.

3 Cut the crusts off the bread and then use a plain pastry cutter to cut out four circles to fit the bottoms of the ramekins. Dip the bread circles into the melted butter and fit them into the dishes. Cut four more circles to fit the tops of the dishes and set aside.

4 Cut the remaining bread into strips, dip into the melted butter, and use to line the sides of the ramekins completely.

5 Divide the plum mixture among the lined dishes and level the tops with the back of a spoon. Place the bread circles on top and brush with the remaining butter. Place the ramekins on a baking sheet and bake for 25 minutes.

6 Make the sauce just before the charlottes are ready. Place the egg yolks and superfine sugar in a large bowl, and whisk them together until pale. Place the bowl over a pan of simmering water and whisk in the Calvados. Continue whisking until the mixture is very light and frothy.

7 Remove the charlottes from the oven and turn out onto warm serving plates. Pour a little sauce over and around the charlottes and serve immediately.

COOK'S TIP
For an extra creamy dessert, serve the desserts with strained plain yogurt or crème fraîche.

PARSNIP CAKE with ORANGE FROSTING

This fabulous vegan cake is similar to the ever-popular carrot cake, but it uses nondairy alternatives to margarine and cream cheese.

SERVES TEN

2¼ cups whole-wheat self-rising flour
1 tablespoon baking powder
1 teaspoon ground cinnamon
1 teaspoon freshly ground nutmeg
9 tablespoons vegan margarine
scant ½ cup unrefined soft light brown
    sugar or rapadura
9 ounces parsnips, coarsely grated
1 banana, mashed
finely grated rind and juice of 1 orange

For the topping
1 cup organic soy cream cheese
3 tablespoons unrefined
    confectioner's sugar
juice of 1 small orange
fine strips of orange peel

1 Preheat the oven to 1350°F. Lightly grease and line the bottom of a 2-pound loaf pan.

2 Sift the flour, baking powder, and spices into a large bowl. Add any bran remaining in the sieve.

COOK'S TIP
If you can't find self-raising wholemeal flour, use ordinary wholemeal flour and add an extra 15ml/1 tbsp baking powder.

VARIATION
Serve the cake as a dessert with a generous spoonful of organic plain yogurt, crème fraîche, or soy cream, flavored with grated orange rind or a little Calvados.

3 Melt the margarine in a saucepan, add the sugar and stir until dissolved. Make a well in the flour mixture, then add the melted margarine and sugar. Mix in the parsnips, banana, and orange rind and juice. Spoon the mixture into the prepared pan and level the top with the back of a spoon.

4 Bake for 45–50 minutes, until a skewer inserted into the center of the cake comes out clean. Let the cake cool slightly before removing from the pan, then transfer to a wire rack to cool completely.

5 To make the topping, beat together the cream cheese, confectioner's sugar, orange juice, and orange peel strips until smooth. Spread the topping evenly over the cake.

COUNTRY APPLE CAKE

This perennial favorite is a great way to take advantage of the season's apple harvest.
There are any number of organic apples available nowadays, including heirloom and
almost-lost local varieties, which makes cooking and eating this cake a real treat.

MAKES ONE 7-INCH CAKE

½ cup soft nonhydrogenated margarine
½ cup unrefined soft light brown sugar
   or rapadura
2 eggs, beaten
1 cup self-rising flour, sifted
½ cup rice flour
1 teaspoon baking powder
2 teaspoons apple-pie spice
   or allspice
1 cooking apple, cored and chopped
scant 1 cup raisins
about 4 tablespoons milk or soy milk
2 tablespoons sliced almonds

4 Turn the mixture into the prepared pan and level the surface. Sprinkle the sliced almonds over the top. Bake the cake for 1–1¼ hours, until risen, firm to the touch, and golden brown.

5 Cool the apple cake in the pan for about 10 minutes, then turn out onto a wire rack to cool. Cut into slices when cold. Alternatively, serve the cake warm, in slices, with custard or ice cream. Store the cold cake in an airtight container or wrapped in foil.

VARIATIONS
• Use golden raisins or chopped dried apricots or pears instead of the raisins.
• A wide variety of organic ice creams is available from independent dairies and supermarkets—vanilla goes particularly well with this cake.

1 Preheat the oven to 325°F. Lightly grease and line a deep 7-inch round, loose-bottomed cake pan.

2 Cream the margarine and sugar in a mixing bowl. Gradually add the eggs, then fold in the flours, baking powder, and spice.

3 Stir in the chopped apple, raisins, and enough of the milk to make a soft, dropping consistency.

OAT and RAISIN DROP SCONES

Serve these easy-to-make organic "scones" as an afternoon treat or a dessert—or even a special breakfast or brunch—with real maple syrup or clear honey.

MAKES ABOUT SIXTEEN

²⁄₃ cup self-raising flour
½ teaspoon baking powder
scant ½ cup raisins
¼ cup fine oatmeal
2 tablespoons unrefined superfine sugar
    or rapadura
grated rind of 1 orange
2 egg yolks
½ tablespoons unsalted butter
    or nonhydrogenated
    margarine, melted
scant 1 cup light cream or soy cream
scant 1 cup water
sunflower oil, for greasing
confectioner's sugar, for dusting

1 Sift the self-raising flour and baking powder together into a large mixing bowl.

COOK'S TIP
Wrap the cooked scones in a clean dish towel to keep them soft.

2 Add the raisins, oatmeal, sugar, and orange rind. Gradually beat in the egg yolks, butter, cream, and water to make a creamy batter.

3 Lightly grease and heat a large heavy skillet or grill pan and drop about 2 tablepsoons of batter at a time onto the skillet or griddle to make six or seven small pancakes.

4 Cook over a moderate heat until bubbles show on the scones' surface, then turn them over and cook for a further 2 minutes, until golden.

5 Transfer to a plate; dust with confectioner's sugar. Keep warm; cook the remaining mixture. Serve warm.

CARAMELIZED ONION and WALNUT SCONES

These "scones" are very good buttered and served with mature cheddar cheese. Make small scones to use as a base for cocktail savories, served topped with a little soft goat cheese.

4 Add the cooked onion and cumin mixture, chopped walnuts, and chopped fresh thyme, then bind to make a soft, but not sticky, dough with the buttermilk.

5 Roll or pat out the mixture to an even thickness of just over ½ inch. Stamp out 10–12 scones using a 2–2½-inch plain round cutter.

6 Place the scones on a floured baking tray, glaze with the milk or soy milk and scatter with a little salt and the remaining cumin seeds. Bake the scones for 12–15 minutes, until well-risen and golden brown. Let cool for a few minutes on a wire rack and serve warm spread with butter, nonhydrogenated margarine, or goat cheese.

MAKES TEN TO TWELVE

7 tablespoons butter or
    nonhydrogenated margarine
1 tablespoon olive oil
1 Bermuda onion, chopped
1 teaspoon cumin seeds,
    lightly crushed
1¾ cups self-raising flour
1 teaspoon baking powder
¼ cup fine oatmeal
1 teaspoon light unrefined
    brown sugar
scant 1 cup chopped walnuts
1 teaspoon chopped fresh thyme
½–⅔ cup buttermilk
a little milk or soy milk
sea salt and ground black pepper

1 Melt 1 tablespoon of the butter with the oil in a small pan and cook the onion gently, covered, for 10–12 minutes. Uncover, then continue to cook gently until it begins to brown.

2 Add half the cumin seeds and increase the heat slightly. Continue to cook, stirring occasionally, until the onion begins to caramelize. Cool. Preheat the oven to 400°F.

3 Sift the flour and baking powder into a large bowl and add the oatmeal, sugar, ½ teaspoon of salt and black pepper. Add the remaining butter or margarine and rub in until the mixture resembles fine breadcrumbs.

FRUIT, NUT, AND SEED QUICK BREAD

Cut into slices and spread with a little butter or nonhydrogenated margarine, jam, or honey, this quick bread makes an ideal breakfast bread. The dried fruit, nuts, and seeds provides a fine source of fiber.

MAKES ONE 2-POUND LOAF

²⁄₃ cup dried dates, chopped
½ cup dried apricots, chopped
1 cup golden raisins
½ cup unrefined soft light brown sugar
 or rapadura
2 cups self-rising flour
1 teaspoon baking powder
2 teaspoons apple pie spice
 or allspice
¾ cup chopped mixed nuts
¾ cup mixed seeds, such as flax,
 sunflower, and sesame seeds
2 eggs, beaten
²⁄₃ cup low-fat milk or
 soy milk

1 Preheat the oven to 350°F. Lightly grease a 2-pound loaf pan. Place the chopped dates and apricots and golden raisins in a large mixing bowl and stir in the sugar.

COOK'S TIPS
• Use whole-wheat self-rising flour for an unbeatable nutty flavor.
• Organic dates have an extremely sweet taste, which makes them wonderful to bake with.
• Try adding hemp seeds to the seed mixture to increase the nutritional value of the quick bread.

2 Place the flour, baking powder, spice, mixed nuts, and mixed seeds in a separate bowl and mix well.

3 Stir the eggs and milk into the fruit mixture, then add the flour mixture and beat together until well mixed.

4 Spoon the mixture into the prepared pan and level the surface. Bake for about 1 hour, until the quick bread is firm to the touch and lightly browned.

5 Let cool the tin for a few minutes, then turn out onto a wire rack to cool completely. Serve warm or cold, cut into slices. Wrap the quick bread in foil to store.

HUNGARIAN FRUIT BREAD

When dried, many of the nutrients and sugars in fruit are concentrated but so, unfortunately, are any pesticide residues. So, to ensure a clear conscience as you tuck into a slice of this delightful light bread, always use organic dried fruit—a much healthier choice.

SERVES EIGHT TO TEN

sunflower oil, for greasing
7 egg whites
scant 1 cup unrefined superfine sugar
   or rapadura
1 cup sliced almonds, toasted
¾ cup golden raisins
grated rind of 1 lemon
1⅓ cups all-purpose flour, sifted,
   plus extra for flouring
6 tablespoons butter or
   nonhydrogenated margarine,
   melted

1 Preheat the oven to 350°F and grease and flour a 2¼-pound loaf pan. Whisk the egg whites until they are very stiff, but not crumbly. Fold in the sugar gradually, then the sliced, toasted almonds, golden raisins, and lemon rind.

2 Fold the flour and butter into the mixture and put it into the prepared pan. Bake for about 45 minutes, until well risen and pale golden brown. Cool for a few minutes in the pan, then turn out and serve warm or cold, in slices.

WINTER

Warming comfort food is the order of the day in cold weather to help keep out winter chills. Root vegetables, such as rutabaga, carrots, turnips, and parsnips, are readily available and can be included in winter soups, stews, and casseroles, such as Chicken Casserole with Winter Vegetables, or Braised Shoulder of Mutton with Pearl Barley and Baby Vegetables.

For vegetarians, substantial main courses include warming ingredients, such as legumes and spices—try Parsnips and Chickpeas in Garlic, Onion, Chile and Ginger Paste, or Barley Risotto with Roasted Squash and Leeks.

Rich, meaty dishes to enjoy during the coldest months of the year include Chile Con Carne and Boeuf Bourguignonne—delicious served with mashed root vegetables and organic red wine.

Fish dishes for the winter season are best served with the addition of well-flavored ingredients. Try Fillets of Brill in Red Wine Sauce or Smoked Haddock with Mustard Cabbage.

Sweet winter treats to enjoy include Baked Maple and Pecan Croissant Pudding, Orange Marmalade Chocolate Loaf, and a fragrant Dried Fruit Compote.

WINTER FARMHOUSE SOUP

Root vegetables form the base of this chunky, minestrone-style main meal soup.
Always choose organic vegetables and vary according to what you have to hand.

SERVES FOUR

2 tablespoons olive oil
1 onion, roughly chopped
3 carrots, cut into large chunks
6–7 ounces turnips, cut into large chunks
about 6 ounces rutabaga,
    cut into large chunks
1 can (14 ounces) chopped Italian
    tomatoes
1 tablespoon tomato paste
1 teaspoon dried mixed herbs
1 teaspoon dried oregano
2 ounces dried bell peppers, washed and
    thinly sliced (optional)
6¼ cups vegetable stock or water
½ cup dried macaroni
1 can (14 ounces) red kidney beans,
    rinsed and drained
2 tablespoons chopped fresh
    flat-leaf parsley
sea salt and ground black pepper
freshly grated Parmesan cheese or premium
    Italian-style vegetarian cheese, to serve

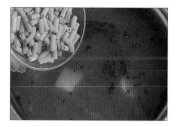

1 Heat the olive oil in a large pan, add the onion, and cook over a low heat for about 5 minutes, until softened. Add the carrot, turnip, and rutabaga chunks, canned chopped tomatoes, tomato paste, dried mixed herbs, dried oregano, and dried peppers, if using. Stir in a little salt and plenty of pepper to taste.

2 Put in the vegetable stock or water and bring to a boil. Stir well, cover the pan, then lower the heat and simmer for 30 minutes, stirring occasionally.

3 Add the pasta to the pan and bring quickly to a boil, stirring. Lower the heat and simmer, uncovered, for about 8 minutes, until the pasta is just tender, or according to the package instructions. Stir frequently.

4 Stir in the kidney beans. Heat through for 2–3 minutes, then remove the pan from the heat and stir in the parsley. Taste the soup for seasoning. Serve hot in warmed soup bowls, with grated cheese handed around separately.

MOROCCAN SPICED MUTTON SOUP

Classic north African spices—ginger, turmeric, and cinnamon—are combined with chickpeas and mutton to make this hearty, warming main-course soup.

SERVES SIX

½ cup dried chickpeas, soaked overnight
1 tablespoon butter or 1 tablespoon
    olive oil
8 ounces mutton, cut into cubes
1 onion, chopped
1 pound tomatoes, peeled and chopped
a few celery leaves, chopped
2 tablespoons chopped fresh parsley
1 tablespoon chopped fresh cilantro
½ teaspoon ground ginger
½ teaspoon ground turmeric
1 teaspoon ground cinnamon
7½ cups water
scant ½ cup green lentils
¾ cup vermicelli or soup pasta
2 egg yolks
juice of ½–1 lemon, to taste
sea salt and ground black pepper
fresh cilantro, to garnish
lemon wedges, to serve

1 Drain the chickpeas and set aside. Heat the butter or oil in a large pan and fry the mutton and onion for 2–3 minutes, stirring, until the mutton is just browned.

2 Add the chopped tomatoes, celery leaves, herbs, and spices and season well with ground black pepper. Cook for about 1 minute, then stir in the water and add the green lentils and the soaked, drained, and rinsed chickpeas.

3 Slowly bring to a boil and skim the surface to remove the froth. Boil rapidly for 10 minutes, then reduce the heat and simmer very gently for 2 hours, or until the chickpeas are very tender.

4 Season with salt and pepper, then add the vermicelli or soup pasta to the pan and cook for 5–6 minutes, until it is just tender. If the soup is very thick at this stage, add a little more water.

5 Beat the egg yolks with the lemon juice and stir into the simmering soup. Immediately remove the soup from the heat and stir until thickened. Put into warmed serving bowls and garnish with plenty of fresh cilantro. Serve the soup with lemon wedges.

COOK'S TIP

If you have forgotten to soak the chickpeas overnight, place them in a pan with about four times their volume of cold water. Bring very slowly to a boil, then cover the pan, remove it from the heat, and let stand for 45 minutes before using as described in the recipe.

CHICKEN, LEEK, and CELERY SOUP

This makes a substantial main course soup with fresh crusty bread. You will need nothing more than a mixed green salad or fresh winter fruit to follow, such as satsumas, tangerines, or apricots.

SERVES FOUR TO SIX

3 pounds chicken
1 small head of celery, trimmed
1 onion, coarsely chopped
1 fresh bay leaf
a few fresh parsley stalks
a few fresh tarragon sprigs
10 cups cold water
3 large leeks
5 tablespoons butter or olive oil
2 potatoes, cut into chunks
⅔ cup dry white wine
2–3 tablespoons light or soy cream
  (optional)
sea salt and ground black pepper
3½ ounces pancetta, broiled until crisp,
  to garnish

4 Meanwhile, set about 5 ounces of the leeks aside. Slice the remaining leeks and the remaining celery, reserving any celery leaves. Chop the celery leaves and set them aside to garnish the soup or reserve a few of the leek pieces.

5 Heat half the butter or oil in a large, heavy saucepan. Add the sliced leeks and celery, cover, and cook over a low heat for about 10 minutes, or until the vegetables are softened but not browned. Add the potatoes, wine, and 5 cups of the stock.

6 Season with a little salt and plenty of black pepper, bring to a boil, and reduce the heat. Part-cover the pan and simmer the soup for 15–20 minutes, or until the potatoes are cooked.

COOK'S TIP
There are a vast number of different varieties of organic potatoes but all fall into two main types: starchy and waxy. Starchy potatoes, such as Russet Burbank and other russets, are ideal for soups, mashing, or baking. Waxy potatoes, such as White Rose or Rose Fir, are delicious boiled and served with butter.

1 Cut the breasts off the chicken and set aside. Chop the rest of the chicken carcass into 8–10 pieces and place in a large saucepan or stockpot.

2 Chop 4–5 of the outer sticks of the head of celery and add them to the pan with the coarsely chopped onion. Tie the bay leaf, parsley stalks, and tarragon sprigs together to make a bouquet garni and add to the pan. Pour in the cold water to cover the ingredients and bring to a boil. Reduce the heat and cover the pan with a lid, then simmer for 1½ hours.

3 Remove the chicken from the pan using a slotted spoon, and cut off and reserve the meat. Strain the stock through a sieve, then return it to the cleaned pan and boil rapidly until it has reduced in volume to about 6¼ cups.

7 Meanwhile, skin the reserved chicken breasts and cut the flesh into small pieces. Melt the remaining butter or oil in a skillet, add the chicken, and fry for 5–7 minutes, until cooked.

8 Thickly slice the reserved leeks, add to the skillet, and cook, stirring occasionally, for a further 3–4 minutes, until they are just cooked.

9 Process the soup with the cooked chicken from the stock in a food processor or blender. Taste and adjust the seasoning, and add more stock if the soup is very thick.

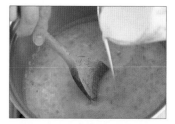

10 Stir in the cream, if using, and the chicken and leek mixture. Reheat the soup gently. Serve in warmed bowls. Crumble the pancetta over the soup and sprinkle with the chopped celery leaves or reserved leek slices.

VARIATIONS
• If you prefer, use ready-cut chicken portions instead of jointing a whole chicken.
• Fatty bacon can be used instead of pancetta to add a delicious flavor to the soup.

SPICED ONION KOFTAS

*These delicious Indian onion fritters are made with chickpea flour, otherwise known as gram
or garbanzo flour, which has a distinctive nutty flavor. Serve with chutney or a yogurt dip.*

3 Add the chickpea flour and baking
powder to the onion mixture in the
bowl, then use your hand to mix all
the ingredients thoroughly.

4 Shape the mixture with your hands
into 12–15 koftas the size of golf balls.

MAKES TWELVE TO FIFTEEN

1½ pounds onions, halved
   and thinly sliced
1 teaspoon sea salt
1 teaspoon ground coriander
1 teaspoon ground cumin
½ teaspoon ground turmeric
1–2 green chiles, seeded and
   finely chopped
3 tablespoons chopped fresh cilantro
¾ cup chickpea flour
½ teaspoon baking powder
sunflower oil, for deep-frying

To serve
lemon wedges (optional)
fresh cilangro sprigs
yogurt and herb dip (see Cook's Tip)

1 Place the onions in a colander, add
the salt, and toss. Place on a plate and
let stand for 45 minutes, tossing once
or twice. Rinse the onions, then squeeze
out any excess moisture.

2 Place the onions in a bowl. Add the
ground coriander, cumin, turmeric, finely
chopped chiles, and chopped fresh
cilantro. Mix well.

COOK'S TIP
To make a yogurt and herb dip to serve
with the koftas, stir 2 tablespoons
chopped fresh cilantro and 2 tablespoons
chopped mint into about 1 cup plain
yogurt. Season to taste with salt, ground
toasted cumin seeds, and a pinch of
brown sugar.

5 Heat the sunflower oil for deep-frying
to 350–375°F, or until a cube of day-old
bread browns in about 30–45 seconds.
Fry the koftas, four to five at a time,
until deep golden brown all over.
Remove with a slotted spoon and drain
each batch on paper towels and keep
warm until all the koftas are cooked.
Serve the koftas warm with lemon
wedges (if using), cilantro sprigs, and
a yogurt and herb dip.

LENTIL DHAL with ROASTED GARLIC

This spicy lentil dhal makes a sustaining and comforting meal when served with brown rice or Indian breads and any dry-spiced dish, particularly a cauliflower or potato dish.

SERVES FOUR TO SIX

3 tablespoons butter or ghee
I onion, chopped
2 green chiles, seeded and chopped
I tablespoon chopped fresh ginger
I cup yellow or red lentils
3¾ cups water
3 tablespoons roasted garlic paste
I teaspoon ground cumin
I teaspoon ground coriander
7 ounces tomatoes, peeled and diced
a little lemon juice
sea salt and ground black pepper
2–3 tablespoons cilantro sprigs,
    to garnish

For the spicy garnish
2 tablespoons sunflower oil
4–5 shallots, sliced
2 garlic cloves, thinly sliced
I tablespoon butter or ghee
I teaspoon cumin seeds
I teaspoon mustard seeds
3–4 small dried red chiles
8–10 fresh curry leaves

I First begin the spicy garnish. Heat the oil in a large, heavy saucepan. Add the shallots and fry them over a medium heat for 5–10 minutes, stirring occasionally, until they are crisp and browned. Add the garlic and cook, stirring frequently, for a moment or two until the garlic colors slightly. Remove the pan from the heat and use a slotted spoon to remove the shallots and garlic from the pan and set aside.

COOK'S TIP
Ghee is clarified butter that has had all the milk solids removed by heating—it was originally made to extend the keeping qualities of butter in India. It is the main cooking fat used in Indian cooking. Because the milk solids have been removed, ghee has a high smoking point and can, therefore, be cooked at higher temperatures than ordinary butter. Look for organic ghee in whole food stores.

2 Melt the 3 tablespoons of butter or ghee for the dhal in the pan, add the onion, chiles, and ginger, and cook for 10 minutes, until golden.

3 Stir in the yellow or red lentils and water, then bring to a boil, reduce the heat, and part-cover the pan. Simmer, stirring occasionally, for 50–60 minutes, until it is the same consistency as a very thick soup.

4 Stir in the roasted garlic paste, cumin, and ground coriander, then season with salt and pepper to taste. Cook the dhal for a further 10–15 minutes, uncovered, stirring frequently.

5 Stir in the tomatoes and then adjust the seasoning, adding a little lemon juice to taste if necessary.

6 To finish the spicy garnish: melt the butter or ghee in a skillet. Add the cumin and mustard seeds and fry until the mustard seeds begin to pop. Stir in the small dried red chiles and fresh curry leaves, then immediately swirl the mixture into the cooked dhal. Garnish with cilantro and the spicy fried shallots and garlic and serve.

JERUSALEM ARTICHOKES with GARLIC

The slightly smoky and earthy flavor of Jerusalem artichokes is excellent with garlic,
shallots, and smoked bacon. These are good with chicken, pork, or a classic nut roast.

SERVES FOUR

4 tablespoons butter or 3½ tablespoons
    olive oil
4 ounces smoked bacon, chopped
1¾ pounds Jerusalem artichokes
8–12 garlic cloves, peeled
4 ounces shallots, chopped
5 tablespoons water
2 tablespoons olive oil
½ cup fresh white or whole-wheat
    breadcrumbs
2–3 tablespoons chopped fresh parsley
sea salt and ground black pepper

1 Melt half the butter or heat half
the olive oil in a heavy skillet, add the
chopped bacon, and cook until it is
brown and just beginning to crisp.
Remove half the bacon from the
skillet and set aside.

COOK'S TIP

If you are unable to find organic shallots,
try using another type of mild and sweet
onion instead, such as red onions. Their
dark color also complements the creamy
artichokes in this dish.

2 Add the artichokes, garlic, and shallots
to the pan, and cook, stirring frequently,
until the artichokes and garlic begin to
brown slightly.

3 Season with salt and black pepper to
taste and stir in the water. Cover and
cook for a further 8–10 minutes, shaking
the pan occasionally.

4 Uncover the pan, increase the heat,
and cook for 5 minutes, or until all the
moisture has evaporated and the
artichokes are tender.

5 In another skillet, heat the remaining
butter or oil with the 2 tablespoons of
olive oil. Add the white or whole-wheat
breadcrumbs and fry over a moderate
heat, stirring frequently with a wooden
spoon, until crisp and golden. Stir in the
chopped parsley and the reserved
cooked bacon.

6 Combine the artichokes with the
crispy breadcrumb and bacon mixture,
mixing well. Season to taste with a little
salt and plenty of ground black pepper,
if necessary. Transfer to a warmed
serving dish and serve immediately.

BRAISED RED CABBAGE with BEETS

Cook this vibrantly colored dish in the oven at the same time as a pork casserole or joint of meat for a simple, easy-to-prepare meal.

SERVES SIX TO EIGHT

1½ pounds red cabbage
1 Bermuda onion, thinly sliced
2 tablespoons olive oil
2 tart eating apples, peeled,
   cored and sliced
1¼ cups vegetable stock
4 tablespoons red wine vinegar
13 ounces raw beets, peeled
   and coarsely grated
sea salt and ground black pepper

COOK'S TIP
When buying any type of cabbage, choose
one that is firm and heavy for its size.
The leaves should look healthy—avoid
any with curling leaves or blemishes.

1 Cut the red cabbage into fine shreds,
discarding any tough outer leaves and
the core, and place in an ovenproof dish.

2 Place the thinly sliced onion and the
olive oil in a skillet and sauté until the
onion is soft and golden.

3 Preheat the oven to 375°F. Stir the
apple slices, vegetable stock, and wine
vinegar into the onions, then transfer
to the dish. Season with salt and
pepper, and cover.

4 Cook the cabbage for 1 hour. Stir in
the beets, re-cover the dish, and cook
for a further 20–30 minutes, or until
the cabbage and beets are tender.

PARSNIPS and CHICKPEAS in GARLIC, ONION, CHILI, and GINGER PASTE

Organic root vegetables, such as parsnips, often have a knobbly appearance that makes them interesting and individual, and their flavors are sweeter and more intense.

SERVES FOUR

1 cup dried chickpeas, soaked overnight in
   cold water, then drained
7 garlic cloves, finely chopped
1 small onion, chopped
2-inch piece fresh ginger, chopped
2 green chiles, seeded and
   finely chopped
scant 2 cups plus 5 tablespoons water
4 tablespoons sunflower oil
1 teaspoon cumin seeds
2 teaspoons ground coriander seeds
1 teaspoons ground turmeric
½–1 tsp chili powder
   or mild paprika
½ cup cashew nuts, toasted
   and ground
9 ounces tomatoes, peeled and chopped
2 pounds parsnips, cut into chunks
1 teaspoon ground roasted cumin seeds
juice of 1 lime, to taste
sea salt and ground black pepper

To serve
fresh cilantro leaves
a few cashew nuts, toasted
plain yogurt
naan bread or chapatis

1 Put the soaked chickpeas in a pan, cover with cold water, and bring to a boil. Boil vigorously for 10 minutes, then reduce the heat so that the water boils steadily. Cook for 1–1½ hours, or until the chickpeas are tender. (The cooking time depends on how long the chickpeas have been stored.) Drain and set aside.

2 Set 2 teaspoons of the finely chopped garlic aside, then place the remainder in a food processor or blender with the onion, ginger, and half the chopped chiles. Add the 5 tablespoons of water and process to make a smooth paste.

COOK'S TIP
Do not add salt to the water when cooking dried chickpeas, as this will toughen them.

3 Heat the oil in a skillet and cook the cumin seeds for 30 seconds. Stir in the coriander seeds, turmeric, chili powder or paprika, and the ground cashew nuts. Add the ginger paste and cook, stirring frequently, until the water begins to evaporate. Add the tomatoes and stir-fry for 2–3 minutes.

4 Mix in the cooked chickpeas and parsnip chunks with the scant 2 cups water, a little salt, and plenty of black pepper. Bring to a boil, stir, then simmer, uncovered, for 15–20 minutes, until the parsnips are completely tender.

5 Reduce the liquid, if necessary, by bringing the sauce to a boil and then boiling fiercely until the sauce is thick. Add the ground roasted cumin with more salt and/or lime juice to taste. Stir in the reserved garlic and green chile, and cook for a further 1–2 minutes. Scatter the fresh cilantro leaves and toasted cashew nuts over and serve straight away with yogurt and warmed naan bread or chapatis.

BARLEY RISOTTO with ROASTED SQUASH and LEEKS

This is more like a pilaff made with slightly chewy, nutty-flavored pearl barley than a classic risotto. Sweet organic leeks and roasted squash are superb with this earthy grain.

SERVES FOUR TO FIVE

1 cup pearl barley
1 butternut squash, peeled, seeded, and
    cut into chunks
2 teaspoons chopped fresh thyme
4 tablespoons olive oil
2 tablespoons butter
4 leeks, cut into fairly thick diagonal slices
2 garlic cloves, finely chopped
2½ cups cremini mushrooms, sliced
2 carrots, coarsely grated
about ½ cup vegetable stock
2 tablespoons chopped fresh parsley
⅔ cup Parmesan cheese or premium
    Italian-style vegetarian cheese,
    grated or shaved
3 tablespoons pumpkin seeds,
    toasted, or chopped walnuts
sea salt and ground black pepper

1 Rinse the barley, then cook it in simmering water, keeping the pan part-covered, for 35–45 minutes, or until tender. Drain. Preheat the oven to 400°F.

2 Place the squash in a roasting pan with half the thyme. Season with pepper and toss with half the oil. Roast, stirring once, for 30–35 minutes, until the squash is tender and beginning to brown.

3 Heat half the butter with the remaining olive oil in a large skillet. Cook the leeks and garlic gently for 5 minutes. Add the mushrooms and remaining thyme, then cook until the liquid from the mushrooms evaporates and they begin to fry.

4 Stir in the carrots and cook for about 2 minutes, then add the barley and most of the vegetable stock. Season well and part-cover the pan. Cook for a further 5 minutes. Add the remaining stock if the mixture seems dry.

5 Stir in the parsley, the remaining butter, and half the cheese, then stir in the squash. Add seasoning to taste and serve immediately, sprinkled with the toasted pumpkin seeds or walnuts and the remaining cheese.

VARIATIONS
• Make the risotto with organic brown rice instead of the barley—cook following the package instructions and continue from step 2.
• Any type of organic mushrooms can be used in this recipe—try sliced portabello mushrooms for a hearty flavor.

PEPPERS FILLED with SPICED VEGETABLES

Indian spices season the potato and eggplant stuffing in these colorful baked bell peppers. They are good with brown rice and a lentil dhal. Alternatively, serve them with a salad, Indian breads, and a cucumber or mint and yogurt raita.

SERVES SIX

6 large evenly shaped red bell or
    yellow bell peppers
1¼ pounds waxy potatoes
1 small onion, chopped
4–5 garlic cloves, chopped
2-inch piece fresh ginger, chopped
1–2 fresh green chiles, seeded
    and chopped
7 tablespoons water
6–7 tablespoons sunflower oil
1 eggplant, diced
2 teaspoons cumin seeds
1 teaspoon kalonji seeds
½ teaspoon ground turmeric
1 teaspoon ground coriander
1 teaspoon ground toasted cumin seeds
pinch of cayenne pepper
about 2 tablespoons lemon juice
sea salt and ground black pepper
2 tablespoons chopped fresh cilantro,
    to garnish

1 Cut the tops off the red or yellow bell peppers, then remove and discard the seeds. Cut a thin slice off the bottom of the bell peppers, if necessary, to make them stand upright.

2 Bring a large saucepan of lightly salted water to a boil. Add the bell peppers and cook for 5–6 minutes. Drain and let stand upside down in a colander.

COOK'S TIP
The hottest part of a chile is the white membrane that connects the seeds to the flesh. Removing the seeds and membrane before cooking gives a milder flavor.

3 Cook the potatoes in lightly salted, boiling water for 10–12 minutes, until just tender. Drain, cool, and peel, then cut into ½-inch dice.

4 Put the onion, garlic, ginger, and green chiles in a food processor or blender with 4 tablespoons of the water and process to a puree.

5 Heat 3 tablespoons of the sunflower oil in a large, deep skillet and cook the diced eggplant, stirring occasionally, until it is evenly browned on all sides. Remove from the skillet and set aside. Add another 2 tablespoons of the sunflower oil to the skillet, add the diced potatoes and cook until lightly browned on all sides. Remove the potatoes from the pan and set aside.

6 If necessary, add another 1 tablespoon sunflower oil to the skillet, then add the cumin and kalonji seeds. Fry briefly until the seeds darken, then add the turmeric, coriander, and ground cumin. Cook for 15 seconds. Stir in the onion and garlic puree and fry, scraping the skillet with a spatula, until the onions begin to brown.

7 Return the potatoes and eggplant to the skillet, season with salt, pepper, and 1–2 pinches of cayenne. Add the remaining water and 1 tablespoon of lemon juice, then cook, stirring, until the liquid evaporates. Preheat the oven to 375°F.

8 Fill the bell peppers with the spiced vegetable mixture and place on a lightly greased baking sheet. Brush the bell peppers with a little oil and bake for 30–35 minutes, until they are cooked. Let cool a little, then sprinkle with a little more lemon juice, garnish with the cilantro, and serve.

COOK'S TIP
Kalonji, or nigella as it is also known, is a tiny black seed. It is widely used in Indian cookery, especially sprinkled over breads or in potato dishes. It has a mild, slightly nutty flavor and is best toasted for a few seconds in a dry or lightly oiled skillet over a medium heat before using in a recipe. This helps to bring out its flavor, as with most spices.

MARMALADE-GLAZED GOOSE

Succulent roast goose is the classic centerpiece for a traditional Christmas dinner.
Red cabbage cooked with leeks, and braised fennel are tasty accompaniments.

SERVES EIGHT

10 pounds goose
1 cooking apple, peeled, cored, and
    cut into eighths
1 large onion, cut into eighths
bunch of fresh sage, plus extra
    to garnish
2 tablespoons ginger marmalade,
    melted
sea salt and ground black pepper

For the stuffing

2 tablespoons butter or olive oil
1 onion, finely chopped
1 tablespoon ginger marmalade
2 cups prunes, chopped
3 tablespoons Madeira
4 cups fresh white or whole-wheat
    breadcrumbs
2 tablespoons chopped fresh sage

For the gravy

1 onion, chopped
1 tablespoon all-purpose or
    whole-wheat flour
⅔ cup Madeira
2½ cups chicken stock

1 Preheat the oven to 400°F. Prick the skin of the goose all over and season it inside and out.

COOK'S TIP
Red cabbage goes well with goose. Cook 1 small leek, sliced, in 6 tablespoons butter or olive oil, add 9 cups shredded red cabbage, with the grated rind of 1 orange, and cook for 15 minutes.

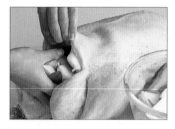

2 Mix the apple, onion, and sage leaves together and spoon the mixture into the parson's nose end of the goose.

3 To make the stuffing, melt the butter or oil in a large saucepan and cook the onion for about 5 minutes, or until softened but not colored. Remove the pan from the heat and stir in the marmalade, chopped prunes, Madeira, breadcrumbs, and chopped sage.

4 Stuff the neck end of the goose with some of the stuffing, then set the remaining stuffing aside in the refrigerator. Sew up the bird or secure it with skewers to prevent the stuffing from escaping during cooking.

5 Place the goose in a large roasting pan. Butter a piece of foil and use to cover the goose loosely, then roast in the preheated oven for 2 hours.

6 Baste the goose frequently during cooking and remove any excess fat from the pan as necessary, using a small ladle or serving spoon. (Strain, cool, and chill the fat in a covered container: It is excellent for roasting potatoes.)

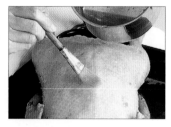

7 Remove the foil from the goose and brush the melted ginger marmalade over the goose, then roast for 30–40 minutes more, or until cooked through. To check if the goose is cooked, pierce the thick part of the thigh with a metal skewer; the juices will run clear when the bird is cooked. Remove from the oven and cover with foil, then let stand for 15 minutes before carving.

8 While the goose is cooking, shape the remaining stuffing into walnut-size balls and place them in an ovenproof dish. Spoon 2 tablespoons of the goose fat over the stuffing balls and bake for about 15 minutes before the goose is cooked.

9 To make the gravy, pour off all but 1 tablespoon of fat from the roasting pan, leaving the meat juices behind. Add the onion and cook for 3–5 minutes, or until softened but not colored. Sprinkle in the flour and then gradually stir in the Madeira and stock. Bring to a boil, stirring continuously, then simmer for 3 minutes, or until thickened and glossy. Strain the gravy and serve it with the carved goose and stuffing. Garnish with fresh sage leaves.

CHICKEN CASSEROLE with WINTER VEGETABLES

A casserole of wonderfully tender organic chicken, winter root vegetables, and lentils, finished with crème fraîche, mustard, and tarragon.

SERVES FOUR

12 ounces onions
12 ounces leeks
8 ounces carrots
1 pound rutabaga
2 tablespoons olive oil
4 chicken portions, about 2 pounds
½ cup green lentils
2 cups chicken stock
1¼ cups apple juice
2 teaspoons cornstarch
3 tablespoons crème fraîche
    or sour cream
2 teaspoons whole-grain mustard
2 tablespoons chopped fresh tarragon
sea salt and ground black pepper
fresh tarragon sprigs, to garnish

1 Preheat the oven to 375°. Prepare and chop the vegetables.

2 Heat the oil in a large flameproof casserole. Season the chicken and brown them in the hot oil until golden. Remove the chicken from the casserole.

3 Add the onions to the casserole and cook for 5 minutes, stirring, until they begin to soften and color. Add the leeks, carrots, rutabaga, and lentils to the casserole and stir over a medium heat for 2 minutes.

4 Return the chicken to the casserole, then add the stock, apple juice, and seasoning. Bring to a boil and cover tightly. Cook in the oven for 50–60 minutes, or until the chicken and lentils are tender.

5 Place the casserole on the stovetop over a medium heat. In a small bowl, blend the cornstarch with about 2 tablespoons of water to make a smooth paste and add to the casserole with the crème fraîche, whole-grain mustard, and chopped tarragon. Adjust the seasoning, then simmer gently for about 2 minutes, stirring, until thickened slightly, before serving, garnished with tarragon sprigs.

COOK'S TIP
Chop the vegetables into similarly sized pieces so that they cook evenly. Organic vegetables do not need to be peeled.

BRAISED SHOULDER of MUTTON with PEARL BARLEY and BABY VEGETABLES

A wonderful variety of organic grains is readily available. In this tasty winter stew, pearl barley absorbs all the juices to become full-flavored with a nutty texture when cooked.

SERVES FOUR

4 tablespoons olive oil
1 large onion, chopped
2 garlic cloves, chopped
2 celery stalks, sliced
a little all-purpose or
    whole-wheat flour
1½ pounds boned shoulder of mutton,
    cut into cubes
3¾–4 cups mutton stock
½ cup pearl barley
8 ounces baby carrots
8 ounces baby turnips
sea salt and ground black pepper
2 tablespoons chopped fresh marjoram,
    to garnish
warm, crusty bread, to serve

1 Heat 3 tablespoons of the oil in a flameproof casserole. Cook the onion and garlic until softened, add the celery, then cook until the vegetables brown.

2 Season the flour and toss the mutton in it. Use a draining spoon to remove the vegetables from the casserole. Add the remaining oil to the juices in the casserole and heat. Brown the mutton in batches until golden.

3 When all the meat is browned, return it to the casserole with the vegetables. Stir in 3¾ cups of the stock and the pearl barley. Cover, then bring to a boil, reduce the heat, and simmer for 1 hour, or until the pearl barley and mutton are tender.

4 Add the baby carrots and turnips to the casserole for the final 15 minutes of cooking. Stir the meat occasionally during cooking and add the remaining stock, if necessary. Stir in seasoning to taste, and serve piping hot, garnished with marjoram, with warm, crusty bread as an accompaniment.

MUTTON SHANKS with BEANS and HERBS

In this hearty winter dish, full-flavored organic mutton shanks are slowly cooked in the oven until tender on a bed of tasty cannellini beans and mixed vegetables.

SERVES FOUR

1 cup dried cannellini, lima, or navy beans,
    soaked overnight in cold water
⅔ cup water
3 tablespoons olive oil
4 large mutton shanks,
    8 ounces each
1 large onion, chopped
1 pound carrots or rutabaga,
    cut into thick chunks
2 celery stalks, cut into thick chunks
1 pound tomatoes, quartered
1 cup vegetable or
    mutton stock
4 fresh rosemary sprigs
2 bay leaves
sea salt and ground black pepper

1 Drain and rinse the soaked cannellini beans and place them in a large saucepan of unsalted boiling water. Bring back to a boil and boil rapidly for 10 minutes, then drain again.

2 Place the ⅔ cup of water in a large casserole, then add the drained cannellini beans. Preheat the oven to 425°F.

3 Heat 2 tablespoons of the olive oil in a large skillet, add the mutton shanks, and cook over a high heat, turning them occasionally until brown on all sides. Remove the mutton shanks from the skillet and set aside.

4 Add the remaining oil to the skillet, then add the onion, and sauté for 5 minutes, until soft and translucent.

5 Add the carrots or rutabaga and celery to the skillet and cook for 2–3 minutes. Stir in the tomatoes and the vegetable or mutton stock and mix well. Transfer the vegetable mixture to the casserole and season well with salt and pepper. Add the fresh rosemary and bay leaves and stir again to combine.

6 Place the mutton shanks on top of the beans and vegetables. Cover the casserole and cook in the preheated oven for about 30 minutes, or until the liquid is bubbling.

7 Reduce the oven temperature to 325°F and continue cooking for about 1½ hours, or until the meat is tender. Check the seasoning and serve on deep, warmed plates, placing each mutton shank on a bed of beans and vegetables.

COOK'S TIP
Mutton shanks are small joints cut from the lower end of the leg. One shank is an ideal-size portion for one. Until recently you would have had to order them from the butcher, but they are now becoming increasingly available, especially from good farmers' markets and home delivery services. To obtain a tender result, shanks should be cooked for a long time at a low temperature.

VARIATIONS
• If you prefer, two cans (14 ounces) cannellini beans can be used in this dish— simply place the drained beans in the casserole with the water and continue from step 3.
• A variety of other organic root vegetables will work well in this recipe— try sweet potatoes, butternut squash, parsnips, or celeriac instead of the carrots or rutabaga. In spring, replace the mutton with spring lamb and add a mixture of baby turnips and baby carrots.

CHILE CON CARNE and RICE

Originally made with finely chopped beef, chiles, and kidney beans by hungry laborers
working on the Texan railroad, this famous Tex-Mex stew has become an international
favorite. Be authentic by using organic ingredients.

SERVES EIGHT

2½ pounds lean braising beef
2 tablespoons sunflower oil
1 large onion, chopped
2 garlic cloves, finely chopped
1 tablespoon all-purpose or
   whole-wheat flour
1¼ cups red wine
1¼ cups beef stock
2 tablespoons tomato paste
sea salt and ground black pepper
fresh cilantro leaves, to garnish
boiled white or brown rice, to serve

For the beans
2 tablespoons olive oil
1 onion, chopped
1 red chile, seeded and chopped
2 cans (14 ounces) red kidney beans,
   drained and rinsed
1 can (14 ounces) chopped tomatoes

For the topping
6 tomatoes, peeled and chopped
1 green chile, seeded and chopped
2 tablespoons chopped fresh chives
2 tablespoons chopped fresh cilantro
⅔ cup sour cream

1 Cut the meat into thick strips and
then cut it diagonally into small cubes.
Heat the oil in a large, flameproof
casserole. Add the chopped onion and
garlic, and cook, stirring occasionally,
for 5–8 minutes, until softened but not
colored. Meanwhile, season the flour
with a little salt and plenty of pepper
and place it on a plate, then toss a batch
of meat in it.

2 Use a draining spoon to remove the
onion from the casserole then add the
floured beef and cook over a high heat,
stirring occasionally with a wooden
spoon until browned on all sides. Remove
from the casserole and set aside, then
flour and brown another batch of meat.

3 When the last batch of meat is
browned, return the first batches with
the onion to the casserole. Stir in the
wine, stock, and tomato paste. Bring to
a boil, reduce the heat, and simmer for
45 minutes, or until the beef is tender.

4 Meanwhile, to make the beans, heat
the olive oil in a skillet and cook the
onion and chile until softened. Add the
kidney beans and tomatoes and simmer
gently for 20–25 minutes.

5 Mix the tomatoes, chile, chives, and
cilantro for the topping. Ladle the meat
onto plates, then add the beans and the
tomato topping. Top with sour cream
and cilantro leaves and serve with rice.

BOEUF BOURGUIGNONNE

The classic French dish of beef cooked in Burgundy style, with red wine, small pieces of bacon, baby onions, and mushrooms, is traditionally cooked for several hours at a low temperature. Using organic top round steak or braising beef reduces the cooking time.

SERVES SIX

6 ounces rindless fatty bacon strips,
    chopped
2 pounds lean braising beef or
    top round steak
2 tablespoons all-purpose or
    whole-wheat flour
3 tablespoons sunflower oil
2 tablespoons butter or
    olive oil
12 shallots
2 garlic cloves, crushed
2½ cups mushrooms, sliced
scant 2 cups robust red wine
⅔ cup beef stock or consommé
1 bay leaf
2 sprigs each of fresh thyme, parsley,
    and marjoram
sea salt and ground black pepper
mashed root vegetables, such
    as celeriac and potatoes,
    to serve

1 Preheat the oven to 325°F. Heat a large flameproof casserole, then add the bacon and cook, stirring occasionally, until the pieces are crisp and golden brown.

2 Meanwhile, cut the meat into 1-inch cubes. Season the flour and use to coat the meat. Use a draining spoon to remove the bacon from the casserole and set aside. Add and heat the sunflower oil, then brown the beef in batches and set aside with the bacon.

COOK'S TIP

Boeuf Bourguignonne freezes well. Freeze for up to 2 months. Thaw overnight in the refrigerator, then transfer to a flameproof casserole and add ⅔ cup water. Stir well, bring to a boil, stirring occasionally, and simmer steadily for at least 10 minutes, or until the meat is piping hot.

3 Add the butter or olive oil to the casserole. Cook the shallots and garlic until just starting to color, then add the mushrooms and cook for 5 minutes. Return the bacon and meat, and stir in the wine and stock or consommé. Tie the herbs together and add to the casserole.

4 Cover and cook for 1½ hours, or until the meat is tender, stirring once or twice. Season to taste before serving with mashed root vegetables.

STEAK, MUSHROOM, and ALE PIE

Organic steak has a great quality and fine texture and flavor—it is delicious in this Anglo-Irish dish. Creamy mashed potatoes or parsley-dressed boiled potatoes and slightly crunchy carrots and green beans or cabbage are perfect accompaniments. French fries and a side salad can be served with the pie.

SERVES FOUR

2 tablespoons olive oil
1 large onion, finely chopped
1½ cups cremini or white mushrooms, halved
2 pounds lean beef in one piece, such as top round steak or braising beef
2 tablespoons all-purpose whole-wheat flour
3 tablespoons sunflower oil
1¼ cups stout or brown ale
1¼ cups beef stock or consommé
1¼ pounds puff pastry, thawed if frozen
beaten egg, to glaze
sea salt and ground black pepper
steamed organic vegetables, to serve

1 Heat the olive oil in a large, flameproof casserole, add the onion, and cook gently, stirring occasionally, for about 5 minutes, or until it is softened but not colored. Add the halved mushrooms and continue cooking for a further 5 minutes, stirring occasionally.

2 Meanwhile, trim the meat and cut it into 1-inch cubes. Season the flour and toss the meat in it.

COOK'S TIP
To make individual pies, divide the filling among four individual pie plates. Cut the pastry into quarters; cover as above. If the pie plates do not have rims, press a narrow strip of pastry around the edge of each one to seal the lid in place. Cook as above, reducing the cooking time slightly.

3 Use a draining spoon to remove the onion mixture from the casserole and set aside. Add and heat the oil, then brown the beef in batches over a high heat to seal in the juices.

4 Replace the vegetables, then stir in the stout or ale and stock or consommé. Bring to a boil, reduce the heat, and simmer for about 1 hour, stirring occasionally, or until the meat is tender. Season to taste and transfer to a 6¼ cup pie plate. Cover and let cool. If you have time, chill the meat filling overnight because this allows the flavor to develop. Preheat the oven to 450°F.

5 Roll out the dough in the shape of the pie plate and about 1½ inches larger all around. Cut a 1-inch strip from around the edge of the pastry. Brush the rim of the pie plate with water and press the pastry strip onto it. Brush the pastry rim with beaten egg and cover the pie with the pastry lid. Press the lid firmly in place and then trim the excess pastry from around the edge of the dish.

6 Use the blunt edge of a knife to tap the outside edge of the pastry rim, pressing it down with your finger as you seal the meat and mushroom filling into the dish. (This sealing technique is known as knocking up.)

7 Pinch the outside edge of the pastry between your fingers to flute the edge. Roll out any remaining pastry trimmings and cut out five or six leaf shapes to garnish the center of the pie. Brush the shapes with a little beaten egg before pressing them lightly in place.

8 Make a hole in the middle of the pie using the point of a sharp knife to allow the steam to escape during cooking. Brush the top carefully with beaten egg and chill for 10 minutes in the refrigerator to rest the pastry.

9 Bake the pie for 15 minutes, then reduce the oven temperature to 400°F and bake for a further 15–20 minutes, or until the pastry is risen and golden brown. Serve the pie hot with steamed organic vegetables.

FILLETS of HALIBUT in RED WINE SAUCE

Forget the old maxim that red wine and fish do not go well together. The robust sauce adds color and richness to this excellent dish.

SERVES FOUR

4 fillets of halibut, about 6–7 ounces
    each, skinned
10 tablespoons chilled butter or
    nonhydrogenated margarine, diced,
    plus extra for greasing
4 ounces shallots, thinly sliced
scant 1 cup robust red wine
scant 1 cup fish stock
salt and ground white pepper
fresh chervil or flat-leaf parsley leaves,
    to garnish

COOK'S TIP

If your baking dish is not flameproof,
put the liquid into a saucepan to cook
on the stove.

1 Preheat the oven to 350°F. Season the fish on both sides with a little salt and plenty of pepper. Generously butter a flameproof dish that is large enough to take all the fish fillets in a single layer without overlapping. Spread the shallots over the bottom and lay the fish fillets on top. Season.

2 Put in the red wine and fish stock, cover the dish, and bring the liquid to just below boiling point. Transfer the dish to the oven and bake for 6–8 minutes, or until the fish is just cooked.

3 Using a spatula, carefully lift the fish and shallots onto a serving dish, cover with foil, and keep hot.

4 Transfer the dish to the stovetop and bring the cooking liquid to a boil over a high heat. Cook it until it has reduced by half. Lower the heat and whisk in the chilled butter or margarine, one piece at a time, to make a smooth, shiny sauce. Season with salt and ground white pepper, set aside, and keep hot.

5 Divide the shallots among four warmed plates and lay the fish fillets on top. Pour the sauce over and around the fish and garnish with the chervil or flat-leaf parsley.

VARIATION

Turbot, sole, or flounder fillets can also be cooked in this way. Make sure that your fish is caught sustainably.

SMOKED HADDOCK with MUSTARD CABBAGE

*A wide range of organic mustards are available—whole-grain is used in this warming
winter dish, but any type can be used instead.*

2 Meanwhile put the smoked haddock
fillet in a large shallow saucepan with the
milk, onion rings, and bay leaves. Add
the lemon slices and white peppercorns.
Bring to simmering point, cover, and
poach until the fish flakes easily when
tested with the tip of a sharp knife. This
will take 8–10 minutes, depending on
the thickness of the fillets. Take the pan
off the heat and set aside until needed.
Preheat the broiler.

3 Cut the tomatoes in half horizontally,
season them with a little salt and plenty
of pepper, and broil until lightly
browned. Drain the cabbage, refresh
under cold water, and drain again.

4 Heat the butter or oil in a shallow
pan or wok, add the cabbage, and toss
over the heat for 2 minutes. Mix in the
mustard and season to taste, then put
the cabbage into a warmed serving dish.

SERVES FOUR

1 savoy cabbage
1½ pounds undyed smoked
    haddock fillet
1¼ cups milk or soy milk
½ onion, peeled and sliced into rings
2 bay leaves
½ lemon, sliced
4 white peppercorns
4 ripe tomatoes
4 tablespoons butter or
    3½ tablespoons olive oil
2 tablespoons whole-grain mustard
juice of 1 lemon
sea salt and ground black pepper
2 tablespoons chopped fresh parsley,
    to garnish

1 Cut the savoy cabbage in half, remove
the central core and thick ribs, then
shred the cabbage. Cook in a saucepan
of lightly salted boiling water, or steam
over boiling water for about 10 minutes,
until just tender. Let stand in the pan or
steamer until required.

5 Drain the haddock. Skin and cut the
fish into four pieces. Place on top of the
cabbage with some of the cooked onion
rings and broiled tomato halves. Pour on
the lemon juice, then sprinkle with
chopped fresh parsley and serve.

SEAFOOD LASAGNE

This dish can be as simple or as elegant as you desire. For an elegant dinner party, you can dress it up with scallops, mussels, or shrimp; for a casual family meal, you can use simple fish, such as haddock and hake. Whatever fish or shellfish you choose, ensure it comes from a sustainable source.

SERVES EIGHT

12 ounces haddock
12 ounces salmon fillet
12 ounces undyed smoked haddock
4 cups milk or soy milk
2¼ cups fish stock
2 bay leaves
1 small onion, peeled and halved
6 tablespoons butter or
    nonhydrogenated margarine,
    plus extra for greasing
3 tablespoons all-purpose or
    whole-wheat flour
2 cups mushrooms, sliced
8–11 ounces fresh lasagne
4 tablespoons freshly grated
    Parmesan cheese or premium
    Italian-style vegetarian cheese
sea salt, ground black pepper,
    freshly grated nutmeg,
    and paprika
arugula leaves, to garnish

For the tomato sauce
2 tablespoons olive oil
1 red onion, finely chopped
1 garlic clove, finely chopped
1 can (14 ounces) chopped tomatoes
1 tablespoon tomato paste
1 tablespoon torn fresh basil leaves

1 Make the tomato sauce. Heat the oil in a saucepan and fry the onion and garlic over a low heat for 5 minutes, until softened and golden. Stir in the tomatoes and tomato paste and simmer for 20–30 minutes, stirring occasionally. Season with a little salt and plenty of black pepper and stir in the basil.

VARIATION
A good selection of organic pastas are available, including a variety of types of lasagne. Choose from classic lasagne, lasagne all'uovo (rich egg pasta sheets), or lasagne verdi (spinach lasagne), which is an attractive dark green color.

2 Put all the fish in a shallow flameproof dish or pan with the milk, stock, bay leaves, and onion. Bring to a boil over a moderate heat; poach for 5 minutes, until almost cooked. Let cool.

3 When the fish is almost cold, strain it, reserving the liquid. Remove the skin and any bones, and flake the fish.

4 Preheat the oven to 350°F. Melt the butter in a saucepan, stir in the flour; cook for 2 minutes, stirring. Gradually add the poaching liquid and bring to a boil, stirring. Add the mushrooms and cook for 2–3 minutes. Season with salt, pepper, and nutmeg.

5 Lightly grease a shallow rectangular ovenproof dish. Spoon a thin layer of the mushroom sauce over the bottom of the dish and spread it out evenly with a spatula. Stir the flaked fish into the remaining mushroom sauce in the pan.

6 Add a layer of lasagne, then a layer of fish and sauce. Add another layer of lasagne, then spread over all the tomato sauce. Continue to layer the lasagne and fish, finishing with a layer of fish.

7 Sprinkle over the grated cheese, then bake for 30–45 minutes, until golden. Before serving, sprinkle with paprika and garnish with arugula leaves.

SPICY PUMPKIN and ORANGE BOMBE

In this fabulous ice cream dessert, the subtle flavor of organic pumpkin is transformed with the addition of citrus fruits and spices. The delicious ice-cream mixture is then encased in syrupy sponge and served with an orange and whole-spice syrup.

SERVES EIGHT

½ cup unsalted butter or nonhydrogenated
    margarine, softened
generous ½ cup unrefined superfine sugar
    or rapadura
1 cup self-raising flour
½ teaspoon baking powder
2 eggs

For the ice cream
1 pound fresh pumpkin, seeded
    and cubed
1 orange
scant 1½ cups unrefined granulated
    sugar or rapadura
1¼ cups water
2 cinnamon sticks, halved
2 teaspoons whole cloves
2 tablespoons orange flower water
1¼ cups extra thick heavy cream or
    soy cream
2 pieces preserved ginger, grated
unrefined confectioners' sugar,
    for dusting

1 Preheat the oven to 350°F. Grease and line the bottom of a 1-pound loaf pan.

2 To make the sponge, beat the butter or margarine, superfine sugar, flour, baking powder, and eggs in a bowl until creamy.

3 Spoon the mixture into the prepared pan, then level the surface and bake in the preheated oven for 30–35 minutes, until firm in the center. Let stand in the pan for a few minutes, then turn out on to a wire rack to cool.

4 Make the ice cream. Steam the cubes of pumpkin for about 15 minutes, or until tender. Drain and blend in a food processor to form a smooth puree. Let cool.

5 Pare thin strips of rind from the orange, scrape off any white pith, then cut the strips into very fine shreds. Squeeze the orange and set the juice aside. Heat the unrefined sugar and water in a small, heavy saucepan until the sugar dissolves. Bring the syrup to a boil and boil rapidly without stirring for 3 minutes.

6 Stir in the orange shreds, orange juice, cinnamon, and cloves and heat gently for 5 minutes. Strain the syrup, reserving the orange shreds and spices. Measure 1¼ cups of the syrup and reserve. Return the spices to the remaining syrup and stir in the orange flower water. Pour into a pitcher and set aside to cool.

COOK'S TIP
If you prefer a smooth syrup, strain to remove the cinnamon sticks and cloves before spooning it over the bombe.

7 Beat the pumpkin puree with ¾ cup of the measured strained syrup until evenly combined. Stir in the cream and ginger. Cut the cake into ½-inch slices. Dampen a 6¼ cup deep bowl and line it with plastic wrap. Pour the remaining strained syrup into a shallow dish.

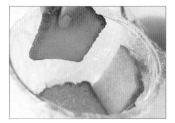

8 Dip the cake slices one at a time briefly in the syrup and use to line the prepared bowl, placing the syrupy coated sides against the bowl.

9 To freeze the ice cream by hand, put the pumpkin mixture into a shallow container and freeze until firm. Scrape the ice cream into the sponge-lined bowl, level the surface, and freeze until firm, preferably overnight. If using an ice-cream maker, churn the pumpkin mixture until very thick, then spoon it into the sponge-lined bowl. Level the surface and freeze until firm, preferably overnight.

10 To serve, invert the bombe onto a plate. Lift off the bowl and plastic wrap. Dust with the confectioner's sugar; serve with the spiced syrup spooned over.

CHOCOLATE MOUSSE with GLAZED KUMQUATS

Bright orange kumquats balance this rich, dark mousse perfectly. There are some excellent organic chocolates available. It is worth spending a little more on them because they have such a luxurious taste and texture, and good fair-trade values.

SERVES SIX

8 ounces bittersweet chocolate, broken into squares
4 eggs, separated
2 tablespoons brandy
6 tablespoons heavy cream or soy cream

For the glazed kumquats
10 ounces kumquats
generous ½ cup unrefined granulated sugar or rapadura
⅔ cup water
1 tablespoon brandy

1 Make the glazed kumquats. Slice the fruit lengthwise and place cut side up in a shallow serving dish.

2 Place the sugar in a saucepan with the water. Heat gently, stirring constantly, until the sugar has dissolved, then bring to a boil and boil rapidly, without stirring, until a golden-brown caramel forms.

VARIATION
If you can't find kumquats, then use peeled and sliced small, seedless organic oranges, pink-fleshed grapefruit, or satsumas instead.

3 Remove the pan from the heat and carefully stir in 4 tablespoons boiling water to dissolve the caramel. Stir in the brandy, then pour the caramel over the kumquats and let cool. Once completely cold, cover and chill.

4 Line a shallow 8-inch round cake pan with plastic wrap. Melt the chocolate in a bowl over a saucepan of barely simmering water, then remove the bowl from the heat.

5 Add the egg yolks and brandy to the chocolate and beat well, then fold in the cream, mixing well. In a separate clean bowl, whisk the egg whites until stiff, then gently fold them into the chocolate mixture.

6 Put the mixture into the prepared pan and level the surface with a spatula. Chill for several hours until set.

7 To serve, turn the mousse out onto a plate and cut into slices or wedges. Serve the chocolate mousse on serving plates and spoon some of the glazed kumquats and syrup alongside.

CHRISTMAS ICE CREAM TORTE

This fruity ice cream cake makes an exciting alternative to a traditional Christmas dessert, but don't feel that you have to limit it to the festive season. Packed with dried organic fruit and nuts, it is perfect for any special occasion and tastes sensational.

SERVES EIGHT TO TEN

¾ cup dried cranberries
scant ½ cup pitted prunes
⅓ cup golden raisins
¾ cup port
2 pieces preserved ginger, chopped
2 tablespoons unsalted butter or
    nonhydrogenated margarine
3 tablespoons light brown sugar
scant 2 cups fresh white or
    whole-wheat breadcrumbs
2½ cups heavy cream or soy cream
2 tablespoons unrefined confectioners'
    sugar
1 teaspoon apple pie spice
    or allspice
¾ cup brazil nuts, finely chopped
2–3 bay leaf sprigs, egg white, superfine
    sugar or rapadura and fresh cherries,
    to decorate

1 Put the dried fruit in a food processor and process briefly to chop roughly. Put the fruit into a bowl and add the port and ginger. Let marinate for 2 hours.

2 Melt the butter in a skillet. Add the brown sugar and heat gently until dissolved. Add the breadcrumbs and fry gently for 5 minutes. Let cool.

3 Put the breadcrumbs into a food processor and process to finer crumbs. Sprinkle one-third into an 7-inch loose-bottomed springform pan and freeze.

4 Whip the cream with the confectioner's sugar and spice to soft peaks. Fold in the nuts and dried fruit mixture.

5 To make sugared bay leaves for decoration, wash and dry the sprigs, then paint both sides with beaten egg white. Dust evenly with sugar. Let dry for 2–3 hours.

6 Spread one-third of the spiced fruit-cream mixture over the frozen breadcrumb base in the pan, being careful not to dislodge any of the crumbs. Sprinkle the cream mixture with another layer of the fine, crispy breadcrumbs. Repeat the layering, finishing with a layer of the spiced fruit-cream mixture. Cover the torte with plastic wrap and freeze it overnight.

7 Remove the torte from the freezer and place in the refrigerator for about 1 hour before serving, decorated with sugared bay leaves and fresh cherries.

DRIED FRUIT COMPOTE

Compotes made with dried fruit are just as wonderful as those made with fresh fruits, especially in winter when fewer organic fresh fruit varieties are in season.

SERVES FOUR

1⅓ cups mixed dried fruit
⅔ cup dried cherries
⅔ cup golden raisins
10 dried prunes
10 dried apricots
hot, freshly brewed fragrant tea, such as
  Earl Grey or jasmine, to cover
1–2 tablespoons unrefined superfine sugar
  or rapadura
¼ lemon, sliced
4 tablespoons brandy

1 Put the dried fruit in a bowl and pour over the hot tea. Add sugar to taste and the lemon slices. Cover with a plate, set aside, and let cool to room temperature.

2 When the fruit is cool, cover the bowl with plastic wrap and chill in the refrigerator for at least 2 hours, but preferably overnight. Just before serving, pour in the brandy and stir well.

MOROCCAN RICE PUDDING

A simple and delicious alternative to a traditional rice pudding. The rice is cooked in almond-flavored milk and delicately flavored with cinnamon and orange flower water.

SERVES SIX

¼ cup almonds, chopped
2¼ cups soft pudding rice
¼ cup unrefined confectioners' sugar
   or rapadura
1 cinnamon stick
4 tablespoons butter or
   nonhydrogenated margarine
¼ teaspoon almond extract
¾ cup milk or soy milk
¾ cup light cream or soy cream
2 tablespoons orange flower water
toasted sliced almonds and ground
   cinnamon, to decorate

1 Put the almonds in a food processor or blender with 4 tablespoons of very hot water. Process until the almonds are finely chopped, then push through a sieve into a bowl. Return the almond mixture to the food processor or blender, add a further 4 tablespoons of very hot water, and process again. Push the almond mixture through the sieve into a pan.

2 Add 1¼ cups water and bring the mixture to a boil. Add the rice, confectioner's sugar or rapadura, cinnamon stick, half the butter, the almond extract, half the milk, and half the cream.

3 Bring to a boil, then simmer, covered, for about 30 minutes, adding more milk and cream as the rice mixture thickens. Continue to cook the rice, stirring, and adding the remaining milk and cream, until the dessert becomes thick and creamy. Stir in the orange flower water, then taste the rice pudding for sweetness, adding a little extra sugar, if necessary.

4 Put the rice pudding into a serving bowl and sprinkle with the toasted sliced almonds. Dot with the remaining butter and dust with a little ground cinnamon. Serve the pudding hot.

BAKED MAPLE and PECAN CROISSANT PUDDING

This variation of the classic English bread and butter pudding uses rich, flaky croissants, topped with a delicious mixture of organic fruit and nuts. Maple-syrup-flavored custard completes this mouthwatering dessert.

SERVES FOUR

scant ½ cup golden raisins
3 tablespoons brandy
4 large croissants
4 tablespoons butter or
    nonhydrogenated margarine,
    plus extra for greasing
⅓ cup pecan nuts, roughly chopped
3 eggs, lightly beaten
1¼ cups milk or soy milk
⅔ cup light cream or soy cream
½ cup maple syrup
2 tablespoons raw sugar
maple syrup, to serve (optional)
half-and-half cream or soy cream,
    to serve (optional)

3 Arrange the croissant slices butter side uppermost and slightly overlapping in the greased dish. Scatter the brandy-soaked golden raisins and the roughly chopped pecan nuts evenly over the buttered croissant slices.

5 Strain the egg custard through a sieve, over the croissants, fruit, and nuts in the dish. Let the pudding stand for 30 minutes so that some of the custard is absorbed by the croissants. Preheat the oven to 350°F.

1 Lightly grease the bottom and sides of a small, shallow ovenproof dish. Place the golden raisins and brandy in a small saucepan and heat gently, until warm. Let stand for 1 hour.

2 Cut the croissants into thick slices and then spread with butter on one side.

4 In a large bowl, beat the eggs and milk together, then gradually beat in the light or soy cream and maple syrup.

COOK'S TIPS
• The main sweetener in this recipe is maple syrup. It is made by tapping the sap of the maple tree. Organic maple syrup is not overprocessed so it retains its natural richness.
• Pecan nuts are an elongated nut in a glossy red oval-shaped shell, but are usually sold shelled. They are native to the USA and have a sweet, mild flavour. Pecans are most commonly used in pecan pie but are also popular in ice creams and cakes. Walnuts can be substituted for pecans in most recipes, and they would be perfect in this one if you don't have any pecan nuts.

6 Sprinkle the raw sugar evenly over the top, then cover the dish with foil. Bake the pudding for 30 minutes, then remove the foil and continue to cook for about 20 minutes, or until the custard is set and the top is golden brown.

7 Let the pudding cool for about 15 minutes before serving warm with extra maple syrup and a little half-and-half cream or soy cream, if you desire.

VARIATION
Thickly sliced one-day-old bread, large slices of brioche, or fruit bread can be used instead of the croissants. Slightly stale one-day-old croissants are easier to slice and butter; they also soak up the custard more easily.

ORANGE MARMALADE CHOCOLATE LOAF

Do not be alarmed at the amount of cream in this recipe—it's decadent but necessary, and replaces butter to make a deliciously mouthwatering moist dark chocolate cake, finished with a bittersweet sticky marmalade filling and topping.

SERVES EIGHT

4 ounces bittersweet chocolate
3 eggs
scant 1 cup unrefined superfine sugar
  or rapadura
¾ cup sour cream
1¾ cups self-rising flour

For the filling and topping
⅔ cup bitter orange marmalade
4 ounces bittersweet chocolate
4 tablespoons sour cream
shredded orange rind, to decorate

1 Preheat the oven to 375°F. Grease a 2-pound loaf pan lightly, then line the bottom with a piece of parchment paper. Break the chocolate into pieces. Melt the chocolate in a heatproof bowl placed over hot water.

2 Combine the eggs and sugar in a separate bowl. Using a handheld electric mixer, beat the mixture until it is thick and creamy, then stir in the sour cream and melted chocolate. Fold in the flour evenly using a metal spoon.

3 Put the mixture into the prepared pan and bake for about 1 hour, or until well risen and firm to the touch. Cool for a few minutes in the pan, then turn out onto a wire rack and let the loaf cool completely.

4 Make the filling: Spoon two-thirds of the marmalade into a small saucepan and melt over a low heat. Break the chocolate into pieces. Melt the chocolate in a heatproof bowl placed over hot water. Stir the chocolate into the marmalade with the sour cream.

5 Slice the cake across into three layers and sandwich back together with about half the marmalade filling. Spread the rest over the top of the cake and let set. Spoon the remaining marmalade over the cake and scatter with shredded orange rind to decorate.

COOK'S TIP
A fantastic variety of different types of organic marmalades are available, including farmhouse and handmade regional varieties.

ORANGE AND NUT SEMOLINA CAKE

In Eastern Mediterranean cooking, semolina is used in many desserts.
Here, it provides a spongy base for soaking up a deliciously fragrant spicy syrup.

SERVES TEN

For the cake
½ cup unsalted butter or nonhydrogenated
    margarine, softened
generous ½ cup unrefined superfine sugar
    or rapadura
finely grated rind of 1 orange, plus
    2 tablespoons juice
3 eggs
1 cup semolina
2 teaspoons baking powder
1 cup ground hazelnuts
plain yogurt, to serve

To finish
1¾ cups unrefined superfine sugar
    or rapadura
2 cinnamon sticks, halved
juice of 1 lemon
4 tablespoons orange flower water
½ cup unblanched hazelnuts,
    toasted and chopped
½ cup blanched almonds,
    toasted and chopped
shredded rind of 1 orange, to decorate

1 Preheat the oven to 425°F. Grease
and line the bottom of a deep 9-inch
square cake pan.

2 Lightly cream the butter in a large
bowl. Add the sugar or rapadura, orange
rind and juice, eggs, semolina, baking
powder, and hazelnuts and beat the
ingredients together until smooth.

3 Put into the prepared pan and level
the surface. Bake for 20–25 minutes,
until just firm and golden. Let cool in
the pan.

4 To make the syrup, put the unrefined
superfine sugar in a small heavy saucepan
with 2½ cups water and the halved
cinnamon sticks. Heat gently, stirring
occasionally with a wooden spoon, until
the sugar has dissolved completely.

5 Bring to a boil and boil rapidly,
without stirring, for 5 minutes. Measure
half the boiling syrup and add the lemon
juice and orange flower water to it. Pour
over the cake. Reserve the remainder of
the syrup in the pan.

6 Let the cake stand in the pan until the
syrup is absorbed, then turn it out onto
a plate and cut diagonally into diamond-
shaped portions. Scatter with the nuts.

7 Boil the remaining syrup until slightly
thickened, then pour it over the cake.
Scatter the shredded orange rind over
the cake to decorate and serve with
plain yogurt.

GREEK FRUIT and NUT PASTRIES

These aromatic sweet pastry crescents are packed with walnuts, which are a really rich source of nutrients. Serve with a cup of organic coffee.

3 Meanwhile, to make the filling, mix the honey and coffee. Add the fruit, walnuts, and nutmeg. Stir well, cover, and let soak for at least 20 minutes.

4 Roll out a portion of dough on a lightly floured surface until about ⅛ inch thick. Stamp out circles using a 4-inch round cutter.

5 Place a heaped teaspoonful of filling on one side of each circle. Brush the edges with a little milk, then fold over and press the edges together to seal. Repeat with the remaining pastry until all the filling is used.

6 Put the pastries on lightly greased baking sheets, brush with milk, and sprinkle with superfine sugar.

7 Make a steam hole in each with a skewer. Bake for 35 minutes, or until lightly browned. Cool on a wire rack.

VARIATIONS
Any dried fruit can be used in this recipe. Try a combination of the following: golden raisins, raisins, currants, apricots, cherries, or prunes.

MAKES SIXTEEN

4 tablespoons clear honey
4 tablespoons strong brewed coffee
½ cup mixed dried fruit, chopped
1 cup walnuts, chopped
¼ teaspoon freshly grated nutmeg
milk, to glaze
superfine sugar or rapadura,
   for sprinkling

For the pastry
4 cups all-purpose flour
½ teaspoon ground cinnamon
½ teaspoon baking powder
10 tablespoons unsalted butter or
   nonhydrogenated margarine
1 egg
½ cup chilled milk or soy milk

1 Preheat the oven to 350°F. To make the pastry, sift the flour, ground cinnamon, and baking powder into a bowl. Rub in the butter until the mixture resembles fine breadcrumbs. Make a well in the center.

2 Beat the egg and chilled milk or soy milk together and add to the well in the dry ingredients. Mix to a soft dough. Divide the dough into two equal pieces and wrap each in plastic wrap. Chill for 30 minutes.

COOK'S TIP
These traditional Greek pastries are known as *moshopoungia* in Greece. Serve them warm with morning coffee or as an afternoon snack with a dollop of whipped cream or crème fraîche.

ORANGE and CORIANDER BRIOCHES

The warm spicy flavor of coriander combines particularly well with orange.
Serve these little muffins with marmalade for a lazy weekend breakfast.

MAKES TWELVE

2 cups white bread flour
½ ounce fresh yeast
½ teaspoon salt
1 tablespoon unrefined superfine sugar
  or rapadura
2 teaspoons coriander seeds, ground
grated rind of 1 orange
2 eggs, beaten
4 tablespoons unsalted butter or
  nonhydrogenated margarine, melted
1 small egg, beaten, to glaze
shredded orange rind, to decorate (optional)

1 Grease 12 individual brioche molds. Blend the yeast with 1½ tablespoon tepid water in a bowl until smooth. Sift the flour into a mixing bowl and stir in the yeast, salt, sugar, coriander seeds, and orange rind. Make a well in the center, pour in 2 tablespoons lukewarm water, the eggs, and melted butter, and beat to make a soft dough. Turn the dough onto a lightly floured surface and knead for 5 minutes. Return to the clean, lightly oiled bowl, cover with plastic wrap, and let stand in a warm place for about 1 hour, or until doubled in bulk.

2 Put the dough onto a floured surface, knead briefly, and roll into a sausage shape. Cut into 12 pieces. Break off one-quarter of each piece and set aside. Shape the larger pieces of dough into balls; place in the prepared molds.

VARIATION
If you prefer, use 2 teaspoons active dried yeast instead of fresh yeast, and add to the flour in step 1.

3 With a floured wooden spoon handle, press a hole in each dough ball. Shape each small piece of dough into a little plug and press into the holes.

COOK'S TIP
These little brioches look particularly attractive if they are made in special brioche tins. However, they can also be made in bun or muffin tins.

4 Place the brioche molds on a baking sheet. Cover with lightly oiled plastic wrap and let stand in a warm place until the dough rises almost to the top of the tins. Preheat the oven to 425°F. Brush the brioches with beaten egg and bake for 15 minutes, until golden brown. Scatter over extra shreds of orange rind to decorate, if you desire, and serve the brioches warm with butter.

SPICED POACHED KUMQUATS

Kumquats are not available throughout the year, but they are undoubtedly at their best
just before the Christmas season. This fruit can be bottled and given as presents.
Its marvelous spicy-sweet citrus flavor complements both sweet and savory dishes.

SERVES SIX

4 cups kumquats
generous ½ cup unrefined superfine sugar
 or rapadura
⅔ cup water
1 small cinnamon stick
1 star anise
a bay leaf, to decorate (optional)

COOK'S TIP
To prepare jars for home preserves,
preheat the oven to 325°F. Wash the
jars in hot soapy water; rinse and dry
thoroughly. Place the jars in the oven
for 10 minutes, then turn off the oven.

1 Cut the kumquats in half and discard
the pips. Place the kumquats in a
saucepan with the sugar, water, and
spices. Cook over a gentle heat, stirring
until the sugar has dissolved.

2 Increase the heat, cover the pan, and
boil the mixture for 8–10 minutes, until
the kumquats are tender. To bottle the
kumquats, spoon them into warm,
sterilized jars, seal, and label. Decorate
the kumquats with a bay leaf before
serving, if you desire.

COOK'S TIP
Serve these delectable treats with baked
ham, roast turkey, or venison steaks.
They would also make a perfect
accompaniment for moist almond or
chocolate cake; or serve with organic
vanilla or chocolate ice cream.

THREE-FRUIT MARMALADE

Seville oranges have a fine flavor and are the best variety for marmalade.
They are only available for a limited time in winter so make the most of them then.

MAKES 2.25KG/5LB

2 Seville oranges
2 lemons
1 grapefruit
7½ cups water
½ cups unrefined granulated sugar
croissants, to serve (optional)

1 Wash the fruit, halve, and squeeze their
juice. Pour into a large heavy saucepan.
Place the pips and pulp in a square of
cheesecloth, gather into a bag, and tie
tightly with string. Tie the bag to the pan
handle so it dangles in the juice.

2 Cut the citrus skins into thin wedges;
scrape off, and discard the membranes
and pith. Cut the rinds into slivers and
add to the pan with the measured water.
Bring to a simmer and cook gently for
2 hours, until the rinds are very tender
and the water has reduced by half. Test
the rinds for softness by pressing a
cooled piece with a finger.

3 Remove the cheesecloth bag from
the pan, squeezing out the juice into the
pan. Discard the bag. Stir the granulated
sugar into the pan and heat very gently,
stirring occasionally with a wooden
spoon, until all the sugar has dissolved.

4 Bring the mixture to a boil, then boil
vigorously for 10–15 minutes, or until the
marmalade reaches 220°F.

5 Alternatively, test the marmalade for
setting by pouring a small amount onto
a chilled saucer. Chill for 2 minutes, then
push the marmalade with your finger;
if wrinkles form on the surface, it is
ready. Cool for 15 minutes.

6 Stir the marmalade and put it into
warm, sterilized jars. Cover with waxed
paper disks. Seal and label when cold.
Store in a cool dark cupboard. Serve
with warm croissants, if you desire.

SAUCES, SALSAS, CHUTNEYS, AND BREADS

You can buy prepared organic sauces, salsas, and breads from farmers' markets, supermarkets, and health food stores. However, homemade varieties are often much better—and by making your own, you can make the most of fresh produce when it's in season. Reasonably priced organic fruits and vegetables are easy to find at farmers' markets and farm stores. As they come into season, start making large quantities of sauces and chutneys, such as Chili Sauce and Apple and Tomato Chutney. Delicious accompaniments, such as Garlic Mayonnaise or Onion Sauce, can transform simply cooked dishes. Take your pick from a wide range of organic flavored breads, such as Pumpkin and Walnut Bread, Wholemeal Sunflower Bread, or Cheese and Onion Cornbread, and serve with organic cheeses and cold meats. Or try making Chapatis to go with your favorite curry, or Pita Bread to dip in a creamy avocado Guacamole.

TAHINI SAUCE

*Made of sesame seeds, spiced with garlic and lemon juice, this is Israel's most famous
sauce. It makes a delicious dip and, when thinned with water, can be spooned over falafel.*

SERVES FOUR TO SIX

⅔–¾ cup tahini
3 garlic cloves, finely chopped
juice of 1 lemon
¼ teaspoon ground cumin
small pinch of ground coriander
small pinch of curry powder
¼–½ cup water
cayenne pepper
sea salt

For the garnish
1–2 tablespoons extra virgin olive oil
chopped fresh cilantro or
    flat-leaf parsley leaves
handful of olives and/or pickled vegetables
a few chiles or a hot pepper sauce

1 Put the tahini and garlic in a bowl
and mix together well. Stir in the lemon
juice, cumin, ground coriander, and
curry powder.

COOK'S TIP
Tahini sauce forms the basis of many of
the salads and dips popular in Middle
Eastern cuisine.

2 Slowly add the water to the tahini,
beating all the time. The mixture will
thicken, then become thin. Season with
cayenne pepper and salt.

3 To serve, spoon the tahini onto a
serving plate, individual plates, or into a
shallow bowl. Drizzle over the oil and
sprinkle with the other garnishes.

CHILI SAUCE

Hot with chiles, pungent with garlic, and fragrant with exotic cardamom, this spicy sauce can be served with rice, couscous, soup, and roast chicken or vegetable dishes.

MAKES ABOUT 2 CUPS

5–8 garlic cloves, chopped
2–3 medium-hot chiles, such as jalapeño,
    seeded and chopped
5 tomatoes, diced
1 small bunch cilantro,
    roughly chopped
1 small bunch flat-leaf parsley, chopped
2 tablespoons extra virgin olive oil
2 teaspoons ground cumin
$\frac{1}{2}$ teaspoon ground turmeric
$\frac{1}{2}$ teaspoon curry powder
seeds from 3–5 cardamom pods
juice of $\frac{1}{2}$ lemon
sea salt
a few sprigs of parsley or cilantro,
    to garnish

COOK'S TIP
There is simply no comparison between the flavor of a freshly picked organic tomato that has been allowed to ripen naturally and the taste of an artificially ripened tomato. Organic growers select the sweetest, tastiest varieties, and whether you buy tiny cherry tomatoes or big beefsteaks, you will not be disappointed.

VARIATIONS
• To make a spicy dip, put 14 ounces chopped fresh tomatoes, or a mixture of chopped fresh and canned tomatoes, in a bowl. Stir in $\frac{1}{2}$ cup of the chili sauce, or to taste, and season with salt, if necessary. Spread the dip onto wedges of flat bread, such as pita bread, or serve in a bowl with strips of raw vegetables for dipping.
• To make a spicy tomato relish, soak 2 tablespoons fenugreek seeds in cold water for at least 2 hours and preferably overnight. Drain, then grind the seeds in a spice grinder or pound them in a mortar with a pestle until they form a smooth paste. In a bowl, combine the paste with 1 tablespoon of the chili sauce and 2 diced tomatoes. Season with salt and black pepper to taste.

1 Put all the sauce ingredients except the salt in a food processor or blender. Process until finely chopped, then season with salt if necessary.

2 Pour the sauce into a bowl, cover, and chill. Garnish with chopped herbs before serving. The sauce can be stored in the refrigerator for 3–4 days.

PEANUT SAUCE

Organic peanuts are an especially good source of iron, protein, and fiber.
This peanut sauce goes well with Indonesian meat or seafood satay.

2 Add the shallots, garlic, ginger, most of the sliced chiles, and the ground coriander to the skillet and cook over a low heat, stirring occasionally, for 4–5 minutes, until the shallots are softened but not at all browned.

3 Transfer the spice mixture to a food processor or blender and add the peanuts, lemon grass, 1 teaspoon of the sugar, the soy sauce, ⅓ cup of the coconut milk, and the fish sauce. Blend to form a fairly smooth sauce.

4 Taste the mixture and add more fish sauce, tamarind paste, seasoning, lime juice, and/or more sugar as necessary.

5 Stir in the extra 2 tablespoons of coconut milk and a little water if the sauce seems thick, but do not make it too runny.

6 Serve the sauce cool or reheat it gently, stirring all the time to prevent it from spitting. Garnish with the remaining sliced chile before serving.

SERVES FOUR TO SIX

2 tablespoons peanut oil
¾ cup unsalted peanuts, blanched
2 shallots, chopped
2 garlic cloves, chopped
1 tablespoon chopped fresh ginger
1–2 green chiles, seeded and
    thinly sliced
1 teaspoon ground coriander
1 lemon grass stalk, tender base only,
    chopped
1–2 teaspoons unrefined light brown
    sugar or rapadura
1 tablespoon dark soy sauce
⅓–½ cup canned coconut milk
1–2 tablespoons Thai fish sauce
1–2 tablespoons tamarind paste
lime juice
sea salt and ground black pepper

1 Heat the oil in a small, heavy skillet and gently fry the peanuts, stirring often, until they are lightly browned. Use a slotted spoon to remove the nuts from the skillet and drain them thoroughly on paper towels. Set aside to cool.

COOK'S TIP
To make tamarind paste, soak 1 ounce tamarind pulp in ½ cup boiling water in a nonmetallic bowl for about 30 minutes, mashing the pulp occasionally with a fork. Then press the pulp through a stainless steel sieve. This paste will keep for several days in a covered container in the refrigerator.

ONION SAUCE

This delicious, dark onion sauce goes really well with organic meat or vegetarian sausages.
It is also good with mashed potatoes, rutabaga, or turnip.

SERVES FOUR

3 tablespoons olive oil
1 pound onions, halved
    and thinly sliced
3 tablespoons all-purpose or
    whole-wheat flour
1²/₃–2 cups vegetable stock
1 fresh thyme sprig
2 teaspoons dark soy sauce
sea salt and ground black pepper

1 Put the oil in a small, heavy saucepan and heat gently. Add the onions and fry, stirring occasionally, for 15–20 minutes, until the onions are soft and beginning to brown.

2 Increase the heat slightly and cook for another 20–30 minutes, stirring occasionally, until the onions are a dark, golden brown.

3 Stir in the flour, then cook for a few minutes, stirring all the time. Gradually stir in 1²/₃ cups of the hot stock. Simmer, stirring, for a few minutes, until thickened, adding a little more stock if the gravy is too thick.

4 Add the thyme, season with salt and pepper, then cook very slowly, stirring frequently, for 10–15 minutes.

5 Stir in the soy sauce and a little more seasoning, if necessary. Add a little more stock if the gravy is too thick, remove the thyme, and serve immediately.

VARIATIONS
• The onions can be browned in the oven instead of on the stove-top. This is best done in sunflower or olive oil rather than butter, which would burn. Place the sliced onions in an ovenproof dish and toss with 45ml/3 tbsp oil. Cook in an oven preheated to 190°C/375°F/Gas 5 for 20 minutes, stirring once or twice, then raise the oven temperature to 220°C/425°F/Gas 7 and cook for a further 15–25 minutes.
• Part of the vegetable stock may be replaced with red wine or dark beer. You may need to add a little extra sugar to balance the acidity of the wine or beer.

GUACAMOLE

Many different types of organic onion are available; this chunky guacamole uses
sweet red onion for flavor and color. Serve as a dip or sauce.

SERVES FOUR

2 large ripe avocados
1 small red onion, very finely chopped
1 red or green chile, seeded and very
    finely chopped
½–1 garlic clove, crushed with a little
    sea salt
finely shredded rind of ½ lime and juice
    of 1–1½ limes
8 ounces tomatoes, seeded and
    chopped
2 tablespoons roughly chopped
    fresh cilantro
½–1 teaspoon ground toasted
    cumin seeds
1 tablespoon olive oil
1–2 tablespoons sour cream (optional)
sea salt and ground black pepper
lime wedges dipped in sea salt
    (optional), to garnish
fresh cilantro sprigs, to garnish

1 Cut one of the avocados in half and
lift out and discard the pit. Scrape the
flesh from both halves into a bowl and
mash it roughly with a fork.

2 Add the onion, chile, garlic, lime
rind, tomatoes, and cilantro and stir
well to mix. Add the ground cumin
and seasoning to taste, then stir in the
olive oil.

3 Halve and pit the remaining avocado.
Dice the avocado flesh and stir it into
the guacamole.

4 Squeeze in fresh lime juice to taste,
mix well, then cover and let stand for
15 minutes so that the flavor develops.
Stir in the sour cream, if using. Serve
with lime wedges dipped in sea salt, if
you desire, and garnish with fresh
cilantro sprigs.

GARLIC MAYONNAISE

Fresh wet organic garlic is available in spring and summer, but try to use dried, cured bulbs because they add a more pungent flavor to this mouthwatering creamy mayonnaise.

SERVES FOUR TO SIX

2 large egg yolks
pinch of dried mustard
1¼ cups mild olive oil
1–2 tablespoons lemon juice, white wine
    vinegar, or warm water
2–4 garlic cloves
sea salt and ground black pepper

1 Make sure the egg yolks and oil are at room temperature before you start. Place the yolks in a bowl with the mustard and a pinch of salt, and whisk together to mix.

2 Gradually whisk in the oil, one drop at a time. When almost half the oil has been fully incorporated, start to add it in a slow, steady stream, whisking all the time.

3 As the mayonnaise starts to thicken, thin it down with a few drops of lemon juice or vinegar, or a few teaspoons of warm water.

4 When the mayonnaise is as thick as soft butter, stop adding oil. Season the mayonnaise to taste and add more lemon juice or vinegar as required.

5 Crush the garlic with the blade of a knife and stir it into the mayonnaise. For a slightly milder flavor, blanch the garlic twice in plenty of boiling water, then puree the cloves before beating them into the mayonnaise.

WATCHPOINT
The very young, the elderly, pregnant women, and those in ill-health or with a compromised immune system are advised against consuming raw eggs or dishes containing them.

VARIATIONS
• To make French Provençal aioli, crush 3–5 garlic cloves with a pinch of salt in a bowl, then whisk in the egg yolks. Omit the mustard but continue as above.
• For spicy garlic mayonnaise, omit the mustard and stir in ½ teaspoon harissa or red chili paste and 1 teaspoon sun-dried tomato paste with the garlic.
• Use roasted garlic puree or pureed smoked garlic to create a different flavor.
• Beat in about ½ cup mixed fresh herbs, such as tarragon, parsley, chervil, and chives.

CONFIT of SLOW-COOKED ONIONS

This jam of caramelized onions will keep for several days in a sealed jar in the refrigerator.
You can use red, white, or yellow onions, but yellow onions will provide the sweetest result.

2 Season with salt and plenty of pepper, then add the thyme, bay leaf, and sugar. Cook slowly, uncovered, for another 15–20 minutes, or until the onions are very soft and dark.

3 Add the prunes, vinegar, and wine with 4 tablespoons of water and cook over a low heat, stirring frequently, for a further 20 minutes, or until most of the liquid has evaporated. Add a little water and reduce the heat if the mixture dries too quickly.

4 Adjust the seasoning, adding more sugar and/or vinegar to taste. Let the confit cool, then stir in the remaining 1 teaspoon of oil. The confit is best stored for 24 hours before eating. Serve either cold or warm.

SERVES SIX TO EIGHT

2 tablespoons olive oil
1 tablespoon butter or
   nonhydrogenated margarine
1 ¼ pounds onions, sliced
3–5 fresh thyme sprigs
1 fresh bay leaf
2 tablespoons unrefined light
   brown sugar or rapadura,
   plus a little extra
¼ cup prunes, chopped
2 tablespoons balsamic vinegar,
   plus a little extra
½ cup red wine
sea salt and ground black pepper

1 Reserve 1 tablespoon of the oil, then heat the rest with the butter in a small, heavy saucepan. Add the onions, cover, and cook gently for 15 minutes, stirring occasionally.

VARIATION
Baby onions with tomato and orange
Gently fry 1 ¼ pounds peeled pearl onions or small *cipollini* in 4 tablespoons olive oil until lightly browned, then sprinkle in 3 tablespoons of unrefined soft light brown sugar or rapadura. Let the onions caramelize a little, then add 1 ½ teaspoons crushed coriander seeds, 1 cup red wine, 2 bay leaves, a few thyme sprigs, 3 strips orange zest, 3 tablespoons tomato paste, and the juice of 1 orange. Cook very gently, uncovered, for 1 hour, stirring occasionally until the sauce is thick and reduced. Uncover for the last 20 minutes of cooking time. Sharpen with 1–2 tablespoons sherry vinegar and serve cold, sprinkled with chopped fresh parsley.

APPLE and TOMATO CHUTNEY

This mellow, golden, spicy chutney makes the most of fresh fall produce.
Any type of organic tomatoes can be used successfully in this recipe.

MAKES ABOUT 4 POUNDS

3 pounds cooking apples
3 pounds tomatoes
2 large onions
2 garlic cloves
1¾ cups pitted dates
2 red bell peppers
3 dried red chiles
1 tablespoon black peppercorns
4 cardamom pods
1 tablespoon coriander seeds
2 teaspoons cumin seeds
2 teaspoons ground turmeric
1 teaspoon sea salt
2½ cups distilled malt vinegar
5¼ cups unrefined granulated sugar
    or rapadura

3 Pour in the vinegar and sugar, then let simmer for 30 minutes, stirring occasionally. Add the red bell peppers and cook for a further 30 minutes, stirring more frequently as the chutney becomes thick and pulpy.

4 Spoon the chutney into warm, dry, sterilized jars. Seal each jar with a circle of wax paper, and cover with a tightly fitting cellophane top. Let cool, then label and store in a cool, dry place.

1 Peel and chop the apples. Peel and chop the tomatoes, onions, and garlic. Quarter the dates. Core and seed the bell peppers; cut into chunky pieces. Put all the prepared ingredients, except the bell peppers, into a preserving pan.

2 Slit the chiles. Put the peppercorns and remaining spices into a mortar and roughly crush with a pestle. Add the chiles, spices, and salt to the pan.

FOCACCIA

This is a flattish bread, originating from Genoa in Italy, made with flour, olive oil, and salt.
There are many variations from many regions, but this is the traditional type.

MAKES 1 ROUND 10-INCH LOAF

1 ounce fresh yeast
3½ cups unbleached white
    bread flour
2 teaspoons sea salt
5 tablespoons olive oil
2 teaspoons coarse sea salt

1 Dissolve the yeast in ½ cup of warm water. Let stand for 10 minutes. Sift the white bread flour into a large bowl, make a well in the center, and add the yeast, salt, and 2 tablespoons of oil. Mix in the flour and add more water to make a dough.

2 Turn out onto a floured work surface and knead the dough until smooth and elastic. Return to the bowl, cover with a cloth, and let rise in a warm place for 2–2½ hours, until doubled in bulk.

3 Knock back the dough and knead again for a few minutes. Press into an oiled 10-inch tart pan, and cover with a damp cloth. Let the dough rise again for 30 minutes.

4 Preheat the oven to 400°. Poke the dough all over with your fingers to make little dimples in the surface. Pour the remaining oil over the dough, using a pastry brush to take it to the edges. Sprinkle with the salt.

5 Bake for 20–25 minutes, until the bread is a pale gold. Carefully remove from the pan and let cool on a rack. The bread is best eaten on the same day, but it also freezes very well.

VARIATIONS
Focaccia is often baked with a selection of different toppings. Before baking, lightly sprinkle over any or a combination of the following: chopped pitted olives, slices of red or yellow bell pepper, sprigs of fresh rosemary, or diced sun-dried tomatoes.

OLIVE BREAD

Variations of this strongly flavored bread are popular all over the Mediterranean.
For this Greek recipe, use rich, oily olives or those marinated with herbs.

MAKES TWO 675G/1½LB LOAVES

2 red onions, thinly sliced
2 tablespoons olive oil
2 cups pitted black or green olives
2 ounces fresh yeast
7 cups white bread flour
1½ teaspoons salt
3 tablespoons each roughly
    chopped parsley, cilantro,
    and mint

1 Fry the onions in the oil until soft.
Roughly chop the olives.

2 Dissolve the yeast in 1 cup warm
water. Let stand for 10 minutes. Put the
flour, salt, and herbs in a large bowl with
the olives and fried onions and add the
yeast mixture.

3 Mix with a round-bladed knife, adding
as much warm water as is necessary to
make a soft dough.

4 Turn out onto a lightly floured surface
and knead for about 10 minutes. Put in
a clean bowl, cover with plastic wrap,
and let stand in a warm place until
doubled in bulk.

VARIATION
Shape the dough into 16 small rolls. Slash
the tops as in step 6 and reduce the
cooking time to 25 minutes.

5 Preheat the oven to 425°F. Lightly
grease two baking sheets. Turn the
dough onto a floured surface and cut
in half. Shape into two rounds and place
on the baking sheets. Cover the dough
loosely with lightly oiled plastic wrap and
let stand until doubled in size.

6 Slash the tops of the loaves two or
three times with a knife, then bake for
about 40 minutes, or until the loaves
sound hollow when tapped on the
bottom. Transfer to a wire rack to cool.

CHAPATIS

More and more types of organic bread are available, but chapatis simply have to be made by hand. These chewy, unleavened breads are eaten throughout Northern India. They are usually served as an accompaniment to spicy dishes.

2 Knead for 5–6 minutes, until smooth. Place in a lightly oiled bowl, cover with a damp dish towel, and let rest for 30 minutes. Turn out onto a floured surface. Divide the dough into six equal pieces. Shape each piece into a ball.

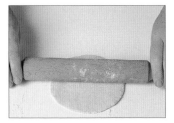

3 Press the dough into a larger round with the palm of your hand, then roll into a 5-inch circle. Stack, layered between plastic wrap, to keep moist.

4 Heat a grill pan or heavy skillet over a medium heat for a few minutes, until hot. Take one chapati, brush off any excess flour, and place on the grill pan or skillet. Cook for 30–60 seconds, or until the top begins to bubble and white specks appear on the underside.

5 Turn the chapati over using a metal spatula and cook for a further 30 seconds. Remove from the pan or skillet and keep warm, layered between a folded dish towel, while cooking the remaining chapatis. If you want, the chapatis can be brushed lightly with melted ghee or butter immediately after cooking. Serve warm.

MAKES SIX CHAPATIS

1½ cups *atta* or whole-wheat flour
½ teaspoon sea salt
about ½ cup water
1 teaspoon sunflower oil
melted ghee, butter or nonhydrogenated
 margarine, for brushing (optional)

COOK'S TIP
Atta or *ata* is a very fine whole-wheat flour that is only found in Indian stores and supermarkets. It is sometimes simply labeled chapati flour. *Atta* can also be used for making rotis and other Indian flat breads.

1 Sift the flour and salt into a large mixing bowl. Add the water and mix to a soft dough using your hand or a round-bladed knife. Knead in the oil, then turn the dough out onto a lightly floured surface.

PITA BREAD

There are many different types of pita breads, ranging from very flat ones, to those with pockets, to a thicker cushiony one, as here. They are fun to make, and look all the better for a little wobbliness around the edges.

MAKES TWELVE

I ounce fresh yeast
5 cups unbleached white bread flour,
    or half white bread flour and half
    whole-wheat flour
I tablespoon sea salt
I tablespoon olive oil I cup water

I Dissolve the yeast in ½ cup of warm water. Let stand for 10 minutes. Put the bread flour and salt in a large bowl and stir in the yeast mixture. Mix together the oil and water, and stir enough liquid into the flour mixture to make a stiff dough.

2 Place the dough in a clean bowl, cover with a clean dish towel, and let stand in a warm place for at least 30 minutes and up to 2 hours.

3 Knead the dough for 10 minutes, or until smooth. Lightly oil the bowl, place the dough in it, cover again, and let rise in a warm place for about 1 hour, or until doubled in size.

4 Divide the dough into 12 equal-size pieces. With lightly floured hands, flatten each piece, then roll out into a circle measuring about 8 inches and about ¼–½ inch thick. Keep the rolled breads covered with a clean dish towel.

5 Heat a large, heavy skillet over a medium-high heat. When smoking hot, gently lay one piece of flattened dough in the skillet; cook for 15–20 seconds. Carefully turn it over and cook the second side for about 1 minute.

6 When large bubbles start to form on the bread, turn it over again. It should puff up. Using a folded clean dish towel, gently press on the bread where the bubbles have formed. Cook for a total of 3 minutes, then remove the bread from the skillet. Repeat with the remaining dough until all the breads are cooked.

7 Wrap the pita breads in a clean dish towel, stacking them as each one is cooked. Serve the pita breads hot while they are soft and moist.

VARIATION
To cook the breads in the oven, preheat the oven to 425°F. Fill an unglazed or partially glazed dish with hot water and place in the bottom of the oven. Alternatively, soak a handful of unglazed tiles in hot water and arrange them in the bottom of the oven. Use either a nonstick baking sheet or a lightly oiled ordinary baking sheet and heat in the oven for a few minutes. Place two or three pieces of flattened dough onto the hot baking sheet and place in the hottest part of the oven. Bake for 2–3 minutes. They should puff up. Repeat with the remaining dough until all the pitta breads are cooked.

SAN FRANCISCO SOURDOUGH BREAD

There are many sourdough bread recipes, but this is a great one to start with. The bread is leavened using a flour and water paste, which is left to ferment with the aid of airborne yeast. If you use unbleached organic flour, the finished loaves will have a moist crumb and crispy crust and will keep for several days.

MAKES TWO ROUND LOAVES

For the starter
½ cup whole-wheat flour
pinch of ground cumin
1 tablespoon milk or soy milk
1–2 tablespoon water
1st refreshment
4 tablespoons water
1 cup white bread flour
2nd refreshment
4 tablespoons water
1 cup white bread flour

For the bread
1st refreshment
5 strong very warm water
⅔ cup unbleached all-purpose flour
2nd refreshment
¾ cup lukewarm water
1¾–2 cups unbleached all-purpose flour

For the sourdough
scant 1¼ cups warm water
5 cups unbleached white bread flour
1 tablespoon sea salt
flour, for dusting
ice cubes, for baking

1 Sift the flour and cumin for the starter into a bowl. Add the milk and sufficient water to make a firm but moist dough. Knead for 6–8 minutes. Return the dough to the bowl, cover with a damp dish towel, and let stand in a warm place, 75–80°F, for about 2 days. When it is ready the starter will appear moist and wrinkled and will have developed a crust.

2 Pull off the hardened crust and discard. Scoop out the moist center (about the size of a hazelnut), which will be aerated and sweet smelling, and place in a clean bowl. Mix in the water for the 1st refreshment. Gradually add the flour and mix to a dough.

3 Cover with plastic wrap and return to a warm place for 1–2 days. Discard the crust and gradually mix in the water for the 2nd refreshment to the starter, which by now will have a slightly sharper smell. Gradually mix in the white flour, cover, and let stand in a warm place for 8–10 hours.

4 For the bread, mix the sourdough starter with the water for the 1st refreshment. Gradually mix in the flour to form a firm dough. Knead for 6–8 minutes, until firm. Cover with a damp dish towel and let stand in a warm place for 8–12 hours, or until doubled in bulk.

5 Gradually mix in the water for the 2nd refreshment, then gradually mix in enough flour to form a soft, smooth elastic dough. Re-cover and let stand in a warm place for 8–12 hours. Gradually stir in the water for the sourdough, then gradually work in the flour and salt. This will take 10–15 minutes. Turn out onto a lightly floured surface and knead until smooth and very elastic. Place in a large lightly oiled bowl, cover with lightly oiled plastic wrap, and let rise, in a warm place, for 8–12 hours.

6 Divide the dough in half and shape into 2 round loaves by folding the sides over to the center and sealing.

7 Place seam side up in flour-dusted *couronnes* bowls or glass bowls lined with flour-dusted dish towels. Re-cover and let rise in a warm place for 4 hours.

8 Preheat the oven to 425°F. Place an empty roasting pan in the bottom of the oven. Dust two baking sheets with flour. Turn out the loaves seam side down on the prepared baking sheets. Using a sharp knife, cut a crisscross pattern by slashing the top of the loaves 4–5 times in each direction.

9 Place the baking sheets in the oven and immediately drop the ice cubes into the hot roasting pan to create steam. Bake the bread for 25 minutes, then reduce the oven temperature to 400°F and bake for a further 15–20 minutes, or until it sounds hollow when tapped on the base. Transfer to wire racks to cool.

COOK'S TIP
If you'd like to make sourdough bread regularly, keep a small amount of the starter covered in the refrigerator. It will keep for several days. Use the starter for the 2nd refreshment, then continue as directed.

PUMPKIN and WALNUT BREAD

Walnuts, nutmeg, and pumpkin combine to yield a moist, tangy, and slightly sweet bread with an indescribably good flavor. Serve partnered with meats or cheese.

MAKES ONE LOAF

1¼ pounds pumpkin, peeled,
   seeded, and cut into chunks
6 tablespoons superfine sugar
1 teaspoon grated nutmeg
¼ cup butter, melted
3 eggs, lightly beaten
3 cups unbleached white bread flour
2 tablespoons baking powder
½ teaspoon sea salt
¾ cup walnuts, chopped

1 Grease and neatly line the bottom of a loaf pan measuring 8½ x 4½ inches. Preheat the oven to 350°F.

2 Place the pumpkin in a saucepan, add water to cover by about 2 inches, then bring to a boil. Cover, lower the heat, and simmer for about 20 minutes, or until the pumpkin is very tender. Drain well, then puree in a food processor or blender. Let cool.

3 Place 1¼ cups of the puree in a large bowl. Add the sugar, nutmeg, melted butter, and eggs and mix. Sift the flour, baking powder, and salt into a large bowl and make a well in the center.

4 Add the pumpkin mixture to the center of the flour and stir until smooth. Mix in the walnuts.

5 Transfer to the prepared pan and bake for 1 hour, or until golden and starting to shrink from the sides of the tin. Turn out onto a wire rack to cool.

COOK'S TIP
If you have more pumpkin puree than you need, use the remainder in soup.

WHOLE-WHEAT SUNFLOWER BREAD

Organic sunflower seeds give a nutty crunchiness to this hearty whole-wheat loaf.
Serve with a chunk of cheese and a rich tomato chutney.

3 Cover the bowl with a damp dish towel and let dough rise in a warm place for 45–50 minutes, or until doubled in size.

4 Preheat the oven to 400°F. Turn out the dough onto a lightly floured work surface and knead for about 10 minutes, until elastic—the dough will still be sticky, but resist the temptation to add more flour.

5 Form the dough into a rectangle and place in the loaf pan. Sprinkle the top with sunflower seeds. Cover with a damp dish towel and let rise again for a further 15 minutes.

6 Bake for 40–45 minutes, until golden. When ready, the loaf should sound hollow when tapped underneath. Let stand for 5 minutes, turn out of the pan, and cool on a wire rack.

MAKES ONE LOAF

1 ounce fresh yeast
4 cups whole-wheat flour
½ teaspoon sea salt
scant ½ cup sunflower seeds,
    plus extra for sprinkling

1 Dissolve the yeast in ½ cup of warm water. Let stand for 10 minutes. Grease and lightly flour a 1-popund loaf pan.

2 Put the flour, salt, and sunflower seeds in a large mixing bowl and stir to combine the ingredients. Make a well in the center and gradually stir in the yeast mixture. Mix vigorously with a wooden spoon, adding sufficient extra warm water to form a soft, sticky dough.

VARIATION
Other seeds would be good in this bread—try sesame seeds, pumpkin seeds, or a mixture of sesame, pumpkin, hemp, and sunflower seeds.

CHEESE and ONION CORNBREAD

Full of flavor, this tasty organic cornbread is delicious served freshly baked, warm, or cold in slices, either on its own or spread with a little butter. It makes an ideal accompaniment to soups, stews, and chiles.

MAKES ONE 2-POUND LOAF

1 tablespoon sunflower oil
1 onion, thinly sliced
1 ½ cups cornmeal
⅔ cup rice flour
¼ cup soy flour
1 tablespoon baking powder
1 teaspoon unrefined superfine sugar
   or rapadura
1 teaspoon sea salt
1 cup coarsely grated sharp cheddar
   cheese
scant 1 cup tepid milk or soy milk
2 eggs
3 tablespoons nonhydrogenated
   margarine, melted

1 Preheat the oven to 375°F. Lightly grease a 2-pound loaf pan. Heat the oil in a skillet, add the onion, and cook gently for 10–15 minutes, until softened, stirring occasionally. Remove the skillet from the heat and set aside to cool.

2 Place the cornmeal, rice flour, soy flour, baking powder, sugar, and salt in a large mixing bowl and combine thoroughly. Stir in the grated cheese, mixing well.

3 In a pitcher, beat together the milk, eggs, and melted margarine. Add to the flour mixture and mix well using a wooden spoon.

4 Stir the cooled, cooked onions into the cornmeal mixture and stir well until the onions are evenly incorporated.

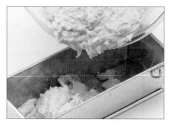

5 Spoon the onion mixture into the prepared pan, level the surface, and bake for about 30 minutes, until the bread has risen and is golden brown.

6 Run a knife around the edge to loosen the loaf. Turn out onto a wire rack to cool slightly and serve warm. Alternatively, let it stand on the rack until completely cold, then cut into slices. To store the loaf, wrap it in foil or seal in a plastic bag.

VARIATIONS
• A wide selection of organic flours is available. In addition to a range of wheat flours, you can choose from buckwheat, rice, rye or maize.
• Reserve a little of the grated cheese and cooked onion and scatter it over the top of the bread before baking.

COOK'S TIP
A loaf pan that has drop-down sides is useful when making cornbread. Because it has a much softer texture than conventional yeast breads, you need to be careful when turning out the cooked bread onto the wire rack.

GLOSSARY

As in every speciality area, organics has its own language. The following is a guide to some of the special terms in common usage.

Agriculture The cultivation of crops and raising of livestock for the production of food and other products.

Agrochemical A chemical or chemical compound used in farming. Also an adjective to describe produce derived from farms that extensively use these chemicals, or the method of agriculture that utilizes agrochemicals.

Aquaculture The farming of fish and other creatures that live in fresh or sea water, such as salmon and shrimp.

Artificial additives Chemicals and chemical compounds added to foods in order to manipulate their taste, color, texture, or shelf life. These include powerful toxins, such as tartrazine, a neurotoxin that is used in beverages to dye them orange. Of the seven thousand additives used in nonorganic food, there are only seven that can be used in organic food.

Biodiversity The wide diversity of plants and creatures that occurs in nature.
Also the ideal of organic systems of farming, biodiversity is a term to describe farms rich in different species of plants and animals, whether intentionally cultivated and bred, or those that occur naturally.

Biodynamics Based on the work of the early twentieth century theosophist Rudolf Steiner, biodynamic farming relies on companion planting, homeopathic preparations, and a seven-year cycle of crop rotation to remain entirely chemical-free. Biodynamic farms are completely self-contained, integrating different crops and livestock to create a mini-ecosystem. The lunar calendar is used as a guide to planting and harvesting crops, with different star constellations signaling the most fruitful times for these activities. Biodynamics is part of the family of organic farming styles.

Certification Each organic certification board has a different code of standards. However, the basic organic standards are legally defined in international law, so every certification board throughout the world must at least comply with these standards. Check details with each certifier if you want to know if they enforce standard organic standards or stricter ones.

Companion planting A method of growing plants in combinations that optimize their beneficial effects while minimizing their negative effects on each other. For example, growing potatoes near tomatoes weakens their resistance to potato blight, so this should be avoided. Growing chamomile and peppermint in proximity is beneficial, as both plants produce more active essential oils in combination. Companion planting is a practical way of conserving and utilizing biodiversity.

Compost Vegetable and animal matter that has been purposefully decomposed (aerobically fermented) to create a natural source of nutrients for growing crops. Encourages good soil quality and beneficial enzyme production. Organic farmers must follow strict procedures to produce composts and

manures. They compost for lengthy periods to ensure that E. coli and other bugs are killed off. Also extensively manufactured and utilized by organic home gardeners.

Crop rotation A traditional method of effectively managing soil fertility on a farm by systematically rotating crops between different fields. This method often includes leaving fields to lie fallow, meaning that they are rested from production to regain their naturally fertile soil.

Fair trade The concept that a fair price will be paid for goods produced by farmers and workers in the developing world. Many poorer farmers are forced to sell their products for much less than is fair if there is no other outlet for them. Fair trade means that a buyer from the developed world will not exploit this opportunity to pay less money than a commodity is worth. Effectively, honorable behavior instead of exploitation. The official Fairtrade Mark prohibits child and forced labor, and guarantees that workers

receive a decent standard of housing, health and safety protection, and employment rights. It also promotes programm for environmental sustainability.

Fertilizers Generally refers to synthetic chemicals and chemical compounds based on synthetic nitrates used by farmers to give plants extra nutrients for growth. An excess of nitrates is known to cause cancer in humans and animals. Organic farming uses natural fertilizers instead, such as manure, seaweed, clays, and rockdust.

Free range A term to describe farm animals and birds that have been able to gain some access to open pastures and skies. When applied to chickens and their eggs, it may simply mean that the chicken house has "popholes" but does not guarantee that the birds will have used these exits, especially if they have been bred in confinement. In Britain, the Soil Association has the highest standards for free-range poultry and eggs—prohibiting debeaking and overcrowding, and ensuring that all birds range properly in daylight. If in doubt, check with your local certification board for details of their guidelines.

Fungicides Chemicals and chemical compounds used to prevent molds growing on crops or food products by killing fungal spores. Organic farming prohibits their use. However, where the whole crop might otherwise be lost to a disease, such as potato blight or mildew, small amounts of traditional chemicals, such as

copper and sulfur compounds, may be used by organic farmers. This practice is restricted to extreme cases, and permission must be granted from an organic certifier.

Gardening The practice of organic gardening is an extremely valuable activity. The United Nations' Food and Agriculture Organisation has calculated that small biodiverse gardens can produce thousands of times more food per acre than large intensive monocultures. Home gardening in Indonesia provides around 40 percent of all food, and in Eastern Nigeria, the 2 percent of land cultivated as domestic gardens provides 50 percent of the food. Gardening provides people in industrialized nations with a connection to the food they eat, whether it is growing herbs in a window box or fruits and vegetables in a garden.

Genetic modification The manipulation of genetic material between different unrelated species of living entities. In agriculture, the creation of crops known as Genetically Modified Organisms (GMOs) or Transgenic Organisms by extracting genes from one species and inserting them in another. GM farming is part of the family of farming styles that makes up agrochemical farming.

GMOs Genetically Modified Organisms (see previous entry).

Herbicides Chemicals and chemical compounds used to kill weeds. Organic farming prohibits their use.

Hydroponics A modern method of agrochemical farming that grows plants in a purely synthetic environment. The plants are suspended in a liquid mixture of

nutrient compounds in a mixture of sand or gravel. Bright lights are often used to stimulate plant growth. Many nonorganic potato and tomato crops are now routinely grown without soil.

Insecticides Chemicals and chemical compounds used to kill insects.

Irradiation The passing of food through a radiation field to preserve it beyond its natural shelf life. The use of ionizing irradiation to preserve food is prohibited under organic standards.

Legumes Crops related to the bean family. Planted extensively in organic agriculture to maintain beneficial levels of nitrogen in the soil. Legumes have the capacity to fix nitrogen from the air into the soil through nodules in their roots. They are often planted as part of the crop rotation system in fallow fields.

Monocultures Agrochemical farms that continually grow only one kind of crop over a vast area. Monocultures are the antithesis of biodiversity, and they are the prevalent form of agriculture in most industrialized nations at the beginning of the twenty-first century. Four

percent of all farms in the United States produce half of the food grown there on huge swathes of land growing only a single species.

Organic A method of farming based on the cultivation of good soil quality and biodiversity. The use of agrochemicals is strictly regulated and kept to the absolute minimum. It prohibits GMOs (even in animal feed), and is a legally binding term defined in international law. The rearing of organic animals must be according to strict welfare standards, and they may only be treated with chemicals, such as antibiotics, as a last resort to cure illness. When the term is used to describe a food product or item, at least 95 percent of its ingredients must be certified organic and it may not be irradiated.

Permaculture This is the design and maintenance of food growing systems that have the diversity, stability, and resilience of natural ecosystems. It is the harmonious integration of the landscape with people, in cities or rural areas. Permaculture can be as small as a city balcony or as large as a forest. It is a way of providing food, energy, shelter, and other material and nonmaterial needs in a sustainable way.

Pesticides Chemicals and chemical compounds used by farmers and gardeners to kill pests. These products often contain organophosphates, which belong to the same family of chemicals as nerve gases. Synthetic pesticides are applied to crops and livestock as a matter of course in agrochemical agriculture for the prevention and treatment of pests. In organic farming, they may only be applied to crops if all other non-chemical actions to tackle a pest problem have failed, and then only with

permission from a certifier. Organic farming relies on biodiversity to provide natural predators to control pests, or uses natural plant-based pesticides. Standards are rigorous and organic farms unfortunate enough to be affected by pesticide drift from neighboring agrochemical properties have on occasion had their licences revoked.

Prevention The method utilized by organic farmers to minimize the use of agrochemicals, hormones, and antibiotics in farming practices. Pesticide use is minimized by careful management, from companion planting to the use of satellite technology to detect potential parasites. Chemical use for livestock is minimized by keeping numbers of animals and fish lower per pen, and encouraging more freedom of movement within the farm or fish tank.

Processed Food Food that has been ready prepared from its raw state for consumption. This can be through a great variety of processes, including boiling, slicing, and baking. Processing food by its very nature removes nutrients and vitality. Seventy percent of all food grown in the United States is processed before it reaches the shops. Only 1 percent of food grown in India is processed before it is retailed. Indian citizens do not eat their produce raw, but simply process the ingredients themselves at home.

Selective Breeding A traditional genetic technique that produces plants or animals with a particular genetic profile. Reasons may include creating a distinctive taste, unusual color, or hardier variety. It is unrelated to modern genetic modification, because selective breeding takes part between plants of the same species through interbreeding instead of between differing species using DNA displacement technology.

SUPPLIERS and INFORMATION SOURCES

United States and Canada

Biodynamic Farming and Gardening Association, Inc.
1 (415) 561–7797
www.biodynamics.com

Canadian Organic Growers
www.gks.com/cog/

Diamond Organics
1 (888) ORGANIC
Ecological Agriculture Projects
http://eap.
mcgill.ca/general/
home_frames.htm

Institute for Agriculture &
Trade's National Organic
Program
1 (202) 720–3252

Organic Grapes into Wine
Alliance
www.isgnet.com/ogwa

Organic Style www.organic-
style.com

Organic Trade Association
www.ota.com

Organic Trading and
Information Center
www.organicfood.com

The Permaculture Institute
P.O. Box 3702
Pojuaque, New Mexico, 87501

Rodale Institute
1 (610) 683–1400
www.rodale.com

Seeds of Change
1 (888) 762–7333
www.seedsofchange.com

Transfair
1 (510) 663–5260
www.transfairusa.org

Whole Foods
1 (512) 477–4455

Wild Oats
1 (800) 494–9453

UK and Eire

Biodynamic Agricultural
Association
+44 (0)1453 759501

British Nutrition Foundation
+44 (0)20 7404 6504

Cambrian Organics
+44 (0)1559 363151
www.cambrianorganics.com

Centre for Alternative
Technology
+44 (0)1654 702400
www.cat.org.uk

Circaroma Organic Skincare
+44 (0)20 7249 9392
www.circaroma.com

Clearspring
+44 (0)20 8740 1781
rudkin@dircon.co.uk

Compassion in World Farming
+44 (0)1730 264208
www.ciwf.co.uk

Fairtrade Foundation
+44 (0)20 7405 5942
www.fairtrade.org.uk

Farmers' World Network
www.fwn.org.uk

Food and Agricultural
Organization (United Nations)
www.fao.org

Fresh and Wild
+44 (0)800 9175 175
www.freshandwild.com

Friends of the Earth
+44 (0)20 7490 1555
www.foe.co.uk

Green Endings
+44 (0)20 7424 0345
www.greenendings.co.uk

Greenfibres
+44 (0)1803 868001
www.greenfibres.com

Green People
+44 (0)1444 401444
www.greenpeople.co.uk

Henry Doubleday Research
Association
+44 (0)120 330 3517
www.hdra.org.uk

Himalayan Green Tea
+44 (0)1895 632409
www.nvspharmacy.co.uk

Irish Organic Farmers and
Growers Association
+353 (0)506 32563
www.irishorganic.ie

Kinvara Irish Organic Smoked
Salmon
+353 (0)916 37489

Llain Farm Fresh Meats
+44 (0)1348 831210

Marine Stewardship Council
+44 (0)20 7350 4000
www.msc.org

National Association of Farmers'
Markets
+44 (0)1225 787914

Neal's Yard Bakery
+44 (0)20 7836 5199
www.nealsyardbakery.co.uk

NHR Organic Oils
0845 310 8066
www.nhr.kz

Organic Wine Company
+44 (0)1494 446557
www.organicwinecompany.com

Permaculture Magazine
0845 458 4150
www.permaculture.co.uk

Pero Organic Pet Foods
+44 (0)1690 710457
pero@perofsbusiness.co.uk

Pesticide Action Network UK
+44 (0)20 7274 8895
www.pan-uk.org

Planet Organic
+44 (0)20 7221 7171
www.planetorganic.com

Race and Race Artisan Foods
+44 (0)1647 277454
raceorganic@aol.com

Ravens Oak Dairy
+44 (0)1270 524210
www.ravensoakdairy.co.uk

Rocombe Farm Organic Ice Cream
+44 (0)1482 575884
icecreamcentre@netscapeonline
.co.uk

Scottish Quality Salmon
+44 (0)1738 587000
www.scottishsalmon.co.uk

Seasoned Pioneers
+44 (0)800 0682348
www.seasonedpioneers.co.uk

Sheepdrove Organic Farm
+44 (0)1488 71659
www.sheepdrove.com
Simply Soaps
+44 (0)1603 720869
www.simplysoaps.com

Slow Food Movement (UK)
c/o The Village Bakery
+44 (0)1768 881515
www.slow-food.com

Soil Association
+44 (0)117 929 0661
www.soilassociation.org
Special Diets News –
+44 (0)20 7722 2866
www.inside-story.com

Solar Homes
+44 (0)1275 540112
www.solarsense-uk.com

Sustain
+44 (0) 7837 1228
www.sustainweb.org

Swaddles
Green Farm
+44 (0)1460
234387
www.swaddles.co.uk

Triodos Bank
+44 (0)117 973 9339
www.triodos.co.uk

UK Register of Organic Food
Standards (UKROFS)
+44 (0)20 7238 5915

Vintage Roots
+44 (0)800 980 4992
www.vintageroots.co.uk

Well Hung Meats
+44 (0)1752 830282
www.carswellfarm.co.uk

Wiggle Wigglers
+44 (0)1981 500391
www.wigglywigglers.co.uk

Willing Workers on Organic
Farms (WWOOF)
+44 (0)1273 476286
www.phdc.com/wwoof

Women's Environmental
Network +44 (0)20 7247 3327
www.gn.apc.org/wen

Australia
Biodynamic Marketing Co Ltd
+61 (3) 5966 7370

Biological Farmers of Australia
Co Op Ltd
+61 (7) 4639 3299

NASSA (National Association
for Sustainable Agriculture)
Australia +61 (8) 8370 8455
www.nassa.com.au

Organic Federation of Australia
www.ofa.org.au

Organic Herb Growers of
Australia (OHGA)
+61 (2) 6622 0100
www.organicherbs.org

Organic Retailers and Growers
Association of Australia
+61 (1800) 356 299
www.orgaa.org.au

Robinvale Organic & Bio-
Dynamic Wines Australia
+61 (3) 5026 3955
www.organicwines.com.au

New Zealand
Bio-Gro New Zealand
www.biogro.co.nz

New Zealand Organics +64 (9)
376 1330 www.nzorganics.co.nz

Author's Acknowledgments

Ysanne Spevack would like to
thank the following people for
their assistance. Without people
like you, this book could never
have happened …

John Barrow at Organic Delivery
Company
Peter Bradford at Fresh & Wild
Lynda Brown
Steve Chandra
Charles, Prince of Wales
Carol Charlton
Caroline Conran
Gilli Davies
The Dkiks
Julie Edgar at Scottish Quality
Salmon
The Finelli-Blowers
Dido Fisher
Jenni Fleetwood
Lou Gibbs
Patrick Holden, Sue Flook, and
Sarah Jeffs at the Soil Association
Peter Kindersley at Sheepdrove Farm
Guy Lafayette and David Lee at
Consultancy for Corporate
Change

Margaret Malone
Mia Manners
Vini Medley
Kate Pengelly
Miriam Polunin
Sarah Ratty
Anita Roddick
Craig Sams
Howard-Yana Shapiro
Brian Spevack
Michael van Straten
Amy Williams at Marine
Stewardship Council
Antony Worrall-Thompson
Joy Wotton

Picture Credits
The Publishers would like to
thank the following for supplying
photographs for use in this book:
Anthony Blake Photo Library: 6 top,
6 bottom, 7, 8 right, 60 bottom left;
A-Z Botanical Collection Ltd: /Bjorn
Svensson 12 right, /Sylvia Sroka 14
right; Science Photo Library: /Simon
Fraser 48 left, Fletcher & Baylis 50
right. Author's portrait on jacket by
Lou Gibbs.

Bibliography

Bissell, Frances – *The Organic
Meat Cookbook* (Ebury Press,
1999)
Boyd, Hilary – *Banishing the Blues*
(Mitchell Beazley, 2000)
Brown, Edward Espe – *Tassajara
Bread Book* (Shambhala,
1970)
Brown, Edward Espe – *Tomato
Blessings and Radish* (Riverhead
Books, 1997)
Brown, Lynda – *Organic Living*
(Dorling Kindersley, 2000)
Charlton, Carol – *Organic Café
Cookbook* (David and Charles,
1999)
Clayton, Dr Paul – *Health Defence*
(Accelerated Learning Systems,
2001)
Elliot, Rose – *Beanfeast* (White
Eagle Publishing Trust, 1975)
Elliott, Renée and Trevillé, Eric –
Organic Cookbook (Dorling
Kindersley, 2000)

Heaton, Shane – *Organic Farming,
Food Quality and Human
Health* (Soil Association,
2001)
Lifespan Community Collective –
Full of Beans (L C C Ltd,
1982)
Lucas, Dr. Caroline MEP – *Stopping
the Great Food Swap* (Earthscan,
2000)
Miller, Mark – *Red Sage* (Ten Speed
Press, 1999)
Shapiro, Howard-Yana and
Harrisson, John – *Gardening for
the Future of the Earth* (Bantam,
2000)
Spevack, Ysanne – *Branding Healthy
Foods* (Reuters Business Insight,
2001)
van Straten, Michael – *Superfoods*
(Dorling Kindersley, 1990)
van Straten, Michael – *Organic
Superfoods* (Mitchell Beazley,
1999)

INDEX

NOTES

NOTES

NOTES

NOTES

NOTES

NOTES

NOTES

NOTES

NOTES

NOTES